D0141884

WHAT IS IT ABOUT GOVERNMENT THAT AMERICANS DISLIKE?

The American public's level of hostility toward government became a major issue in the 1990s. In this edited volume, twenty-four of the country's leading students of public attitudes toward government in the United States address the reasons for this hostility. In fourteen original chapters, the authors explain why people's approval of government dropped so precipitously in the late 1960s, why some parts of the government (such as the Supreme Court) are better liked than others (such as the Congress), and why certain actions by political elites are particularly upsetting to much of the American public. Uniting several of the contributions is the theme that dissatisfaction with government occurs not just when people dislike governmental policies but also when they dislike the manner in which those policies are made. Another unifying theme is the potential danger of a public with nothing but disdain for its own political system.

John R. Hibbing is Professor of Political Science at the University of Nebraska–Lincoln, where he has taught since 1981, specializing in the American Congress and American public opinion. He has been a NATO Fellow in Science in Great Britain, a Fulbright scholar in Spain, and a Visiting Professor in Hungary, and he has also edited the *Legislative Studies Quarterly*. His most recent book, *Congress as Public Enemy: Public Attitudes toward American Political Institutions* (with Elizabeth Theiss-Morse), won the APSA's Fenno Prize in 1996 as the best book on legislatures.

Elizabeth Theiss-Morse is Associate Professor of Political Science at the University of Nebraska–Lincoln. She has published research on citizen participation, political tolerance, and public attitudes toward government, and is a co-author of two award-winning books: *Congress as Public Enemy: Public Attitudes toward American Political Institutions* (awarded the APSA's Fenno Prize in 1996 for the best book published on legislatures) and *With Malice Toward Some: How People Make Civil Liberties Judgments* (awarded the APSA's Best Book in Political Psychology Prize in 1996).

Cambridge Studies in Political Psychology and Public Opinion

This series has been established in recognition of the growing sophistication in the resurgence of interest in political psychology and the study of public opinion. Its focus ranges from the kinds of mental processes that people employ when they think about democratic processes and make political choices to the nature and consequences of macro-level public opinion.

Some of the works draw on developments in cognitive and social psychology and relevant areas of philosophy. Appropriate subjects include the use of heuristics, the roles of core values and moral principles in political reasoning, the effects of expertise and sophistication, the roles of affect and emotion, and the nature of cognition and information processing. The emphasis is on systematic and rigorous empirical analysis, and a wide range of methodologies are appropriate: traditional surveys, experimental surveys, laboratory experiments, focus groups, and in-depth interviews, as well as others. These empirically oriented studies also consider normative implications for democratic politics generally.

Politics, not psychology, is the primary focus, and it is expected that most works will deal with mass publics and democratic politics, although work on nondemocratic publics is not excluded. Other works will examine traditional topics in public opinion research, as well as contribute to the growing literature on aggregate opinion and its role in democratic societies.

Other books in the series

Asher Arian, *Security Threatened: Surveying Israeli Opinion on Peace and War*

James DeNardo, *The Amateur Strategist: Intuitive Deterrence Theories and the Politics of the Nuclear Arms Race*

Series list continues on page following the Index

WHAT IS IT ABOUT GOVERNMENT THAT AMERICANS DISLIKE?

EDITED BY

JOHN R. HIBBING
University of Nebraska–Lincoln

ELIZABETH THEISS-MORSE
University of Nebraska–Lincoln

PUBLISHED BY THE PRESS SYNDICATE OF THE UNIVERSITY OF CAMBRIDGE
The Pitt Building, Trumpington Street, Cambridge, United Kingdom

CAMBRIDGE UNIVERSITY PRESS
The Edinburgh Building, Cambridge CB2 2RU, UK
40 West 20th Street, New York, NY 10011-4211, USA
10 Stamford Road, Oakleigh, VIC 3166, Australia
Ruiz de Alarcón 13, 28014 Madrid, Spain
Dock House, The Waterfront, Cape Town 8001, South Africa

http://www.cambridge.org

First published 2001

Printed in the United States of America

Typeface Sabon 10/12 pt. *System* QuarkXPress [BTS]

A catalog record for this book is available from the British Library.

Library of Congress Cataloging in Publication data

What is it about government that Americans dislike? / edited by John R. Hibbing, Elizabeth Theiss-Morse.
p. cm.—(Cambridge studies in political psychology and public opinion)
Includes bibliographical references and index.
ISBN 0-521-79181-2 – ISBN 0-521-79631-8 (pb.)
1. Public administration—United States. 2. Public opinion—United States. 3. Political culture—United States. 4. Political psychology. I. Hibbing, John R. II. Theiss-Morse, Elizabeth. III. Series.
JK2443.W483 2001
320.973–dc21 00-054665

ISBN 0 521 79181 2 hardback
ISBN 0 521 79631 8 paperback

Contents

Figures

Figures

Tables

Contributors

John R. Alford is Associate Professor of Political Science at Rice University.

Stephen Earl Bennett is Professor of Political Science at the University of Cincinnati.

Jeffrey L. Bernstein is Assistant Professor of Political Science at Eastern Michigan University.

David W. Brady is Professor in the Graduate School of Business at Stanford University.

Virginia A. Chanley is Assistant Professor of Political Science at Florida International University.

Jack Citrin is Professor of Political Science at the University of California–Berkeley.

Jack Dennis is Professor of Political Science at the University of Wisconsin–Madison.

Amy Fried is Assistant Professor of Political Science at the University of Maine.

Carolyn L. Funk is Associate Professor of Political Science at Virginia Commonwealth University.

Chris Sissie Hadjiharalambous is Assistant Professor of Political Science at Northern Iowa University.

Douglas B. Harris is Visiting Assistant Professor of Political Science at the University of Texas–Dallas.

Marc J. Hetherington is Assistant Professor of Political Science at Bowdoin College.

John R. Hibbing is Professor of Political Science at the University of Nebraska–Lincoln.

David J. Houston is Associate Professor of Political Science at the University of Tennessee.

Samantha Luks is a graduate student in Political Science at the University of California–Berkeley.

John D. Nugent is a graduate student in Political Science at the University of Texas–Austin.

Diana Owen is Associate Professor of Government at Georgetown University.

Wendy M. Rahn is Associate Professor of Political Science at the University of Minnesota.

Lilliard E. Richardson, Jr., is Associate Professor of Public Administration at the University of Missouri.

Thomas J. Rudolph is a graduate student in Political Science at the University of Minnesota.

Elizabeth Theiss-Morse is Associate Professor of Political Science at the University of Nebraska–Lincoln.

Sean M. Theriault is a graduate student in Political Science at Stanford University.

Tom R. Tyler is Professor of Psychology at New York University.

Eric M. Uslaner is Professor of Government at the University of Maryland.

Introduction
Studying the American People's Attitudes Toward Government

JOHN R. HIBBING AND ELIZABETH THEISS-MORSE

Government is supposed to make the lives of people better. It helps them to "form a more perfect union, establish justice, insure domestic tranquility, provide for the common defense, promote the general welfare, and secure the blessings of liberty." But Americans do not approve of their government. In recent years, only one out of five expressed confidence in the federal government, with state and local levels receiving only slightly higher support (*Washington Post* 1997). Why are people so dissatisfied with something that was intended to do so much good? Has American government failed in its purposes? Or are people upset with government even though it is basically doing the things it is supposed to do? Are Americans inherently dissatisfied with collective action of the sort government embodies or are there things government could be doing that would improve the public's opinion of it? If the latter, should reforms be undertaken in order to lessen the people's disapprobation of government or is disapprobation of the current system preferable to the style of government that would make the people happy?

These are vital questions both for understanding people and for understanding the limitations and potential of political institutions and of politicians in the current environment. Public attitudes toward government clearly influence what government does and how it does it. Public negativity, for example, can affect who runs for, and who stays in, public office (see Fowler and McClure 1989; Theriault 1998), the extent to which new policy initiatives are undertaken by those in office (see Hess 1998), and even the extent to which people comply with the output emanating from those in office (see Tyler 1990).

Given the importance of understanding what it is about government that so upsets people, it is unfortunate that scholarly interest in the topic has not been greater. Perhaps because it has not been seen to culminate in a well-defined behavioral act (such as voting rather than not voting, or voting for Candidate A rather than voting for Candidate B), research on public attitudes toward government lags far behind research on participation and vote choice in terms of the scholarly resources (grant money, journal space, etc.) devoted to it.

Still, interest in public attitudes toward government has been growing of late. The chapters in this volume speak to this renewed interest and, we hope, will serve as a stimulus to even more research. The chapters are united in the goal of trying to understand what it is about government that Americans dislike. While this is the core motivation, the chapter authors pursue this single goal in wonderfully diverse fashions, reflecting the breadth of useful approaches to the topic. We place these individual approaches into three larger groups and organize the volume into three parallel parts (plus a concluding, summary section).

The impression often given in the popular press is that the people "hate" government and that is that. But the truth of the matter is that there have been times when people are more favorable toward government than others, not all institutions of government are disliked by the people in equal measure, and not all actions of public officials are viewed negatively by the public. In fact, it is this variation that allows scholars to gain some compass on the reasons for the generally high levels of public dissatisfaction with government in the United States. By scrutinizing the times government is most disliked, the disliked parts of government, and the disliked actions of governmental officials, important conclusions can be drawn about what causes so many people to be so dissatisfied with their government so much of the time.

The first part of the volume includes the papers that focus on the variations in public approval of government over time, thereby trying to understand public attitudes toward government by seeing when those attitudes are more favorable or less. The second part includes the papers that compare the approval of some parts of government to the approval of other parts, thereby trying to determine if there is a particular institutional arrangement that might be better than others in terms of public approval. And the third part looks not at institutional structure but at the activities of elected officials within those institutions to see if their actions might be responsible for public unhappiness.

Americans' level of satisfaction with government is anything but constant. While all the talk tends to be of scandalously low approval ratings, the reality is that there have been time periods when the public was quite favorable toward government, most notably in the early to mid-1960s. What is it about these periods that leads the public to be more approving of government? Likewise, by noting the common features of periods of public disapproval, perhaps slumping economic conditions, it may be possible to draw conclusions about the larger reasons for public attitudes. In other words, accounting for longitudinal variations in public attitudes could hold the key to understanding what it is that people like and, more often, dislike about government. The first part of the book is composed of four studies that adopt this approach.

Just as it is erroneous to leave the impression that the public's displeasure with government has been constant across time, so too is it erroneous to leave the impression that the public is equally unhappy with all parts of government. The American political system includes a welter of institutions thanks to the federal as well as the power-separating instincts of the founders. The four articles in the second part of this collection take advantage of this wide institutional variation. Specifically, they seek to understand the phenomenon of public disapproval of government by paying careful attention to the institutions (and institutional arrangements) of government that are more or less likely to engender unfavorable reactions. If, say, the public displays a fondness for judicial rather than legislative institutions or for state as opposed to federal institutions that would be valuable information for those eager to understand the reasons for public dissatisfaction.

As important as they are, institutions constitute only part of the American governmental system. After all, within these institutions flesh and blood politicians speak and act in ways likely to have great effects on the public's perceptions of government. The three chapters in the third part of this collection utilize variations in the activities of politicians to determine the kinds of things that heighten public dissatisfaction with government. Perhaps politicians consciously encourage dissatisfaction with government in the hopes of achieving personal political gain, or perhaps they do so unwittingly either by the extreme positions the public sees them expounding or by the unsavory nature of debate on those positions. If so, the solution to public unhappiness may be achievable. We just need to get politicians to behave better.

Appropriately, in the fourth and final part of this volume the contributors step back to reflect on the larger enterprise; the direction it is going and should go. Suggestions are made regarding the measurement of public dissatisfaction with government, the need to do more by way of considering the consequences of public dissatisfaction, and the appropriate theoretical framework for interpreting public dissatisfaction. Together, the essays in this section should be of some assistance to those planning to engage in future research on public attitudes toward government.

Whether the approach taken is to observe the temporal conditions, the institutions, or the politicians, all fourteen of the chapters provide food for thought on the reasons the American public tends to be negative toward its government. Further, they demonstrate the variety of manners in which analytical leverage can be brought to bear on the topic. As such, we hope that they might serve not only as a guide for future research on the topic but as a stimulus for such research. All scholars contributing to this volume are united not just by the desire to understand public attitudes toward government but by the belief that understanding these attitudes is vital in a political system where the people have such potential to shape and to change governmental arrangements. Knowing people's policy positions is not enough. We must also come to grips with their preferences for the processes by which authoritative policy decisions are made. It is in the spirit of this important undertaking that we offer this collection of original research.

Part I

When Do Americans Tend to Be Dissatisfied with Government?

The public's attitude toward government can be measured in a variety of ways, and while in most research endeavors measurement decisions can exercise great influence over the final results, there is one finding that is seemingly impervious to measurement choices. Regardless of the precise wording of the survey questions, results indicate that between 1965 and 1975 Americans became much less favorable toward government. In the mid-1960s and several other earlier time periods, people were actually quite approving and supportive of government. Even after Watergate, there have been times when the public was fairly positive. The mid-1980s is the most notable period, but there was another, briefer one in the late 1990s after the balanced budget agreement and before the impeachment proceedings against President Clinton. The most common public attitude toward government is clearly discontent, but there are enough instances to the contrary to invite scholarly efforts to identify explanations for these ups and downs.

The four contributions in Part I take up the challenge of accounting for longitudinal variations in public attitudes toward government. Every two years, the National Election Studies of the University of Michigan asks a national sample of adults how much of the time "the government in Washington can be trusted to do what is right," and whether they believe "that the government is pretty much run by a few big interests looking out for themselves or is run for the benefit of all people." In the volume's first chapter, Jack Citrin and Samantha Luks attempt to determine why American attitudes as indicated by these two measures have fluctuated the way they have. They document the key trends in public approval of government and demonstrate that these trends seem to be consistent across virtually every demographic group in the country. Whatever causes approval to go up and down, it apparently is a broad force. This finding encourages Citrin and Luks to turn toward such independent variables as economic conditions. "The most obvious basis for increasing trust [in government] would be consistently effective performance, particularly in the economic domain," they write. But they wisely note that what they call a "cultural revolution . . . has shattered older traditions of deference to authority." This along with media practices that accentuate the negative make it unlikely that, even with good economic conditions, public attitudes in the future will return to the levels of the mid-1960s.

John Alford uses data very similar to Citrin and Luks and, not surprisingly, identifies very similar patterns. Like Citrin and Luks, Alford is taken with the consistency of the trends across demographic groups. In fact, he concludes that "the most striking pattern . . . is the breadth and similarity of the trend in trust across all groups." Obviously, the changes in mean level of government approval are not being driven merely by certain subgroups. Thus, Alford, too, is forced to search for a broad explanatory variable. Interestingly, rather than focus on fluctuations in the economy, Alford posits an alternative explanation. Admitting that it is speculative at this point, he reminds us of the strong social psychological evidence of the ability of an external threat to pull people together. Perhaps the end of the Vietnam War, declining interest in foreign-policy matters, and the end of the Cold War has deprived government of the outside threat that in the past has served to unite Americans behind their leaders and their government.

Rather than attempt to explain all of the ups and downs of public attitudes toward government, Stephen Bennett chooses to focus on a brief but fascinating period; specifically, just before the massive decline in public approval. Bennett quite rightly wonders about the accuracy of accepted wisdom that this was a golden era in public attitudes toward government. Since survey data are not available for portions of this period, data must be taken wherever they can be found, so in addition to the occasional survey finding, Bennett creatively utilizes newspaper accounts and published works on American culture of the era. While going to great pains to note that Americans seem to have always had ambivalent feelings toward government, his basic conclusion is that, indeed, attitudes were far more rosy in the late 1950s and early 1960s than they have been since. He even goes so far as to state that "if there was one brief shining moment to Americans' views about their political system, 1960 seems to be that time." No doubt Alford would claim that all the talk of a missile gap successfully conjured up an outside threat that in turn generated more positive views of government.

Part I concludes with Virginia Chanley, Thomas Rudolph, and Wendy Rahn's more detailed study of changes in public attitudes toward government over time. Using a sophisticated process of combining different results from different questions and different surveys, Chanley, Rudolph, and Rahn are able to compute and chart *quarterly* measurements of public attitudes, a substantial departure from the other works in this section that use either years (Citrin and Luks and Alford) or eras (Bennett). Their data cover the period of 1980 to 1997 and show a pattern consistent with that produced by other procedures; namely, favorable attitudes in the mid-1980s and unfavorable attitudes in the early to mid-1990s. Their techniques allow them to probe for the causal direction of relationships. Their findings suggest that trust of the government is an attitude that should be viewed as a variable that *causes* other things and not as something that needs to be explained. For example, they believe that a trusting attitude toward government will increase the chances that a person will become a policy liberal, whereas conventional wisdom probably would have theorized that liberal policy attitudes would increase the likelihood that a person would trust government. In general, like Citrin and Luks, they interpret their findings to support the view that outcomes such as a prosperous economy are important, albeit indirect, influences on attitudes toward government.

1

Political Trust Revisited: Déjà Vu All Over Again?

JACK CITRIN AND SAMANTHA LUKS

A good politician is quite as unthinkable as an honest burglar.

—H. L. Mencken

INTRODUCTION[1]

Trust, once again, is the word on everyone's lips. In the early 1990s, polls recorded a new decline in confidence in America's politicians and government institutions (Lipset 1995; Nye 1997). To many observers (Burnham 1997; Tolchin 1996), the electoral tremor of 1994 expressed feelings of deep anger that subsequent partisan bickering and legislative gridlock would surely reinforce. Good economic times seemed to stop the rot in trust, but with Bill Clinton's travails, Cassandra-like predictions abounded about how a new rise in cynicism toward politics would affect the capacity to govern (Apple 1998).

Such worries are not new, of course. Domestic turmoil in the late 1960s and early 1970s fueled similar anxieties about "the alienated voter" (Schwartz 1973), confidence "gaps" (Lipset and Schneider 1987), and a "crisis of competence" (Sundquist 1980). These convulsive events also spawned empirical research into the causes and significance of political trust (Miller 1974a; Citrin 1974; Citrin et al. 1975; Wright 1976; Hart 1978; Craig 1993). While no one disputed that confidence in government had declined after 1964, the meaning of this trend was controversial from the outset (Miller 1974a; Citrin 1974). The so-called Miller–Citrin debate (1974) centered on two issues: (1) Whether the drop in trust recorded by the American National Election Studies (ANES) signified a growing rejection of the political *regime*, in Easton's

1 An earlier version of this chapter, titled "Revisiting Political Trust in an Angry Age," was presented at the 1997 Annual Meeting of the Midwest Political Science Association.

(1965b) sense of the term (Miller), or just more dissatisfaction with *incumbent* authorities (Citrin); and (2) Whether the main source of rising mistrust was disapproval of the *policies* of *both* main parties (Miller) or unhappiness with the *performance* of the sitting national administration (Citrin).

The recent oscillations in the public's outlook—the loss of trust between 1988 and 1994 and the upward bounce between 1994 and 1996—thus provide an opportunity to reconsider these conflicting interpretations and to formulate a unifying account of the entire pattern of change. The present inquiry explores continuity and change in the foundations of political trust and cynicism by analyzing the ANES surveys from 1964 to 1996 and the 1992–94–96 Panel Study.[2] We begin by commenting on the literature concerning the meaning of political trust. Next, we propose and test a modified version of the model proposed by Citrin and Green (1986) to explain cross-sectional variations in trust between 1980 and 1996. The principal modification is to incorporate attitudes toward Congress as a predictor. This provides a more comprehensive assessment of the influence of performance evaluations and helps identify the effects of changes in the *political* as well as the economic context on the institutional focus of mistrust.

SUPPORT FOR THE SYSTEM OR TRUST IN INCUMBENTS?

This argument about the "object" of the conventional trust in government measures seems settled (Norris 1998; Craig 1993). Easton (1965b) assumed that support for the regime would be more enduring and pervasive than support for incumbent authorities or their policies. He also maintained that the implications of an erosion of support would vary depending on the level of the system. The concept of regime refers to the polity's core principles and values and to its operating rules. Yet the items making up the standard survey indicators of political trust and confidence explicitly ask about the "government in Washington," "administrators," or the "people running" the government or a particular branch of it. Many Americans who give cynical responses to these items nevertheless express pride for "our system of government" (Citrin 1974; Lipset 1995). Additional evidence that these questions stimulate opinions about incumbents is that Republicans consistently are more trusting than Democrats when their party occupies the White House, and vice versa (Pew Research Center 1998; Luks and Citrin 1997). Finally,

2 These data were obtained from the InterUniversity Consortium for Political and Social Research and UC DATA, Survey Research Center, University of California, Berkeley.

between 1980 and 1986, favorable beliefs about the incumbent president's performance and character along with an improved economy triggered an across-the-board rise in trust (Citrin and Green 1986). More generally, the trend in political trust closely tracks changes in the national mood, as indicated by questions about whether or not the country is "on the right track" (Pew Research Center 1998). From Easton's theoretical perspective, the fluctuating impact of short-run events is seen as falling more heavily on evaluations of current office-holders than on support for the political regime as a whole (Norris 1998).

At a minimum, the ANES trust index fails to discriminate between "alienated" cynics, who truly reject the political system, and "performance" or "partisan" cynics, who merely dislike the party in power, the incumbent president, or current government policies. But it seems clear that the latter group is the more numerous. For one thing, to say that one can trust the government to do what is right "only some of the time" hardly bespeaks a desire to transform existing processes or institutions.

On the other hand, political trust and presidential popularity are not identical. Many who approve of the president express mistrust of government "in general;" there is no evidence that trust soared when George Bush's approval rating reached 91 percent just after the Gulf War. One explanation for the sluggishness in political trust is that a component of people's responses to the usual measures is a "ritualistic" disdain for politicians as a class (Citrin 1974). Another is that "the government in Washington" means more than just the president, so his short-run success need not mitigate disapproval of how other institutions, such as Congress, are performing. And to the extent that mistrust reflects a perceived gap between democratic values and entrenched practices, the persistence of low levels when presidential approval climbs arguably indicates that there has been some loss of support for regime processes (Norris 1998).

Upon reflection, the debate between Miller and Citrin probably posed too stark a distinction between support for the political system and trust in the government of the day. It is not simply that these attitudes are empirically interrelated, even in a stable regime like the United States (Citrin et al. 1975). In addition, *both* concepts have multiple referents. For example, the desire to reform the two-party system is a criticism at the regime level, even if it does extend to rejection of other institutional arrangements. Similarly, in the American political system, the key incumbents include both executive and legislative actors. Citrin and Green (1986) argue that feelings about the president drive changes in the level of political trust in part because the presidency dominates news coverage of current politics (Graber 1997). However, they do not explicitly consider the role of attitudes toward Congress, which Feldman (1983) concludes is the cognitive focus of the ANES trust in government questions.

Since "the government in Washington" encompasses both president and Congress, the specific actors whose conduct provokes one's overall level of political trust may vary across individuals or time. Hibbing and Theiss-Morse (1995) argue that the public does make distinctions in how they evaluate individual institutions. Furthermore, divergent attitudes toward the president and Congress may be more prevalent in a period of divided government. These considerations prompt our attention to how the political context may condition the *relative* influence of feelings about president and Congress on one's overall sense of trust in government.

If many streams flow in (or out) of the reservoir of political trust, then whether feelings about the president or about Congress have the heavier impact should depend on how people allocate responsibility for national successes or failures. In other words, reactions to events, doubtless mediated by news coverage, may determine the institutional focus of political trust as well as its overall level. For example, it is plausible that congressional scandals and follies, including the abortive effort at a pay raise, widespread check kiting, and misuse of campaign funds, contributed to the rise in cynicism between 1990 and 1992.

Whatever the institutional focus of mistrust at any given time, the particular aspect of either presidential or congressional conduct that elicits public disaffection is another significant empirical question. For example, is it perceptions of the president's perceived job performance, policies, or personal character that most strongly influence overall feelings of trust in government? Disentangling the relative influences of these beliefs is complicated, since they are inevitably interrelated. Politicians use statements about policy to convey messages about their personal qualities, so someone who approves of the administration's generous attitude toward the poor is likely to view the president as compassionate. Similarly, approval of a forceful foreign policy should reinforce beliefs that the president is a strong leader. Competence and integrity generally are cited as critical for favorable assessment of political institutions and leaders, but, as the trajectory of opinion toward President Clinton indicates, positive ratings on these traits do not always go together. Thus, in this analysis, we shall explore how the political and economic context may affect the chosen criteria for assessing the government's trustworthiness.

HYPOTHESES, DATA, AND METHOD

Trust refers to expectations of future behavior and is based on beliefs about the trustee's competence and sense of fiduciary responsibility

(Barber 1983). Accordingly, one can conceive of mistrust as resulting from a gap between expectations and perceived outcomes. Orren (1997) distinguishes between long-term influences on mistrust, such as the suspicion of power endemic to American political culture and the lack of deference to authority that comes with modernization, and short-run influences, such as national conditions, evaluations of the government's performance, dissatisfaction with policy, and media coverage of scandals and government corruption. The explanation developed here focuses on the role of the more immediate political factors. Our special concern is the stability, at the theoretical level, of the causes of political trust. We ask whether the same factors explain trust when the aggregate level is rising as when it is falling, when a Democrat is president as when a Republican, and when government is unified as when it is divided.

Our starting point is the model of political trust proposed by Citrin and Green (1986). They emphasize the role of presidential leadership and evaluations of the nation's economy in causing the rise in trust during the early 1980s. Our expectation is that these factors remain significant in the 1990s too. However, we modify the Citrin–Green account to consider the influence of evaluations of congressional performance. Since the cognitive association of Congress and "the government in Washington" is natural, satisfaction with this institution also should predict political trust.

The biennial ANES data make it possible to track changes in the focus of popular discontent. The nature of the political environment and the flow of information about current reality should affect which institutions and what specific aspects of their behavior are salient when respondents are asked about their overall level of trust in government as a whole. For example, news about corruption in government may concentrate on members of Congress. If "priming" effects are potent (Iyengar and Kinder 1987), then when one asks about trust in government, widespread exposure to this information should result in a stronger causal influence for attitudes toward Congress as opposed to feelings about the incumbent president. In Zaller's (1992) terms, the accessibility of stored information about Congress will make it an important consideration in forming opinions about the government's trustworthiness.

Turning to methodological issues, the data we analyze are the ANES surveys. In tracking aggregate trends, we start with the 1964 election study. The multivariate analysis begins with the 1980 survey, however, because the earlier surveys did not include measures of key explanatory variables such as presidential character and attitudes toward Congress. We follow Citrin and Green (1986) in using a two-item version of the Trust in Government Index rather than the five-item measure previously used by Miller (1974a) and Citrin (1974). The truncated measure simply sums responses to the questions "How much of the time do you think that the government in Washington can be trusted to do what is right?" and "Would you say that the government is pretty much run by a few big interests looking out for themselves or that it is run for the benefit of all people?"[3] Finally, in reporting trends in trust we employ the summary Percentage Difference Index, which is computed by subtracting the proportion of cynics (two cynical responses) from trusting (two trusting answers) respondents in each designated group. In estimating the multivariate model of trust in government, we use ordinary least squares regression.

SOCIAL AND POLITICAL CONTOURS OF CHANGE IN POLITICAL TRUST

The "Reagan recovery" in political trust ended during his second term, due in part to the corrosive effects of the Iran-Contra revelations (Krosnick and Kinder 1990; Citrin, Green, and Reingold 1987). Trust continued to crumble through the Bush presidency. The decline was variously attributed to the bickering and gridlock characteristic of divided government, the deteriorating economy, Bush's lack of charisma when compared to his predecessor, and congressional scandals. The 1992 election brought unified government, but no end to gridlock, investigations of official malfeasance, or economic anxiety. President Clinton's first two years in office witnessed another upsurge in mistrust, with scores on the ANES index reaching their nadir in 1994. Just as in 1984, sustained economic growth and increased presidential popularity produced a rise in trust between 1994 and 1996.

Table 1.1 compares the trend in political trust among major social and political groups. These data have theoretical relevance in that the pattern of social cleavages is a clue to the motivational basis of mistrust. For example, if rich and poor or black and white move in opposite directions, an implication is that ideological disagreement over distributional issues are salient. On the other hand, if most groups move in the same direction, it is more likely that perceptions of performance on "valence"

3 The resultant three-point index clearly is highly correlated with the earlier, longer measure. Citrin and Green initially employed the truncated version because some of the other items were not included in the surveys they analyzed. In addition, the items about "wasting our tax money" and "crooked administrators" omitted from the short version have a ritualistic flavor and somewhat different objects that on their face are more specific and less "regime-like." In addition, replication of the analysis using the longer version of the trust in government index does not affect the results.

Table 1.1. *Trends in Political Trust, 1964–96*

	1964	1966	1968	1970	1972	1974	1976	1978	1980	1982	1984	1988	1990	1992	1994	1996
Total Sample	47	31	19	–1	–6	–36	–41	–44	–52	–35	–14	–27	–47	–50	–58	–40
Race																
White (not Latino)	47	29	16	2	–2	–35	–33	–46	–55	–33	–11	–23	–50	–53	–59	–42
Black (not Latino)	47	47	36	–26	–42	–59	–46	–35	–35	–46	–38	–48	–54	–51	–56	–33
Party Identification																
Strong Democrat	59	47	38	–16	–28	–38	–60	–26	–33	–42	–30	–47	–54	–46	–36	–19
Weak Democrat	52	43	19	–1	–10	–36	–41	–42	–49	–37	–17	–33	–48	–50	–59	–32
Independent Democrat	58	33	15	0	–25	–39	–62	–42	–54	–49	–41	–32	–55	–62	–59	–43
Independent	31	21	–14	–12	–5	–48	–46	–50	–61	–41	–10	–36	–50	–61	–72	–55
Independent Republican	23	14	13	0	14	–17	–28	–64	–69	–31	–9	–22	–40	–47	–64	–50
Weak Republican	47	21	20	12	12	–32	–27	–46	–59	–10	–3	–11	–43	–40	–57	–48
Strong Republican	19	5	13	26	18	–24	–5	–51	–53	–21	10	1	–27	–43	–66	–55
Congressional Approval																
Approve									–30	–5	5	–7	–22	–13	–31	–24
Neutral									–60	–39	–27	–46	–48	–46	–55	–53
Disapprove									–65	–54	–39	–50	–62	–66	–73	–53
Presidential Job Performance																
Strongly Approve									–23	–9	12	–3	–24	–29	–35	–18
Not Strongly Approve									–37	–25	–5	–17	–44	–40	–54	–39
Not Strongly Disapprove									–60	–40	–41	–44	–57	–49	–64	–55
Strongly Disapprove									–68	–60	–49	–54	–77	–65	–75	–70

(continued)

Table 1.1 *(continued)*

	1964	1966	1968	1970	1972	1974	1976	1978	1980	1982	1984	1988	1990	1992	1994	1996
Personal Financial Situation Compared to Last Year																
Better		44	30	9	–2	–31	–28	–30	–45	–20	1	–15	–36	–40	–51	–30
Same		30	16	–4	–6	–36	–44	–47	–48	–33	–19	–29	–53	–50	–59	–43
Worse		13	6	–3	–28	–41	–51	–56	–61	–47	–32	–44	–55	–57	–67	–53
Affect Toward Major Parties																
Positive–Positive	48		43		29		–12	–17	–46	–12	14	–9	–17	–25	–44	–20
Positive–Neutral	61		27		4		–25	–36	–43	–23	–6	–20	–18	–35	–38	–27
Positive–Negative	46		18		–11		–44	945	–52	–42	–25	–30	–63	–54	–62	–43
Neutral–Neutral	52		18		–1		–36	–42	–52	–26	–4	–29	–45	–44	–56	–32
Negative–Neutral	36		8		–33		–51	–57	–62	–49	–27	–27	–63	–64	–70	–49
Negative–Negative	0		12		–32		–69	–75	–77	–49	–45	–46	–77	–66	–84	–70

Note: Entries are percentage difference index scores: the percentage of respondents giving two trusting responses to the trust government and big interest items, minus the percentage giving two cynical responses.
Source: American National Election Studies.

questions such as peace and prosperity are motivating responses about trusting the government.

Our results support the latter interpretation. Just as in earlier decades, the recent data find few demographic fault-lines in the public's outlook. The decline in trust after 1986 was an across-the-board phenomenon (Alford, this volume; Pew Research Center 1998). Blacks and whites, men and women, young and old, rich and poor consistently moved in the same direction. Table 1.1, however, also points to the influence of support for the incumbent president on trust in government. During the Reagan-Bush years, whites expressed more trust than blacks; with Clinton in office, the opposite is true.

The evidence of strong period effects in Table 1.1 indicates that whatever one's party affiliation or ideological identification, one swims with the cynical (or trusting) tide. For example, both strong Democrats and strong Republicans became more trusting between 1994 and 1996. But there is also a partisan component in changing attitudes. All groups became more trusting during Reagan's first term, but the largest shift took place among Republican identifiers. With Clinton in the White House, Democrats changed the most. Nevertheless, we do find that respondents who are negative about *both* major parties tend to be more cynical than any other group, including those who like the "ins" and dislike the "outs."[4]

Table 1.1 also supports earlier findings about the significance of economic conditions in influencing the level of trust in government (Citrin and Green 1986; House and Mason 1975). In the 1990s, as earlier, people whose financial situations are improving express more political trust than those whose circumstances are worsening. Interestingly, this relationship seemed relatively weak in 1994, perhaps because economic issues were less salient during an election dominated by the Republican attack on the size and ineffectiveness of the federal government.

PRESIDENT AND CONGRESS?

The bivariate relationships reported in Table 1.1 also show that approval of how *both* the president and Congress are doing is associated consistently with generalized feelings of political trust. This relationship persists in the 1990s, when the level of public approval of Congress dropped sharply. Moreover, as shown in Table 1.2, the size of the correlations between trust in government scores and approval of the

4 This analysis was based on Wattenberg's (1996) technique of summing the number of "likes" and "dislikes" expressed in open-ended responses about the Democratic and Republican parties (Luks and Citrin 1997).

Table 1.2. *Correlations Between Political Trust and Approval Ratings*

	1980	1982	1984	1988	1990	1992	1994	1996
Presidential Approval	0.24	0.26	0.30	0.27	0.25	0.18	0.20	0.25
Congressional Approval	0.22	0.28	0.25	0.25	0.26	0.34	0.32	0.19
Approval of Own Representative	0.04*	0.10	0.10	0.14	0.08	0.08	0.11	0.03*
Correlation Between Congressional Approval and Presidential Approval	0.24	0.19	0.08	0.02*	0.14	0.11	0.30	–0.07*

Note: * Not significant at $p < .05$.

president's and Congress's performance, respectively, generally are very similar, even when the relationship between evaluations of the executive and legislative branches diminishes, understandably, during years of divided government. In 1992 and 1994, however, the link between attitudes toward Congress and political trust seemed distinctively strong, congruent with accounts that the public's anger was aimed at incumbent legislators at that time (Mann and Ornstein 1994).

Overall, these trends suggest important continuities in the causes of political trust over more than three decades. Events matter, exerting a potent and similar influence on the attitudes of every social and political group. Political trust, as conventionally measured, taps a diffuse orientation toward government founded on evaluations of incumbent authorities. But it is not just the president whose performance is critical for trust. The public desires peace, prosperity, and a modicum of honesty in government, and Table 1.2 indicates that the public tends to hold each of the major policy-making branches jointly and severally responsible for how well the country is doing on these "valence" issues.[5]

There also is a partisan component of political trust. Even during periods of divided government, a lack of affiliation with the party controlling the presidency lowers one's level of trust. But if partisan effects are strong, it is puzzling that approval of each branch of a divided government contributed *independently* to overall trust. One explanation may be that there are differences between groups with convergent and divergent evaluations of the president and Congress, respectively. In fact, Table 1.3 reveals an intriguing difference in the level of political aware-

5 This conclusion is buttressed by the finding that respondents' feelings about their own representative, as opposed to Congress as a whole, have only weak and inconsistent associations with trust in government.

Table 1.3. Correlation Coefficients Between Presidential Approval and Congressional Approval by Political Awareness

	1992	1994	1996
Low Awareness	0.24	0.31	0.15
Medium Awareness	0.10	0.31	–0.07*
High Awareness	–0.13	0.26	–0.33

Note: Entries are Pearson Coefficients; * not significant at 0.05 level.

ness among these groups of respondents.[6] In 1994, when the Democrats controlled both institutions, approval of the president and Congress were positively correlated all along the continuum of political sophistication. When partisan control of "the government in Washington" was divided in 1992 and 1996, this relationship still prevailed among those with little political awareness. Among the politically knowledgeable, however, approval of the president and Congress were negatively associated, particularly in 1996 when the ideological confrontation between the two branches was intense. This pattern suggests that for those lacking political interest and information, "government" is a relatively undifferentiated object that is evaluated as a whole on the basis of global events. The politically sophisticated, by contrast, have a more complex image of government that differentiates among specific institutions. Since this group is more likely to know and care about "position" issues, it is here that policy preferences should have a relatively stronger influence on evaluations of incumbent authorities and, ultimately, on political trust.

THE CAUSES OF TRUST THROUGH POLITICAL TIME

In charting the contours of trends in political trust, we have described a series of overlapping correlations. To determine the robustness of these relationships and the interplay among the hypothesized causes of political trust, we turn to the multiple regression analysis reported in

6 Political awareness is measured by an index comprised of the interviewer's rating of the respondent and correct answers to questions about current politicians, party differences, and constitutional provisions. Because the items varied from one year to the next, the low, middle, and high groups are trichotomies of the distribution of index scores, with about 30% in the low group, 40% in the middle, and 30% in the high awareness group. A full discussion of these measures can be found in Luks (1998).

Table 1.4.[7] The model estimated revises the Citrin and Green (1986) equation by adding the respondent's approval of Congress as a predicted variable and by coding age as a series of categorical variables. Feldman (1983) maintains that trust in government reflects evaluations of institutions (such as Congress) more than reactions to individual leaders (such as the president). Yet the capacity of the average citizen to make the distinction between institution and incumbent is an open question. In any event, since neither feelings about the presidency as an institution nor approval of specific congressional leaders are measured, this hypothesis cannot be tested directly.[8]

The main finding of Table 1.4 is continuity in the underpinnings of political trust. Whether a Republican or Democrat is president, whether there is unified or divided partisan control of national government, and whether times are good or bad, the underlying structure of causality is essentially the same. As one would predict, the effects of demographic group membership on political trust generally are mediated by the influences of political predispositions or beliefs about presidential or congressional performance. More significantly, the causal influences of both party affiliation and ideological orientation also are explained by the intervening role of approval of incumbent authorities.

The inclusion of evaluations of Congress as a predictor does not alter the finding that both the president's job performance and his personal image significantly affect trust in government (Citrin and Green 1986). Table 1.4 also shows that economic judgments retain a significant independent effect on political trust in the full model, even after we controlled for the impact of beliefs about the performance of incumbent authorities. The model includes both reports about one's own and the nation's economic situation as predictors; in every year, one or both of these interrelated indicators has a significant causal influence. Finally, these data confirm the speculation that approval of Congress has an influence on political trust, independent of how one evaluates the president, and that the relative causal impact of these feelings is roughly the same.[9]

7 The table reports results for the presidential election years of 1980, 1984, 1988, 1992, and 1996. The surveys before 1980 did not include questions about approval of presidential or congressional performance. In addition, we include the off-year 1994 study because of our interest in assessing the contextual influence of events focusing on the performance of Congress.

8 When the question about how respondents evaluate their own member of Congress is added as a predictor, this variable fails to achieve a statistically significant effect on trust in government.

9 The presidential approval variable is scaled from 1 to 5, whereas approval of congress is scaled from 1 to 3, making the magnitude of its unstandardized regression

Table 1.4. *Explaining Political Trust*

	1980		1984		1988		1992		1994		1996	
	Unstd. Coeff.	Std. Coeff.	Unstd. Coeff.	Std. Coeff.	Unstd. Coeff.	Std. Coeff.	Unstd. Coeff.	Std. Coeff.	Unstd. Coeff.	Std. Coeff.	Unstd. Coeff.	Std. Coeff.
Presidential Approval (strongly disapprove = 1 to strongly approve = 5)	0.04*	0.09	0.09***	0.17	0.06**	0.12	0.04**	0.09	0.02	0.04	0.04*	0.08
	(0.02)		(0.02)		(0.02)		(0.01)		(0.02)		(0.02)	
President Moral (strongly disagree = 1 to strongly agree = 4)	0.03	0.04	0.07*	0.07	0.14***	0.13	0.02	0.02	0.07*	0.90	0.15***	0.17
	(0.03)		(0.03)		(0.03)		(0.02)		(0.03)		(0.03)	
President Strong Leader (strongly disagree = 1 to strongly agree = 4)	0.13***	0.16	0.07*	0.07	0.00	0.00	0.05*	0.06	0.07*	0.90	0.10**	0.11
	(0.03)		(0.03)		(0.03)		(0.02)		(0.03)		(0.03)	
Approval of Congress	0.11***	0.15	0.19***	0.21	0.22***	0.26	0.23***	0.30	0.18***	0.25	0.16***	0.21
(disapprove = 1 to approve = 3)	(0.02)		(0.02)		(0.02)		(0.02)		(0.02)		(0.02)	
Party Identification (strong Dem. = 1 to strong Rep. = 7)	0.02	0.05	–0.01	–0.01	0.02	0.06	0.00	–0.01	0.01	0.04	0.02	0.05
	(0.01)		(0.01)		(0.01)		(0.01)		(0.01)		(0.01)	
R Liberal/Conservative (strong liberal = 1 to strong conservative = 7)	–0.01	–0.02	0.01	0.01	–0.01	–0.02	–0.01	–0.01	0.01	0.01	0.00	0.01
	(0.02)		(0.02)		(0.02)		(0.01)		(0.02)		(0.02)	
Personal Financial Situation	0.04	0.06	0.06*	0.05	0.06*	0.06	0.04	0.05	0.06*	0.08	0.04	0.04
(worse = 1 to better = 3)	(0.02)		(0.03)		(0.03)		(0.02)		(0.02)		(0.03)	
National Economy (much worse = 1 to much better = 5)	0.06*	0.07	0.03	0.04	0.04	0.05	0.04*	0.06	0.04*	0.07	0.07***	0.11
	(0.03)		(0.02)		(0.02)		(0.02)		(0.02)		(0.02)	

(continued)

Table 1.4 *(continued)*

	1980		1984		1988		1992		1994		1996	
	Unstd. Coeff.	Std. Coeff.	Unstd. Coeff.	Std. Coeff.	Unstd. Coeff.	Std. Coeff.	Unstd. Coeff.	Std. Coeff.	Unstd. Coeff.	Std. Coeff.	Unstd. Coeff.	Std. Coeff.
Age												
17–29	–0.03	–0.02	0.02	0.01	0.01	0.00	0.11*	0.06	–0.17**	–0.11	–0.03	–0.01
	(0.06)		(0.07)		(0.06)		(0.05)		(0.06)		(0.07)	
30–44	0.04	0.02	0.01	0.00	–0.13*	–0.08	0.05	0.03	–0.12*	–0.09	0.03	0.02
	(0.07)		(0.06)		(0.06)		(0.04)		(0.05)		(0.06)	
45–59	–0.12	–0.07	0.03	0.01	0.03	0.02	0.07	0.04	–0.08	–0.05	0.14*	0.08
	(0.07)		(0.07)		(0.06)		(0.05)		(0.06)		(0.06)	
Female	–0.08*	–0.06	0.09*	0.06	–0.04	–0.02	0.02	0.02	0.02	0.01	–0.05	–0.03
	(0.04)		(0.04)		(0.04)		(0.03)		(0.04)		(0.04)	
Nonwhite	0.03	0.02	–0.03	–0.01	–0.09	–0.04	0.01	0.00	–0.13*	–0.06	–0.07	–0.03
	(0.07)		(0.07)		(0.06)		(0.05)		(0.06)		(0.06)	
Non-South	0.00	0.00	–0.06	–0.04	0.03	0.02	–0.01	–0.01	0.09*	0.06	–0.07	–0.04
	(0.05)		(0.05)		(0.04)		(0.03)		(0.04)		(0.04)	
Education	0.02	0.03	0.02	0.03	0.04*	0.06	0.00	0.00	0.00	0.00	0.02	0.03
(low = 1 to high = 5)	(0.02)		(0.02)		(0.02)		(0.02)		(0.02)		(0.02)	
Income	0.00	–0.01	–0.02	–0.02	0.05*	0.06	–0.02	–0.03	–0.02	–0.03	–0.02	–0.03
(low = 1 to high = 5)	(0.02)		(0.02)		(0.02)		(0.02)		(0.02)		(0.02)	
Constant	0.60		0.48		0.17		0.67		0.55		0.20	
	(0.17)		(0.15)		(0.15)		(0.12)		(0.17)		(0.18)	
R-squared	0.10		0.15		0.18		0.14		0.13		0.14	
N	1,002		1,403		1,350		1,790		1,102		1,292	

Note: Entries are unstandardized and standardized OLS coefficients; standard errors in parentheses. * $p < .05$. ** $p < .01$. *** $p < .001$.
Source: American National Election Studies.

The increased influence of the approval of Congress variable in the 1992 and 1994 data supports our contention that events channel attention to the trustworthiness of specific institutions. The political context also may influence which dimensions of presidential character inspire trust. Citrin and Green (1986) hypothesized that during periods of crisis and national pessimism, the public craves direction and strong leadership. Table 1.4 shows that in the 1988, 1994, and 1996 surveys, the belief that the president was moral was a strong influence on trust in government. In 1992, however, no such relationship emerged, but the image of the president as a strong leader did matter. We speculate, therefore, that while scandals such as Iran-Contra or Whitewater may prime people to tie confidence in government to their leader's integrity, when the state of the economy is the most salient political issue, trust is based more strongly on perceptions of the president's competence than his moral rectitude.

DISCUSSION

We have revisited earlier debates about the meaning of political trust by examining public opinion in the early 1990s when the nation's dominant mood seemed angry and disillusioned. Deja vu. Now, as before, dissatisfaction with the state of the nation, filtered through evaluations of incumbent authorities, underpins a loss of generalized confidence in government. Whatever the roots of political trust in early socialization (Easton and Dennis 1969; Jennings and Niemi 1981), lifelong openness corresponds most to this attitude toward government. When opinion moves, people of all ages and background tend to shift in the same direction.

While our analysis relies exclusively on the ANES Trust in Government items, the General Social Survey Confidence in Institutions questions produce similar results (Brehm and Rahn 1997). The 1998 Pew Survey confirms that the performance of government and opinions about the dishonesty and self-interestedness of political leaders are the main causes of distrust. This study also speculates that worry about the moral health of American society is suppressing the rise in political

coefficients appear larger. In addition, the presidential approval, president moral, and president strong leader variables are interrelated, of course, and including all three as predictors "splits" the variance accounted for by any one. If one rescales these variables and compares the standardized coefficients, approval of Congress generally has an apparently stronger effect than any single one of the three indicators concerning the president although not stronger than their joint effect, except in 1992 and 1994.

confidence engendered by a thriving economy. Nevertheless, most citizens with mistrusting attitudes view themselves as frustrated, not deeply angry.

The foundations of trust in government, then, are largely political in nature. Though fundamentally correct, the account proposed by Citrin and Green (1986) is incomplete. Approval of Congress, an excluded variable in their original model, turns out to be a robust predictor of trust in government scores. A broader view of the institutional focus of political trust permits a more nuanced explanation of shifts in the public's outlook. Attitudes toward Congress seemingly were more important sources of political trust in the early 1990s than previously, we believe, because of heightened attention to its performance during a period of intense executive–legislative conflict and the involvement of prominent legislators in a series of scandals.

One obvious task for future research, therefore, is to identify the ingredients of generalized approval of Congress, much as Citrin and Green decomposed evaluations of the president into beliefs about performance, policy, and personality. In the same vein, is approval of Congress based upon ideological agreement with the majority party's policies, opinions about prominent leaders such as the speaker of the House, or judgments about the fairness of internal rules and procedures?

A second question to explore concerns the manner in which people combine their attitudes toward the presidency and Congress, respectively. For the less politically engaged segment of the public, an undifferentiated image of government seems to prevail, fueling an apparent tendency to project feelings about one institution onto the other. More generally, the impact of divided government on the foundations of political trust deserves additional study. By impeding change and enhancing the need to compromise, this circumstance increases the frustration of those at both ends of the ideological spectrum. This may accentuate the impact of policy dissatisfaction on confidence in government, although the institutional focus of mistrust would differ for liberals and conservatives.

Our explanation of trends in the level and focus of political trust emphasizes the role of "contextual" factors. This broad term, however, fails to specify what features of the political environment are salient and when. Indeed, a faint odor of tautology emanates from the proposition that satisfaction with the conduct of incumbent authorities is the proximate cause of trust in government. We therefore need to probe the nature of earlier links in the causal chain. The economy matters for approval of the president, but it is not all that matters; the erosion of political trust began in the mid-1960s when times were good (Lawrence 1997). A comprehensive account of political trust should consider the role of economic and social conditions, the public's perceptions of the nation's problems, and citizens' expectations of government in shaping evaluations of political leaders. Clearly too, there may be group differences in these expectations and perceptions that depend on people's underlying values and interests. The Pew Study (Pew Research Center 1998) concluded that cynicism about the honesty of leaders is especially critical to distrust among Americans who came of age after Vietnam and Watergate, while performance failures are more important to older generations.

How people interpret the current state of the nation is also a function of what and how they learn about political events and outcomes. Here the interplay between "reality" and "mediality" is significant. Do real-world cues or media frenzies change or reinforce opinions about the trustworthiness of government? The Reception–Acceptance model's axioms regarding the impact of prior attitudes and political sophistication on one's susceptibility to news stories (Zaller 1992) is a useful starting point for addressing this question. For example, some have speculated that the reason that allegations about President Clinton's perjury and adultery had a limited impact is that cynicism about all political leaders is already deeply entrenched.

IMPLICATIONS

Anxiety about the consequences of declining political trust is one motivation for diagnosing its causes. In addressing the "so what" question, it is important to disentangle the specific objects of eroding trust. Since so many Americans mistrust politicians as a class while remaining deeply attached to the political community and to underlying democratic principles, a drop in confidence, even if sustained, poses little threat to the stability of existing institutions. Moreover, to some degree the long-run increase in political cynicism reflects a change in how people speak about politics. The dominant discourse is critical. From talk shows to *Saturday Night Live*, no one hesitates to mock and denigrate the nation's top leaders. But as linguistic standards change, so may the emotional significance and behavioral implications of verbal expressions of mistrust.

Criticism of the political process does not necessarily imply disengagement. Political cynicism, at least as measured by the ANES items, does not stimulate voter apathy (Luks and Citrin 1997). There is no relationship between trust and turnout at the individual level, and the politically cynical and trusting are equally likely to engage in more intense forms of electoral participation such as attending rallies or displaying bumper stickers (Citrin and Luks 1998).

Political mistrust stimulates voice rather than exit. There is a strong association between mistrust and voting against the incumbent president or his party's candidate. This anti-incumbent effect remains statistically significant even after one imposes a rigorous set of controls (Hetherington 1997; Luks and Citrin 1997). Thus, rising mistrust, if based on realistic assessments of governmental performance, may contribute to the maintenance of democratic accountability through electoral change.

On a day-to-day level, government functions smoothly when citizens voluntarily obey the law, even when it entails personal sacrifice. For example, belief in the fairness of authorities boosts compliance in paying taxes (Scholz and Pinney 1995) and a willingness to comply with government-sponsored restrictions on water usage (Tyler and Degoey 1995). This implies that widespread trust facilitates the mobilization of citizens when the government proposes policies requiring cooperation and sacrifice. Still, there is little evidence that lower levels of political trust have produced a nation of scofflaws.

In bemoaning the decline of trust in the 1960s and 1970s, several theorists "blamed the victim" (Crozier, Huntington, and Watanuki 1975); weakening confidence was due to the excessive demands of citizens rather than the failures of ruling elites. Today, a populist perspective seems more appropriate. Trust is a gamble that others will act responsibly on one's behalf. So continued trust is rational only if it is earned (Hardin 1993). It may be wise to give someone with an established reputation the benefit of the doubt, but foolish to entrust one's interests to a proven failure.

The political relevance of declining trust in government may lie in how a suspicious climate of opinion shapes the decisions of politicians rather than the actions of ordinary citizens. It is often argued that when the reservoir of trust is low and people are unwilling to give their leaders the benefit of the doubt, the government becomes timid, shunning innovation and failing to make necessary, if potentially costly, commitments. A president who lacks credibility cannot use his bully pulpit effectively. Whether this is worrisome, however, depends on the wisdom of the proposed undertakings.

A cynical climate of opinion probably emboldens opposition forces, fueling demands for changes in public policy. The erosion of trust in recent decades almost certainly contributed to the passage of conflict of interest regulations, changes in campaign finance rules, ethics committees in Congress, term limits in many states, and even the independent prosecutor law. Taken together, these measures significantly altered how government functions, without constituting a revolution in the normal sense of that term.

Political Trust Revisited

Since a return to the confidence levels of the 1960s seems unlikely, the fact that mistrust is not always malign is comforting. The most obvious basis for increasing trust would be consistently effective performance, particularly in the economic domain. The belief that government has a universal realm and must deal with virtually every important problem, however, makes setbacks inevitable. Moreover, the proliferation of combative social movements and the ideological polarization of the political parties undermine the development of a consensus on how to solve these problems. Add to this the cultural revolution that has shattered older traditions of deference to authority and media practices that accentuate the negative about politics. In sum, the cynical zeitgeist is unlikely to vanish.

In this context, shared values are another potential basis for boosting trust. People are more likely to trust authorities whose personal characteristics imply this mutuality of interests. The American dilemma is reaching common ground in a diverse society where every faction can advocate its particular viewpoint. Finally, trust may be based on the belief that institutional *processes* encourage dutiful conduct and punish wrongdoing. Reforms that demonstrate commitment to these norms thus can have symbolic as well as substantive importance. As this suggests, political trust is never fully realized; its production is an ongoing process of exchange between citizens and authorities.

2

We're All in This Together
The Decline of Trust in Government, 1958–1996

JOHN R. ALFORD

Ideologies separate us. Dreams and anguish bring us together.
—Eugene Ionesco

Decline has played a central role in the postwar study of American politics. Party decline, the decline in marginal House districts, and the decline in voting turnout, have all been detailed and commented on extensively as descriptive trends. The search for the causes and consequences of these major shifts has produced a large and diverse empirical literature. Recently, the decline in trust in government has re-emerged as a major topic in both public and scholarly debate. The fact that we lack experimental control over most of our interesting independent variables undoubtedly accounts for much of the importance that these declines have played in the research literature. Each decline represents stochastic variation on a grand scale. Even if the subject matter of these shifts had been relatively trivial, the impulse to analyze the resulting variation would have been powerful. As it happens, all of these shifts, including the decline in trust, have been of substantial theoretical and practical significance. The decline in trust seems to have struck a particularly responsive nerve, with a rising chorus of vocal concern about its impact on the future of American political life, not only from scholars, but also from journalists, politicians, and the public. While modern political science is often criticized for a lack of relevance to the real world, the decline in trust represents a major example of an issue that has generated both scholarly *and* real-world concerns. The empirical questions of what happened, why it happened, and what the likely impacts will be are not merely intellectual puzzles, they are questions of genuine import.

The intention here is to address in some detail the pattern of decline in trust in government over time. A careful look at the nature of a change can often help in our search for its cause, or at the least allow us to rule out some of the potential suspects. Much of what follows is similar in spirit to earlier analyses in this area, most notably that of Miller (1974a), Citrin (1974), and later Lipset and Schneider (1987). While very much in the spirit of these excellent earlier explorations, the analysis here covers a broader time span and focuses more exclusively on a visual analysis of how the time lines for different demographic and political subgroups compare over this period.

The value of this approach is twofold. Much of what we think we know about the cross-sectional correlates of trust in government may be time-bound. A look across forty years should provide a clearer picture of what is perennial and what is ephemeral. Turning to explaining the decline in trust, explanations for the decline in trust that are difficult to reconcile with a detailed look at the actual pattern of decline must be considered suspect. Details of both timing and of subgroup impact should mesh with the proffered causes.

MEASURING TRUST IN GOVERNMENT OVER TIME

While many available survey measures contained in many diverse surveys offer a view of trust in government, I will limit my attention to a single measure. The Center for Political Studies' American National Election Study (ANES) series of election surveys provides the longest stable time series for a key trust measure: "How much of the time do you think you can trust the government in Washington to do what is right?"[1] The question is preceded by an introduction that explicitly directs the respondents away from "Democrats or Republicans in particular" and toward "government in general." This is the best match among the ANES questions to the general thrust of what we mean when we say trust in government has declined and is superior to a "trust index" that combines other extraneous concerns.[2] This question is also a good time-series indicator, since

1 The source for all the data used in this chapter is: Miller, Warren E., and the National Election Studies. American National Election Studies Cumulative Data File, 1948–1996 (computer file). 9th ICPSR version. Ann Arbor, MI: University of Michigan, Center for Political Studies (producer), 1998. Ann Arbor, MI: Inter-University Consortium for Political and Social Research (distributor), 1998.

2 Four additional measures of regard for the government have been asked with some regularity in the ANES series; a question about whether government "is pretty much run by a few big interests looking out for themselves or . . . it is run for the benefit of all," whether respondents believe that the government is run by smart people who mostly know what they are doing, how much of our tax money the respondent thinks the government wastes, and respondents' perception of how many of the people running government are crooked. None of these represent as complete a time series as the general trust question and the trends for each are very

it has been asked with essentially no variation beginning in 1958 and again in 1964 and then in every election year since.[3]

THE TREND IN TRUST OVER TIME

Figure 2.1 shows the trend in trust over time using all four of the response categories. Looking first at the two extreme categories should provide a measure of comfort. The proportion of the American public that has no trust in the government is very small and has been throughout this period. This may account for the fact that the widely discussed collapse of trust in government has not produced the sort of severe negative consequences that some have envisioned. At the other extreme, trusting the government "just about always" peaked at only 18% in 1966, immediately dropped below 10% in 1968, and hasn't been out of single digits since. Thus even at its peak, trust in government over this period never reached a level that suggested a dangerous excess of trust, as over 80% of the public retained a measure of skepticism about Washington. Figure 2.1 also makes it clear that the real shift has been one from a public that largely trusted its government "most of the time" to a public that largely trusts its government only "some of the time."

For the purposes of the rest of this analysis we can simplify the over-time picture of trust by combining the two categories that broadly indicate trust ("most of the time" and "just about always") into one "trusting" category. This has become common practice and simplifies the picture without sacrificing a clear delineation of the shift in levels of trust over this period. The remaining two categories combined into a "nontrusting" category would simply be the reflex of the line for the combined "trusting" category and so can be eliminated from the figures without any loss of information.

What does the broad trend in combined trust alone tell us? Trust was high in the late 1950s and early 1960s, with three-quarters of the public in one of the two trusting categories. By the late 1960s a decline in trust was clearly underway. This decline bottomed out in 1980, with three-quarters of the public in one of the two nontrusting categories. In just fifteen years the country went from one dominated by public trust to a mirror image dominated by public mistrust. Clearly, Watergate can't bear the blame for triggering this slide in trust. True, the largest two-year drop

similar over this time period to that discussed here for the general trust in government question.

3 An additional response category of "almost never" was offered in 1966, but this was not used in any other year, and its impact is minimized by the collapsed categories used here.

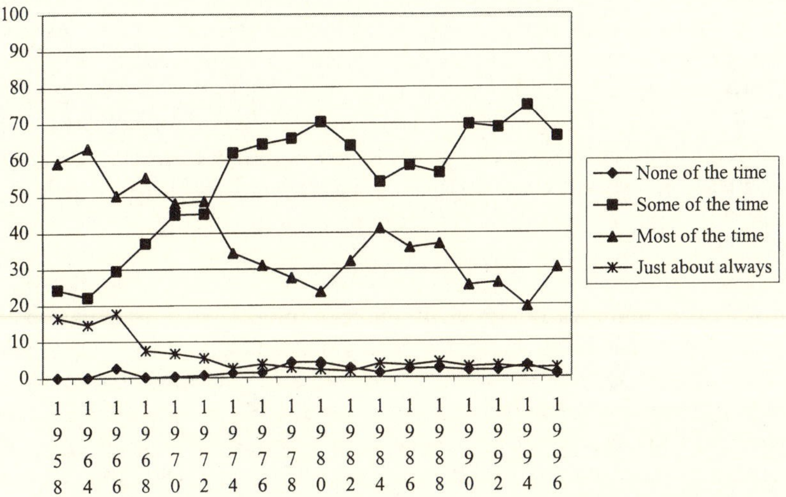

Figure 2.1. Trust Government in Washington to Do What Is Right.

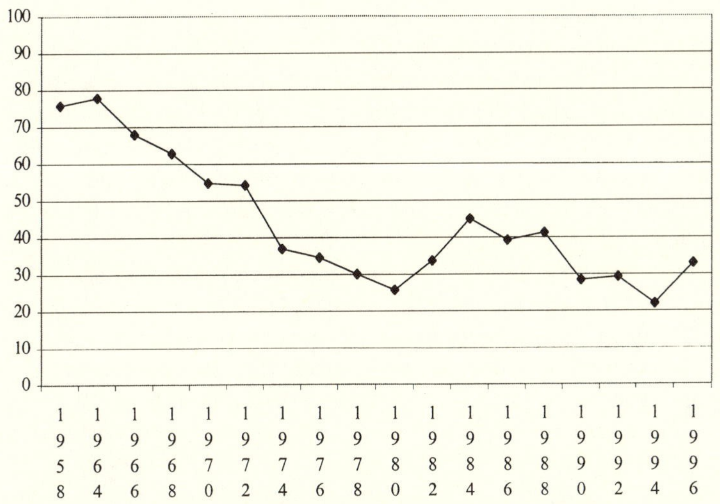

Figure 2.2. Trust Government in Washington Most or All of the Time.

(seventeen percentage points) came between 1972 and 1974, but trust was already twenty-three points below its 1964 high by then. Indeed, the steep drop in trust is essentially linear from its inception around 1963 until it began to slow its decline after 1974, dropping only another eleven points before halting its decline in 1980. By 1980, trust had dropped over fifty percentage points. The recovery of trust in the first Reagan administration was significant (nearly twenty points in four years), but too brief to even carry trust back to the 50% level, and a new downturn was already underway by the end of Reagan's second term. By 1994 that downturn would carry trust to its lowest point in the thirty-eight year history of the survey question. The nearly eleven point jump between 1994 and 1996 could be the start of second rebound in trust, but must await the 1998 and 2000 survey results for confirmation.

SUBGROUP ANALYSIS

Just as the timing can help to eliminate some potential explanations of changes in trust in government, so can careful analysis of patterns of trust across different subgroups of the public. What kinds of patterns are we looking for here? If trust is driven by reactions to the policy choices made in Washington, then we should see some evidence of divergent trends in trust. We could argue, for example, that the Great Society programs, while boosting trust among liberals, African Americans, urban dwellers, the poor, and Democrats, simultaneously reduced trust among conservatives, rural residents, the wealthy, and Republicans.[4] The overall level of trust would drop if the benefitted group was smaller than the offended group, or if the level of impact on trust was greater for one side. The latter would be a variant of the asymmetry of likes and dislikes argument, in which trust among the supporters and beneficiaries of a policy would remain unchanged or increase only slightly, while trust among the angry opponents of the policy would show a decided decline. The net effect would be a policy related decline in overall levels of trust.

If, on the other hand, basic demographic or attitudinal shifts are behind the changes in levels of trust in government, then we would expect a quite distinct pattern. Such a compositional change in trust would arise if two groups had very different, but basically stable, levels of trust, and the relative size of the two groups changed over time. For example, we might find that higher levels of formal education were

4 Note that this use of demographic and attitudinal groups is distinct from the simple rejection of group sources of trust notable in both Miller (1974a) and Citrin (1974). The idea here is not to look simply at static levels of trust but rather at the entire political cycle of trust across nearly forty years. Policy dissatisfaction in the sense that both Miller and Citrin meant it cannot easily be thought of as remaining constant in its arrangement across groups for such a long and varied policy history. The very policy responses that they credit with causing distrust would have to lead eventually to some predictable group variations in levels of trust.

associated with fairly stable low levels of trust across this period, while in contrast, low levels of formal education were associated with fairly stable high levels of trust. This would mean that some major part of the decline in the overall level of trust could be attributed to the increasing levels of formal education over this period. In terms of trend lines, if we find trend lines that are essentially level for each subgroup across this period, then we have the visual hallmark of compositional change. A set of flat lines for subcategories on one of these charts would be the equivalent of forcing variation to the marginals in a cross tabulation with controls.

Several other patterns provide useful indications. If the trend lines for the subgroups move together and are closely intertwined, then the characteristic that defines the subgroups is unrelated to both the level of trust and to changes in the level of trust. For example, we might well expect that the trend lines for various astrological signs would not show any particular degree of separation either over time or at any given point in time. In contrast, if we see a consistent gap between essentially "parallel" trend lines, then we have subgroups that do have real and persistent differences in their baseline levels of trust, but these subgroups share a common trust dynamic in that their levels of trust rise and fall together. Liberals, for example, might always be substantially more trusting in government than conservatives, but both groups might share parallel declines in trust over time. Both the "intertwined" pattern and the "parallel" pattern suggest that the cause of the variation in levels of trust over time would have to be irrelevant to the characteristic that defines the subgroups. In statistical terms the causal variable would be orthogonal to the group variable.

With this in mind, examining a broad set of subgroup patterns for key demographic and attitudinal variables should allow considerable insight into the nature of the cause of the decline in trust in government. A varied set of results across figures should allow us to zero in on specific government-policy concerns and/or compositional shifts that are related to the decline in trust. A more uniform set of results across figures would suggest the elimination of an entire class of explanations.

DEMOGRAPHICS AND THE DECLINE IN TRUST

Race

Racial differences in a wide variety of opinion areas and political behaviors are well documented in the literature. It seems likely that these differences would extend to trust in government. Beginning in the mid-sixties, the Federal government took on a strong role in advancing civil

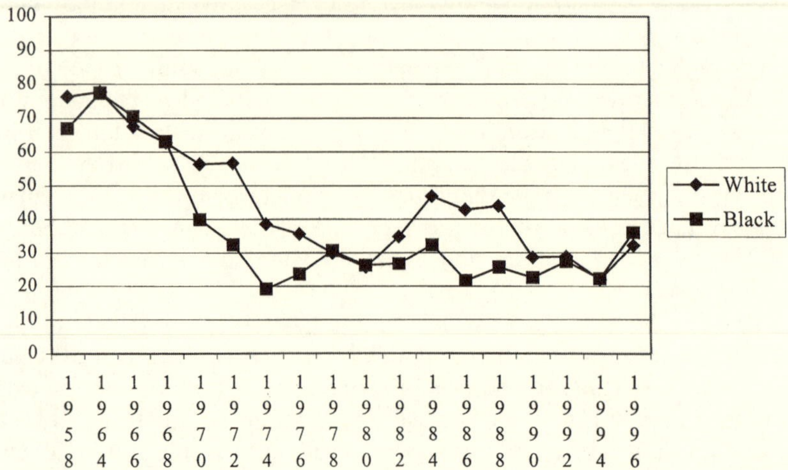

Figure 2.3. Trust Government in Washington Most or All of the Time by Race.

rights, often in direct conflict with the wishes and policies of state and local governments. Discussion of a "white backlash" was prominent in the seventies, and the "angry white male" is a fixture of the nineties. If the commitment of the Federal government to the cause of civil rights led to increased trust in the government in Washington among blacks, but with an opposite and perhaps more powerful reaction among whites, then the relatively larger proportion of whites in the population would have yielded a net decline in trust. Figure 2.3 shows the over-time trend in trust in government for blacks and whites.[5]

Remarkably, the patterns are essentially the same for blacks and whites across this time period. Trust in the government in Washington declined for both races during the civil rights era. Far from becoming more trusting over the period, trust among blacks declined even more precipitously than among whites.[6] Whatever produced the broad decline in trust, it has acted with largely equal force on both blacks and whites.

Education

Education, particularly at the college level, is often criticized for eroding the trust in government that is natural to young children and reinforced

5 The typical sample size across this period does not allow for analysis of any other racial or ethnic breakdowns beyond black and white.

6 This pattern remains clear even with controls for party.

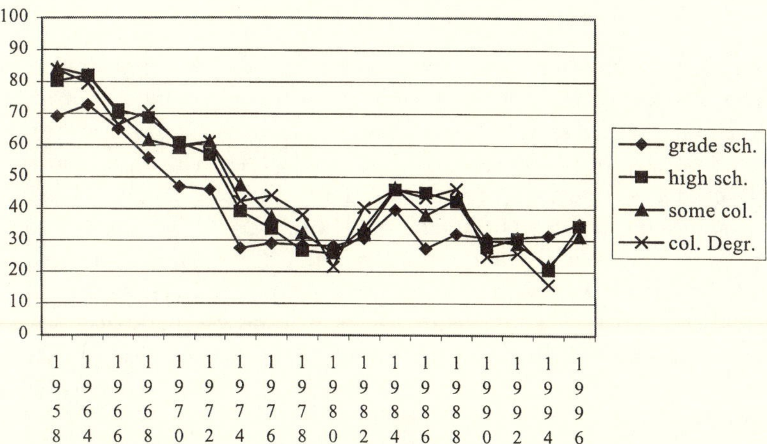

Figure 2.4. Trust Government in Washington Most or All of the Time by Education.

by their grade-school socialization. An emphasis at the college level on developing more critical thinking, as well as a less "civics" orientated approach to teaching in history and political science, are thought to reduce a somewhat naive tendency toward automatic trust in the government. If this is true, we should see higher levels of education associated with lower levels of trust. This pattern, combined with the general increase in formal education across the period, is a potential compositional explanation for the decline in trust. Figure 2.4 shows the over-time trend in trust in government for four levels of education: grade school (0–8), high school (9–12), some college, and college graduate. All respondents were placed in one of the four groups according to the highest grade level they had completed.

The patterns are, in the broad sense, the same for all four levels of education across this time period. Looking at the differences that do exist, it is clear that for most of this period higher levels of education have not been associated with lower levels of trust. In fact the pattern is the reverse. As with income, 1980 and the 1990s are the only exception to this pattern. Also notable is close tracking of high school and college education. Clearly, the trend toward more universal college education did not make any significant contribution to the decline in levels of trust.[7]

7 A full explication will have to await a cross-sectional time series analysis, but some preliminary poking around in the data suggests that the education impact may be the more important of the two variables.

Age

At least since the mid-sixties, the lack of regard and respect for government among young people has been the cause of much alarm, and hand wringing. Today, concern about the "Hippies" has been replaced by concern about "Gen-X." If in fact the period since the mid-sixties has been characterized by an unusually low level of trust in government among the young, then this effect could be cumulating to produce the general decline in trust. Figure 2.5 shows the over-time trend in trust in government for two age groupings. Again, the patterns are in the broad sense the same for both levels of age across this time period. But contrary to so much popular knowledge, young people are generally *more* trusting of government than their elders throughout this period.

Income

With even a modestly elite-centered view of who really runs things in Washington, it would be easy to argue that the poor should trust government far less than the rich. On the other hand, given the volume of rhetoric regarding the overly generous "Robin Hood" nature of the Federal government, it would be easy to see why the poor should trust the government far more than the rich. As was argued for civil rights policy, the social welfare policy initiatives of Lyndon Johnson's Great Society could well have polarized the rich and the poor in terms of trust

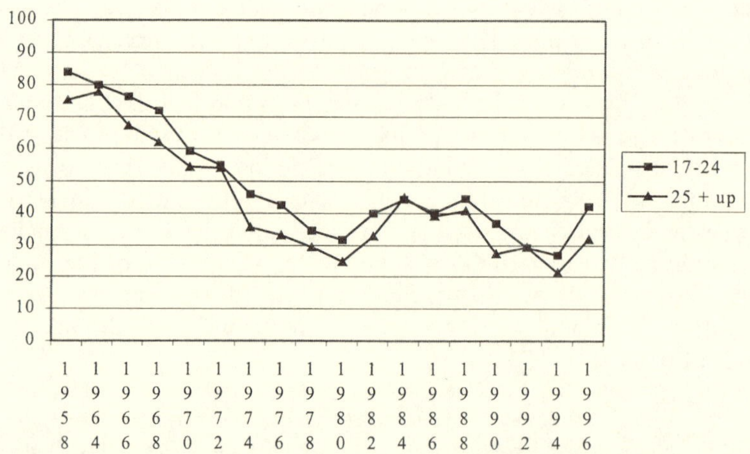

Figure 2.5. Trust Government in Washington Most or All of the Time by Age.

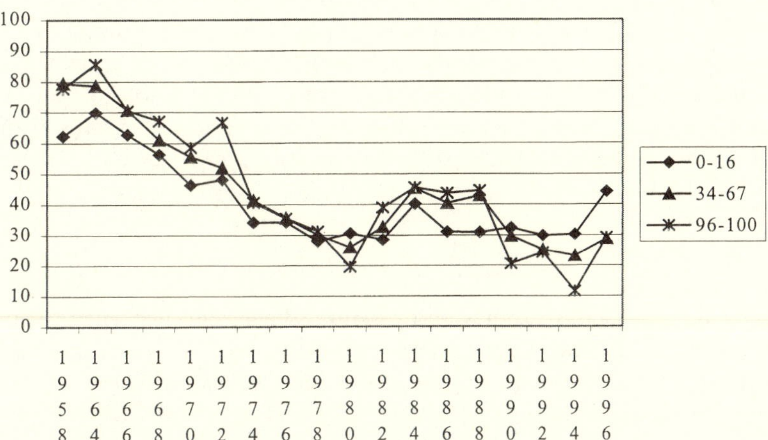

Figure 2.6. Trust Government in Washington Most or All of the Time by Income.

in the government in Washington. Figure 2.6 shows the over-time trend in trust in government for those with incomes in the sixteenth percentile and below (what I will call the poor), those with incomes in the thirty-fourth through the sixty-seventh percentiles (what I will call the middle class), and those with incomes in the ninety-sixth percentile or above (what I will call the rich).[8]

Again, the patterns are in the broad sense the same for the poor and the rich across this time period. Trust among the poor, the middle class, and the rich declined in tandem from 1964 to 1980. Up until 1990, the poor generally trusted government in Washington less than the rich, with 1980 being the lone exception. Beginning in 1990, the rich and poor traded places, with the poor currently solidly more trusting than the rich.

The rich and the poor are not the entire income picture. The great middle class is as much a part of political myth and rhetoric as either extreme. One slightly jaundiced view of the role of the middle class can be paraphrased as "Republicans steal from the middle class and give to the rich—Democrats steal from the middle class and give to the poor." This sort of view of the overtaxed and under-appreciated middle class could lead to the expectation that the middle class would trust

8 The actual income levels in dollars varied across this time period, but as a fairly current example, in 1996 the sixteenth percentile and below was equal to an annual income of less than $12,000, while the ninety-sixth percentile and up was equal to an annual income of over $105,000.

government even less than either the rich or the poor. In contrast, a focus on what we commonly reference by the phrase "solidly middle-class" might lead us to the opposite conclusion. Solidly middle-class values include a high level of basic respect for and trust in government. The actual picture is a much more literal one. The middle class tracks in the middle, threading its way between the rich and poor regardless of their relative positions.

Gender, Region, and Urbanity

The remaining demographics will be discussed briefly without presenting the actual figures, as the pattern should be clear by now. Gender differences in voting turnout, support for Republicans, and "use of force" policy issues have been well documented. Is there a gender gap in trust? The answer is no. Whatever produced the broad decline in trust, it acted with equal force on both women and men. There is a slight tendency for men to be more trusting in government, but the average over this period is only just above one percentage point, and the gap never exceeds five percentage points.

Turning to regional differences, both the south and the west have been characterized as regions with deep suspicion of the government in Washington; the South more so in the sixties and the West more so in the eighties and nineties. A regional difference in trust levels, combined with the rapid shift in population to the least trusting regions of the south and west, could account in a compositional manner for the decline in overall levels of trust. The fact is that no region shows any consistent tendency to be significantly more or less trusting for any length of time. The South does average about three percentage points less trust than the rest of the nation for the period from 1958 to 1974, but this is a minor gap, and the South is slightly more trusting on average in the period from 1976 to 1996. The West never shows any distinctive pattern in trust at all.

Perhaps region is less important to trust than urban–rural distinctions. Are city dwellers more trusting of government than the more self-reliant rural population? Are the suburbs characterized by tax-fueled upper–middle class resentment of government? Again, as was the case for all the other demographic characteristics, the patterns are essentially the same for residents of all three areas. There was a slight tendency for rural dwellers to be less trusting from 1958 to 1970, and a slight tendency for suburban residents to be a bit more trusting throughout, but the notion that any one type of area has been distinctive in its level of trust or in the pattern of change in trust is simply not supportable.

Summary of Demographic Patterns

The most striking pattern across these demographic variables is the breadth and similarity of the trend in trust among all groups. Trust was high in the late fifties and early sixties, dropped precipitously over the next fifteen years, recovered slightly in the eighties, gave up some ground in the early nineties, and may be moving up a bit in the late nineties. This is a good summary of the overall pattern and is also a good summary for every subcategory of the population identified here.

POLITICAL ORIENTATION

Party Identification

On the basis of New Deal ideology, Democrats should show the highest levels of trust for the government in Washington, Republicans should exhibit the lowest levels of trust in government, and independents should fall somewhere in between. Within this pattern, members of the two major parties should show some tendency to be more trusting when their party is in control of the White House. A modification, based on the notion that the perception of needless conflict is what drives down trust (Hibbing and Theiss-Morse 1995), might suggest that independents would be the least trusting, with major party identifiers arrayed as suggested above. For party identifiers, a battle between the two parties could be seen as a necessary, even welcome, fight between good and evil. For independents, the same dispute might just look like another brawl between two self-interested sets of party elites. If this is indeed the pattern, then the increase in the proportion of independents over this period could be a major contributing factor to the decline in trust. Figure 2.7 shows the over-time trend in trust in government for these three partisan groupings.

Clearly, the pattern for independents fails to conform to the conflict scenario previously suggested. Independents are in between the two major parties two-thirds of the time and don't represent a distinct source for compositional decline in trust. On the other hand, there is modest support for the conflict notion. In the one-third of the cases that independents are not in the middle, they are uniformly at the bottom. Thus independents are never the most trusting party category. Independents, while most often falling between the two major parties in terms of trust, tend to track most closely with whichever party exhibits the least trust. If we ignore time for a moment and simply pool all the respondents from these eighteen studies, the proportion trusting government in Washington most or all of the time is 38% for independents, 44% for

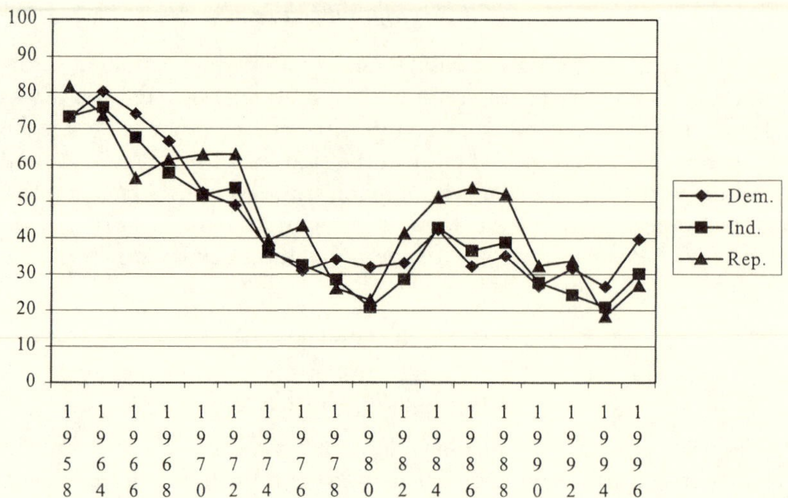

Figure 2.7. Trust Government in Washington Most or All of the Time by Party Identification.

Democrats, and 46% for Republicans. These pooled figures lend some support to our expectations for independents, but they also highlight the importance of looking at the actual trend lines rather than simply pooling respondents as some other studies have done.

Like the pooled figures, the trend lines for the two major parties in Figure 2.7 also disconfirm our basic expectation as to the relative levels of trust between the two parties. Democrats do not show any sustained tendency to be more trusting of Washington despite all of the differences in rhetoric, policy, and ideology that would suggest this. Indeed the pooled analysis suggests that Democrats are slightly less trusting than Republicans. Generally, the two major party lines seem to cross back and forth fairly freely as Republicans and Democrats flip their relative position on trust while generally tracing the same historical pattern. However, even a cursory look suggests that the relative positions are not random. The party that holds the presidency seems to be the more trusting party. Democrats are the more trusting group in 1964, 1966, 1968, 1978, 1980, 1994, and 1996; all years in which the Democrats held the White House. Republicans are the more trusting group in 1958, 1970, 1972, 1974, 1976, 1982, 1984, 1986, 1988, 1990, and 1992; all the years in which the Republicans held the White House. The slightly more trusting average for the Republicans in the pooled figures can thus be attributed simply to the fact that Republicans controlled the White House in nine of these years, while Democrats held the White House in

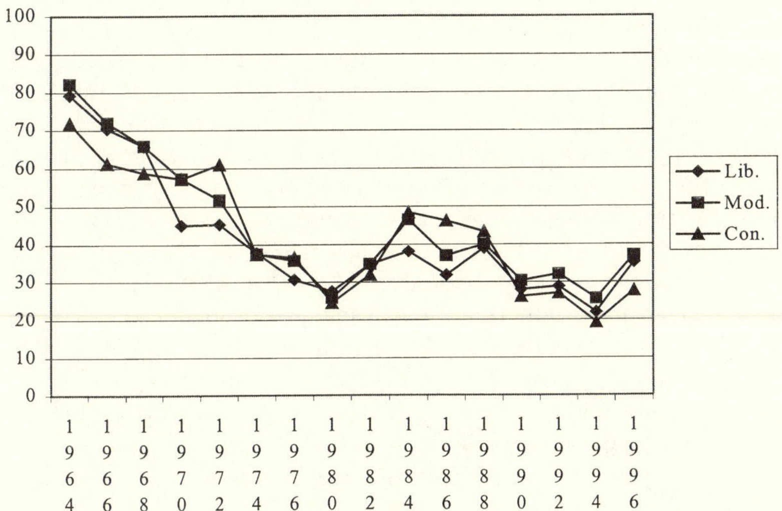

Figure 2.8. Trust Government in Washington Most or All of the Time by Ideology.

only seven. These party flips in trust, combined with the tendency for the out-party to track with independents, suggests that the impact of controlling the White House is mostly centered in a positive effect on trust for the in-party.

Despite all the rhetoric to the contrary, Republicans are no less trusting of the government in Washington than Democrats. Moreover, the general trend in trust over time has been similar for both parties. Both Democrats and Republicans lost trust across the Johnson and Nixon administrations, both recovered some trust in the first Reagan administration, and both had given back those gains by the middle of Clinton's first term.

Ideology

The pattern for ideology should be clear. Beliefs about the appropriate size and power of the government in Washington are by far the most salient characteristics of modern American political ideology. Liberals should consistently show the highest levels of trust for the government in Washington, conservatives should consistently exhibit the lowest levels of trust, and moderates should fall somewhere between.[9] Figure 2.8

9 The measure used here is the one that is based on the respondents' thermometer ratings of liberals and conservatives.

shows the over-time trend in trust in government for these three ideological groupings.

Clearly, our expectations are not fulfilled. In fact the expected pattern appears in only two years, 1974 and 1980. In both cases the range from conservative to liberal in terms of trust is very small, only half a percentage point in 1974, and only three-and-a-half percentage points in 1980. The reverse pattern, with conservatives the most trusting and liberals the least trusting, occurs in five years, most dramatically in 1972, 1984, and 1986. Clearly, who occupies the White House is far more important than any broad ideological affect toward Washington. Liberals, for all their purported and much maligned confidence in Washington, show no distinct tendency to trust the government in Washington. Likewise, conservatives show no distinct tendency to distrust the government in Washington. Even in the face of Reagan's constant rhetorical attacks on government in Washington, conservatives' trust in that same government rose sharply during his terms in office.

THE SUMMARY PICTURE

These findings should not be surprising. Read broadly, past research also suggests little more than sporadic, time-bound success at disaggregating the decline in trust. The more common pattern has been one of similar declines across assorted demographic and attitudinal subgroups. The problem with the past literature is that this nonfinding has not been taken seriously when researchers turn to speculating on the causes of decline. Despite clear evidence that the decline in trust has occurred across institutions, researchers offer institution-specific explanations for the decline such as a coincidental series of weak or flawed presidents or an argumentative Congress. Despite evidence that the decline in trust has occurred across party, ideology, race, income, and region, researchers offer policy-specific explanations for the decline, such as the rapid growth of the federal government, the Vietnam War, civil-rights legislation, or Great Society social policies, that clearly were viewed differently across at least some of these subgroups. The typical response to this observation has been to offer a farrago of explanations to cover various subgroups. So we are told that "the war turned off this subgroup," while "civil rights turned off that subgroup," and so on until all the groups are covered. Lack of parsimony and improbability aside, such a combined impact explanation is simply not supported by appropriate evidence of differential timing and degree in the declines in trust across various subgroups. In short, my argument here is that it is time to take the details of the actual trends in trust seriously and to stop asserting that we all know why trust in government declined in the sixties and seventies when in fact we have no explanation that is compatible with the details of what we know about the decline itself.

Large-scale changes in the levels of trust in government take place for all of us in the same way and at the same time. It is difficult to imagine how factors related to actual specifics of government policy, performance, or personnel could strike such a diverse nation in such a uniform fashion. Put another way, if our trust in government to make the right choice most of the time was related to our assessment of the quality of the actual choices being made, then our reactions would have to be much more diverse. Clearly, Hibbing and Theiss-Morse (2001) are right—this just isn't about policy. Even more broadly, we need to keep in mind Lipset and Schneider's (1987) observation that the decline in trust occurred across a diverse set of public institutions, not just government.

If trusting government to make the right choice isn't primarily about whether the choices government makes are right, then what is it about? Tyler and Degoey (1996) contrast what they call "instrumental" trust with what they call "relational" trust. The former resembles trust based on government making the right choices (competence), while the latter is more related to trusting in good intentions (good faith and fairness). Relational trust is, in this context, the rough equivalent of believing that the government's heart is in the right place. This view would allow for considerable variation in policy outputs and outcomes, without any necessary direct impact on trust. If we accept this view, then we should be focusing our attention on what accounts for variation in our tendency to believe that the government, and public institutions in general, have our best interests at heart.

EXPLAINING THE DECLINE

We know what does not fit, but what sort of explanation *is* compatible with the details of what we know about the decline in trust? Clearly we are looking for a change with an impact that was broad, pervasive, and largely undifferentiated. This suggests something that could have altered the way an individual viewed government, without interacting with or being filtered by an individual's existing preferences, orientations, or capabilities. This means thinking much more broadly than we have in the past.

Cynicism

One sufficiently broad and systemic explanation is a general rise in cynicism. The decline in trust in government might not be directly related to government itself, or even to the broader performance of public institutions in general, but instead might be due to a rise in public cynicism that colored the public's view of everything, including public institutions. This would of course raise the question of what might account for such a rise in cynicism. The potential answers would clearly shift things to a very different realm of explanation. The nature of postmodern life, globalization, and the general decline in social capital are the sorts of trends we might look to if general cynicism is in fact the proximate cause of the decline in trust in government.

Unfortunately, the ANES survey does not have a complete time series for a suitable measure of broad cynicism. The best available measure is a question that taps the respondent's belief that people are generally trustworthy. This question was asked regularly only in the period from 1964 to 1976, but happily this time period covers much of the most dramatic decline in trust in government. What does the trend in cynicism look like? The actual pattern for trust in other people is amazingly flat. Between 1964 and 1976 the proportion of the public with positive expectations about whether you could trust other people dropped less than *two* percentage points. By comparison, over this same period, trust in government dropped over *forty-three* percentage points. Put another way, in 1964 people were about twenty percentage points more likely to trust the government than each other. By 1976 people were about twenty percentage points less likely to trust the government than each other. A significant rise in general cynicism simply did not take place in the period in which trust in government was in a free fall.

Now we have an even tougher puzzle. What kind of change could drive trust in government, as well as other public institutions, down so rapidly, while leaving our trust in other people virtually untouched? The discussion of cynicism provides a useful clue. Note that of the two end points (1964 and 1976), it is the relative trust levels in 1964 that seem unnatural. It is easy to accept that in 1976 we trusted government less than other people. It is harder to accept as natural the 1964 situation in which we trust government so much more than our fellow citizens.

We began with a discussion of decline, and the whole scholarly and popular discussion of trust in government has been colored by the negative connotation of this term. Perhaps a reversal of perspective would be useful. Suppose that distrust of government, and indeed of all large social institutions, is the natural state. Occasionally circumstances arise that lift us to rare, and perhaps even dangerous, heights of trust.[10] These

10 Citrin (1974) suggests such a view in his discussion of the fashionable nature of cynicism, and in his conclusion that high levels of trust may not be such a positive thing. This would also fit nicely with a stream of research that has followed Citrin's lead in demonstrating very little substantive impact for low trust. For a

trusting times are typically short lived, and in the absence of these uncommon protrust circumstances, we relax without any need of specific negative forces back to our natural untrusting equilibrium.

External Threat

The question then becomes, "What could drive up trust in collectives, while leaving trust in individuals untouched?" I offer one possible explanation: external threat. In the face of a broadly perceived national threat, competition and criticism would shift from internal targets to an external one. This is the essence of what is commonly termed a "rally round the flag" effect in regard to presidential popularity. In terms of social psychology, this is the effect of an outside threat on in-group behaviors. This is also similar to Tyler and Degoey's (1996) observations on the importance and nature of internal trust when organizations face a crisis. This would have both a direct impact on individual levels of collective trust and an indirect impact on trust through its suppression of critical rhetoric among elites and the press.

Unfortunately, the ANES surveys do not offer any questions that directly track individual perception of external national threat over time. Nor do the ANES surveys offer any variables that track intervening attitudinal variables such as patriotism (or national chauvinism if you prefer a more pejorative term). What is available is a question regarding the number-one problem facing the nation. Figure 2.9 plots two trends on one graph; the familiar trust in government trend from Figure 2.2 and the proportion of respondents that cite foreign policy or defense as the number-one problem facing the nation.

In 1960 over 60% of the respondents cite foreign policy or defense as the number one problem. By 1974 this has fallen into single digits and remains there through 1978. Likewise, trust in government takes its dramatic plunge over this same period. Concern for foreign policy and defense rebounds in the eighties, though only to about half the level it was in 1960. As we have noted before, trust also rebounds in this period. Foreign policy and defense concerns return to single-digit levels in the nineties, and trust slumps once again as well.[11] Thus the broad patterns are compatible with

recent example see Kazee and Roberts (1998). Note however that the fact that general cynicism about other people did not fall during this period would seem to undercut Citrin's argument that the rise in distrust was mostly due to a common use of cynical language.

11 Chanley, Rudolph, and Rahn (this volume), using a very different methodology, note a similar effect of defense concerns on confidence in government, though not for trust in government. Lipset and Schneider (1987) offer a related explanation

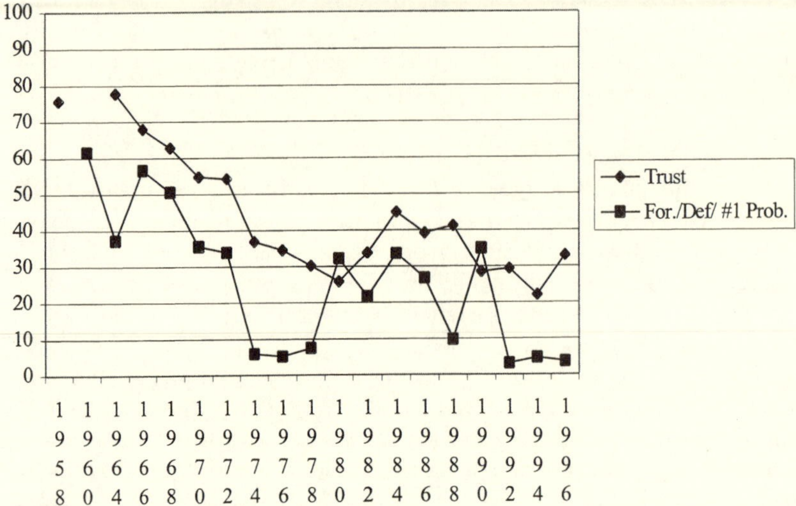

Figure 2.9. Trust and Proportion Citing Foreign Affairs or Defense as the Number One Problem.

an explanation of trust in government that begins with the presumption that trust is typically low and assigns a key role to external threat in accounting for increases in levels of trust. Much more analysis will need to be done to support this role for external threat, but at least it has the virtue of being compatible with what we know to be the actual trends in general and subgroup trust in government over time.

CONCLUSION

A careful look at the long-term trends in trust in government strongly suggests that we have not yet adequately explained large scale over-time variation in levels of trust. Most of what has been offered as explanation is simply not compatible with the actual pattern and detail of change over time. The main argument developed here is that it would be profitable to give some sustained attention to the possibility that rather than declines in trust, it is the occasional historically *high* levels of trust in government that need explaining, and that the explanation is not likely to be found in specific policies or presidents. External threat is one possibility.

for shifts in trust that focuses on economic concerns as the key causal variable. However, the trend lines for the economy as the number one problem are far less clearly and appropriately associated with the trust trend, and in a multivariate analysis, foreign policy and defense clearly dominate the economy as an explanation for the trend in trust over this period.

3

Were the Halcyon Days Really Golden?
An Analysis of Americans' Attitudes about the Political System, 1945–1965

STEPHEN EARL BENNETT

This chapter seeks to determine whether Americans really were as favorably disposed toward national political leaders and institutions during the twenty years after the end of World War II as some researchers claim.[1] Moreover, what light does understanding Americans' "basic political orientations" (Stokes 1962) between 1945 and 1965 shed on the factors behind choleric views of government and political elites during most of the last twenty-five years?

It is now commonplace to characterize Americans' attitudes toward their government and political leaders as very cynical (Craig [1993, 1996] summarizes the evidence). Some analyses of today's cynicism observe that Americans' attitudes about government and politicians used to be very positive, and that the halcyon days were between 1945 and the mid-1960s (see, e.g., Lane 1965; Lipset and Schneider 1987). Although some historians disagree (e.g., Goulden 1976; Oakley 1990; Rose 1999), others characterize the period as "the proud decades" (Diggins 1988) and "the years of confidence" (O'Neill 1986).

Those who believe the first twenty years after World War II were a "golden era" may be thinking of Gabriel Almond and Sidney Verba's seminal study *The Civic Culture* (1963) that, as Peter Natchez noted (1985), profoundly affected students of U.S. politics. Relying on a survey conducted in June 1960, Almond and Verba found that most Americans viewed their government and public officials favorably. Americans also had a well-developed sense that they should take part in public affairs,

1 Picking 1945 as the starting point seems natural. As Theodore White (1982) noted, "[f]or a proper historian of our times there was only one overtowering beginning—the Year of Victory, 1945. . . . The intoxication of that victory . . . lasted for a generation." 1965 also seems a fitting ending point. Not only did the Watts riot signify a turning point in race relations, the first major battle of the Vietnam War took place in 1965.

and that if they did, their efforts would bear fruit. Almond and Verba (1963) described the American political culture in the twilight of the Eisenhower Era as "allegiant and participant."

Was Almond and Verba's description accurate? Re-assessing Almond and Verba's work after the passage of nearly two decades filled with "assassinations, war, racial conflict, political scandals, and economic dislocation," Alan Abramowitz (1980, 180) nonetheless concluded that "the portrait of American political attitudes contained in *The Civic Culture* does appear to be accurate for the time period in which the research was conducted: the late 1950s and early 1960s."

It is difficult to recall a time when nationwide surveys were rarely conducted. Even when a survey was done between 1945 and the mid-1960s, queries about ordinary people's views of government and politicians were seldom asked. We face, therefore, a paucity of nationwide survey data with which to plumb public opinion about government and politicians throughout much of the period between 1945 and 1965.

Nevertheless, several nationwide surveys shed some light on Americans' views of government and politicians during these years. The American National Election Studies of 1958 and 1964 contain helpful information. I will also analyze the June 1960 survey conducted by NORC for Almond and Verba (1963).[2]

None of these surveys covers the years before 1958. Several published sources report nationwide survey data from the late 1940s and early 1950s (Erskine 1973–4; Hyman and Sheatsley 1954; McClosky 1964; McClosky, Hoffman, and O'Hara 1960; Mitchell 1959), thereby enabling us to flesh out a picture of Americans' attitudes about government and public officials.

Studies of American political culture lead one to anticipate Americans held mixed views about government and political leaders.[3] On the one hand, they have long expressed a special pride in being Americans and in virtually everything connected with America (Sniderman 1981). At the same time, however, and perhaps because of our revolutionary experience with the British crown (Almond and Verba 1963), Americans have

2 The 1960 NORC survey, done as part of the "Five Nation Study," was released by the Inter-University Consortium for Political and Social Research. The 1952–1964 NESs were conducted by the University of Michigan's Survey Research Center, and the data were released by the ICPSR. Mark Carrozza assisted in securing the data. I am responsible for all analyses and interpretations.

3 If Samuel P. Huntington's cyclical theory of the ebbs and flows of American opinion about the political order is correct, the years between 1945 and 1965 constituted a "consensus" period.

long been suspicious of politicians; they therefore subject almost all facets of public affairs to popular control (Almond and Verba 1963), efforts that often end in frustration (Morone 1990).

AMERICANS' ATTITUDES ABOUT POLITICS AND POLITICIANS, 1945–1965

Evidence from Published Studies

Herbert Hyman and Paul Sheatsley (1954) were among the first to assay public opinion about government and public officials during the early post-war era. Their main finding was that Americans' views were ambivalent. Although regarding political occupations highly, "the public reveals a fundamental cynicism which seems far removed from the view that public service is an honorable career" (p. 40). At the same time, however, polls found great pride in national governmental institutions. Hyman and Sheatsley concluded that "[p]erhaps the explanation of the apparent inconsistencies of survey findings . . . lies in the fact that *the public combines a deep respect for American institutions and offices with a healthy skepticism about the men* [sic] *who fill them*" (p. 41; italics added).

The best evidence for ambivalent views of government and politicians during the late 1940s and 1950s can be found in William Mitchell's 1959 article. Drawing on a 1946 NORC survey, he detailed Americans' tendency to hold several types of governmental occupations in high esteem. Indeed, although the survey did not inquire about certain types of elected jobs, such as the presidency, vice presidency, and Congressmember, NORC's survey found that the public rated many governmental occupations—such as Supreme Court justice, foreign service diplomat, U.S. Senator, state governor, and big-city mayor—higher than any other class of occupations. On a scale where 100 designated the highest prestige, the 1946 NORC survey reported that the governmental occupations received an average rating of 90.8.

As Mitchell pointed out, however, when a 1944 NORC survey asked if respondents would like to see their son enter politics, only 18% answered "yes," while 69% said "no," and the remainder answered either that "it depends" or were undecided (see also NORC 1944).[4]

4 Can a 1944 poll help understand post-war dispositions? Even though the poll was conducted before D-Day and the U.S. armed forces' return to the Philippines, few Americans doubted the conflict's eventual outcome. Moreover, by 1944—given the successes U.S. military forces had experienced on battlefields around the globe—one might assume that government and politicians should have been basking in a

Those from the upper socioeconomic orders were more favorably disposed toward a son entering politics than were persons from lower socioeconomic backgrounds.

When the 1944 NORC survey asked why people opposed a son choosing a career in politics, half mentioned something related to graft or dishonesty. Mitchell noted that the same NORC survey found that 48% of adult Americans agreed that "it is almost impossible for a man to stay honest if he goes into politics," while 42% disagreed and 10% were undecided. Other polls from the late 1940s and 1950s would reveal similar concerns about honesty and corruption (Erskine 1973–4).

As had Hyman and Sheatsley, Mitchell concluded that "Americans hold ambivalent attitudes toward politics and those who make it an occupation" (1959, 691). He proffered a theory to account for this ambivalence. Noting the Jacksonian Era's belief that ordinary men were qualified to hold political offices that wielded great power and responsibility, Mitchell contended that Americans have long held contradictory feelings about government. On the one hand, they admire people in powerful positions. (Gallup polls annually rank the president, regardless of what else people may think of the individual personally, as one of the "ten most admired men in the world.") On the other hand, large slices of the public deprecate and disparage power (see also Almond and Verba 1963; Huntington 1981). Mitchell concluded that "[i]mpression suggests that Americans appear to be cynical about politics and quite idealistic about certain politicians, especially dead ones, and about certain [governmental] offices" (1959, 695). At bottom, according to Mitchell, "the American tends to expect the worst in politics but hopes for the best."

Finally, Herbert McClosky's January 1958 "Political Beliefs and Attitudes" survey also found evidence of ambivalence. Although the poll overrepresented the well-educated (McClosky, Hoffman, and O'Hara 1960), McClosky found that roughly 90% of the Eisenhower Era public agreed that they "usually have confidence that the government will do what is right" (McClosky 1964, 320). Only a third thought that "the laws of this country" "are almost always 'rich-man's' laws." Almost three-fifths (59%) opined that "most politicians can be trusted to do what they think is best for the country" (1964, 320).

Nevertheless, McClosky (1964) concluded that Americans held ambivalent views about government and politicians. Although many felt "hopelessly ineffectual politically," the overwhelming bulk of the late 1950s public expressed confidence that the government will do what is

warm glow of public approval. At the very least, data from 1944 provide a backdrop against which to judge post-war views.

right. McClosky concluded that Americans may have been cynical about the political system's operation, but they did not question its legitimacy.

Did Anything Change Between 1945 and 1965?

Did Americans' basic political orientations change significantly between 1945 and 1965? Lisle Rose (1999) claims to detect a profound shift in public sentiment that occurred in 1950. Rose believes that the almost giddy optimism that characterized Americans' political attitudes in the immediate aftermath of World War II ended when the Cold War came to main-street America and, moreover, that not even prosperity during the Eisenhower years could overcome pessimism and doubt brought on by the threat of Soviet Communism and global nuclear war.

Philip Converse (1972) provided survey-based evidence of changing opinions about public affairs in the 1950s and 1960s. Utilizing American National Election Studies data from 1952 to 1968, he found belief that ordinary people could influence politicians' decisions rose between 1952 and 1960, largely because of increased exposure to higher education. Thereafter, however, belief in the average person's political clout fell, and the decline occurred across all levels of formal schooling. Converse ticked off several events that began in 1963 and continued throughout the rest of the 1960s and concluded that "[t]his sequence of national catastrophes, disruptions, and blunders seems adequate to account for a considerable loss of confidence in the government and politics on the part of the public" (p. 330).

Summarizing Views of Government and Politicians from 1945 to the Late 1950s

It is probable that most Americans continued a pattern stretching well back into the past of holding ambivalent views about government and politics. On the one hand, they were proud to be Americans and accorded great respect to those occupying high government positions. At the same time, they viewed certain types of political figures with thinly disguised bemusement. Think of Jack S. Fogbound, Al Capp's creation as the congressmember from "Dog Patch." Capp's imaginary blowhard, corrupt pol must have resonated with at least a segment of the populace.

An interesting tidbit appears to buttress views of a trusting public at this time. As Donald Devine (1972) noted, surveys from the late 1940s through the mid-1960s found that most Americans believed other people were altruistic. In 1948, for example, 66% of an NORC survey said "yes" that "most people can be trusted." In 1964, the figure was 77%

(1972). Proponents of the "declining social capital" thesis, such as Robert Putnam (1995a, 1995b), argue that waning belief in their fellow citizens' altruism has covaried with declining trust in government officialdom during the last quarter century.[5] If that is true, then relatively high levels of altruistic beliefs between 1948 and the mid-1960s may have been connected to relatively high levels of trust in government.

It is also important to note significant shifts in Americans' views of government during these years. If we can generalize from Converse's findings regarding political efficacy beliefs, public opinion toward government became more positive after Eisenhower became president in 1953, the Korean War ended, McCarthyism became, according to one wag, "McCarthywasm," and—save for the recession of 1957–8—the economy expanded significantly. Rosy views of government and politicians probably came from victory in World War II and the dramatic economic expansion during the late 1940s and throughout the 1950s. Even if Rose (1999) is right that giddy optimism right after World War II gave way to pessimism in 1950, his thesis seems to founder on the shoals of survey data in the late 1950s and early 1960s.

But can we say with certainty that confidence and trust in government changed much during the period? Since external political efficacy beliefs and trust in government—as tapped by the SRC items—are linked (Mason, House, and Martin 1985), it seems reasonable to see if Americans' trust in government also changed between the late 1950s and early 1960s.

EVIDENCE FROM THE 1958 AND 1964 ANESS

Those who seek to analyze Americans' political dispositions between the late 1950s and mid-1960s concentrate on three nationwide surveys: the 1958 and 1964 ANESs, and the 1960 NORC data for Almond and Verba's "Five Nation Study." We turn first to the 1958 and 1964 ANESs because they contain the only battery of items probing Americans' perceptions of the federal government's trustworthiness to appear on more than one national survey during the twenty years after World War II.

As Donald Stokes noted, the Survey Research Center introduced five items on the 1958 ANES that were intended to tap "basic evaluative orientations toward the national government," including ethical dimensions of official honesty as well as "the ability and efficiency of government

5 As the 1964 NES shows, for example, a three-item misanthropy index resonated with the three-item trust in government index at $r = .22$.

officials and the correctness of their policy decisions" (1962, 64). Three items, including one tapping belief that citizens can trust the federal government "to do what is right," a query probing perceptions of officials' honesty, and another tapping beliefs about the national establishment's tendency to waste tax monies (Miller, Miller, and Schneider 1980), have appeared on many subsequent ANESs, and they will be the focus of attention for this section.[6]

The three items were combined into a "trust in government index." The index had a Cronbach's coefficient alpha of .60 in 1958 and .63 in 1964 (Zeller and Carmines 1980) suggesting that the items formed a satisfactory composite index in both years. The data thus confirm Stokes' observation that "a single dimension of attitude toward government was found to embrace the various criteria of evaluation implicit in the [SRC's] questions" (1962, 64). Table 3.1 depicts distributions on the three-item trust in government index in 1958 and 1964.

Two things are striking about Table 3.1. First, Americans' views of governmental trustworthiness, as tapped by the three SRC items, evidenced a great deal of diversity in the late 1950s and early 1960s. Judged by these data, one could not say that Americans were consensually trusting in their opinions about the federal government (cf. the data in Table 3.1 with those in Miller, Miller, and Schneider 1980). Second, in both years, a sizable portion of the public held cynical views about the national government. While it is true that only a minority of the public could be classified as "extremely cynical" in 1958 or 1964, more Americans distrusted the national establishment than trusted it in both years.

Still, two points need to be made. First, scores on the ANES's trust in government index were remarkably similar in the late 1950s and the mid-1960s. Although trust fell slightly and cynicism rose, in both instances the changes were relatively minor. More important, judged by ANESs after 1972, the 1958 and 1964 data look positively rosy. Indeed, the 1996 ANES shows that over half the public (56%) were "extremely cynical" on the same three-item index that is depicted in

6 A fourth item, probing perceptions of government's equal treatment of all citizens, did not again appear in its 1958 format. In 1964, another item appeared seeking to tap the same component of trust in government. But, since its wording is much different from the 1958 version, this item will be ignored. A fifth, asking for opinions about how "smart" government officials were, was eventually found to suffer from a fundamental methodological flaw, and no longer appears on the NES. Despite differences over what the items tap (*cf.* Miller 1974a, 1974b with Citrin 1974), and questions about their quality (Weatherford 1988), the ANES's "trust in government" battery remains useful.

Table 3.1. *Americans' Trust in Government, 1958 and 1964*

Trust in Government[a] Category	1958	1964
Very Trusting	10.2%	7.0%
Slightly Trusting	18.3	13.8
Neutral	24.4	29.4
Slightly Cynical	21.6	21.8
Very Cynical	25.5	28.0
N	1,285	1,360

Note: [a] A Composite index built from how much of the time respondents trust the government in Washington to do what is right, how much they think the national government wastes tax dollars, and how many government officials respondents believe are "a little crooked."

Source: University of Michigan's Survey Research Center's National Election Studies.

Table 3.1, while another one-quarter (24%) were "slightly cynical," and only 5% were either "very" or "slightly" trusting. In short, just as Converse (1972) found for external efficacy, it appears that trust in the national government quickly fell after 1964, and the decline had already begun by 1966.

Although by no means overwhelmingly trusting of the national government, the American public between the late 1950s and mid-1960s was far more positive in its views of the federal government than people were from the 1970s onward. Multivariate analyses suggest that the public's perceptions of Washington's trustworthiness between 1958 and 1964 were shaped by perceptions of the country's position in the world, race, and education. By 1964, partisanship had also become a factor (data not shown). At that, however, none of these factors was strongly related to trust in government in either year.

THE "CULPRIT" APPREHENDED

If the data in Table 3.1 are a fair characterization of public sentiment about government's trustworthiness before public opinion soured, what accounts for scholars' belief that post-1964 trends represented a profound break with the past? The answer is not hard to find. Look at the American data from Almond and Verba's "Five Nation Study" (1963), one of the most widely read studies of political culture in the post-war era.

NORC's survey of 970 voting-age Americans conducted in June 1960—the twilight of the Eisenhower Era—found a public overwhelmingly positive in its views of the U.S. political system. The majority (85%) of the citizenry said they were aware of government's impact on their personal lives. Three-quarters (76%) of those people viewed government's impact as positive. Only a trace element among the public (3%) opined that America would be better off without the national government (Almond and Verba 1963). When asked what made them most proud of the country, 85% said "the government" or some "political institution." Most Americans expected to be treated fairly by government agencies, and roughly four-fifths believed their views would be given at least some attention by a government office. Most Americans also viewed their fellow humans as altruistic, which undoubtedly buttressed rosy views of government and public officials.

Almond and Verba offered one warning about American political culture. Americans had guarded views about officials' responsiveness to public opinion. For this reason, according to Almond and Verba, Americans tended "to subject all governmental institutions, including the judiciary and bureaucracy, to direct popular control" (1963, 441). Thus, the American political culture was "imbalanced" toward citizens' participation to the detriment of governmental effectiveness.

One cannot prove that Almond and Verba's characterization of Americans' attitudes toward government and public officials is the reason why authors after the mid-1960s harked back to a halcyon era of positivity. Still, a prima facie case can be made. *The Civic Culture* quickly became a highly regarded example of the then-emerging behavioral movement in political science. As Natchez later noted (1985, 125), "among American political scientists, *The Civic Culture* was a most welcome addition to the literature, for it seemed to capture the qualities that made American politics distinctive and triumphant." Eventually Almond and Verba's tome would come under methodological and theoretical assault (see, e.g., Lijphart 1980; Natchez 1985; Pateman 1980; Wiatr 1980). To scholars looking for a baseline against which to judge changing American attitudes toward government after the mid-1960s, however, *The Civic Culture* was an ideal source.

One caveat is necessary. The queries put to the respondents of NORC's 1960s survey are not the same as those the Survey Research Center developed in the early 1950s to tap political efficacy, or those introduced on the 1958 ANES to measure trust in government. An individual can say she is proud of American government and political institutions and still be wary of those currently serving in national office.

Nevertheless, the disconnect is far from complete. One wonders how those in 1960 who claimed the federal government's impact on them was positive could also hold jaundiced views of people in government leadership roles. In short, perhaps driven by economic abundance (Gitlin 1987; Weatherford 1984), perhaps because of Eisenhower's presidential stewardship (Citrin and Green 1986), perhaps because the perception of a Soviet threat led many to "rally around the flag" (Alford, this volume), perhaps because the dominant news media tended to put a positive "spin" on political coverage (Fallows 1996), the public in 1960 viewed the federal government favorably. If there was "one brief shining moment" to Americans' views about their political system, 1960 seems to be that time.

SUMMARY AND CONCLUSIONS

The goal has been to assay Americans' views of government and public officials during the first two decades after World War II ended. Why would a study such as this be worthy? First, given a tendency among students of present discontents to assume that public opinion about government and politicians was different before the mid-1960s from what it has since become, it is important either to establish the fact or to determine how, when, and why attitudes during the halcyon days differed from how they are now recalled. If it should turn out that public opinion in the golden era was less overwhelmingly positive than most have been inclined to assume, then many of the explanations for trends since the mid-1960s ring hollow. On the other hand, some views of public opinion after the mid-1960s, particularly those stressing partisan ties, social strains stemming from racial discord, and possibly fall-out from economic distress, may yet prove worthwhile.

There is a second reason to look anew at public opinion about government during the years between 1945 and 1965. After a time in the doldrums, concepts and theories connected to the notion of "political culture" are once again in vogue (see, e.g., Huntington 1996; Lipset 1990, 1996; Seligman 1992; Shafer 1997; Thompson, Ellis, and Wildavsky 1990; Woshinsky 1995). A major component of a nation's political culture is its people's views of political leaders and institutions (Almond and Verba 1963, 1980). If experiences in Africa and Asia following colonialism's end in the 1950s and 1960s (see, e.g., Shils 1960) and after Communism collapsed in Eastern Europe and the former Soviet Union in the late 1980s (see, e.g., White, Rose, and McAllister 1997) have taught us anything, it is that the institutional trappings of democracy mean little where patterns of political culture are not conducive to a democratic way of conducting public affairs. Studying how Americans felt about their national political leaders and institutions between 1945 and 1965—a period noted for stability—can broaden scholars' understanding of the linkage between basic political orientations and political life in the United States and possibly elsewhere.

As we have seen, a major problem is paucity of public opinion data before the late 1950s. To flesh out evidence derived from polls, the student of public opinion in the late 1940s and 1950s will have to turn to impressionistic sources, such as letters to editors—which pose their own methodological problems (see, e.g., Converse, Clausen, and Miller 1965)—and other published and unpublished indicators of how Americans felt about government and politicians. An example, albeit only as one means of tapping the reading public's views, is to look at publishers' data on best-selling novels and nonfiction books about government and politics. If the best-selling political novel of 1958 was Alan Drury's *Advise and Consent*—it was—then the image of politicians and politics Drury developed may provide clues about what at least a portion—albeit an important one—of the American public was willing to think about at that time. Expressions of popular culture as disparate as movies and comics often provide useful clues about how the public felt about government and politicians. The 1946 award-winning film *The Best Years of Their Lives* may tell a good deal about how an important slice of American society felt about the costs of victory in World War II. That, in turn, may shed useful light on how some Americans felt about government, politics, and politicians.

Using print and electronic sources such as newspapers, news magazines, novels, nonfiction books, comic strips, and movies to gauge public opinion is risky, but historians have been making good use of these materials to gauge public opinion for eras in which no poll data exist. As someone who began his academic career seeking to become an historian, a return to the assumptions and methods of history may be gratifying indeed.

Historian James Patterson provides an appropriate ending. Explaining why he entitled the book *Grand Expectations*, Patterson writes that "the majority of the American people during the twenty-five years following the end of World War II developed ever-greater expectations about the capacity of the United States to create a better world abroad and a happier society at home" (1996, vii). If true, we have the backdrop against which to understand both relatively benign—albeit mixed—views of government and politicians between 1945 and 1965 *and* growing negativity since. A victorious people, enjoying what seemed to be unparalleled prosperity twenty years after the "good war" ended, could only look upon the events that have transpired since 1965 with shock and growing anger. If a generation of political leaders, tempered by wartime fires and themselves beneficiaries of that paragon of national recognition—the GI Bill—could point with pride to their accomplishments during the first two decades after 1945, is it any surprise that as the accomplishments grew few and far between, and the catalogue of blunders, catastrophes, and scandals amassed, people who once thought all was well came to blame the national government and its leaders?

4

Public Trust in Government in the Reagan Years and Beyond

VIRGINIA A. CHANLEY, THOMAS J. RUDOLPH, AND WENDY M. RAHN

Public evaluations of the U.S. government have grown increasingly negative in recent decades. Survey data indicate that public trust and confidence in government are lower than at almost any point in the period for which data exist. Nonetheless, government continues to function. Short of total disintegration of government, however, public cynicism is understood to have consequences. Voter turnout hovers at around 50% in presidential elections and is significantly lower for off-year elections. Public opinion polls reveal that President Clinton's military actions were viewed as diversions: a Machiavellian effort by the president to deflect attention from his personal and political troubles. Although polls also show public support for these military actions, the cynical evaluation of the president's motivation undercuts the validity of these and future actions.

In democracies, citizen trust in government is necessary for political leaders to make binding decisions and to commit resources to attain societal goals (Gamson 1968). It is also necessary to secure citizen compliance without coercion (Levi 1997; Tyler 1990). For example, Scholz and Lubell (1998) found in a study of taxpaying compliance that taxpayers' trust in the federal government was much more important in deterring cheating on tax returns than was fear of getting audited by the IRS. Thus, levels of citizen trust in government have considerable consequences for government's ability to raise needed revenue for public programs. The research reported in this chapter is designed to contribute to our understanding of the causes and consequences of citizens' views of government based on a time series examination of changes in trust and other dimensions of public evaluations of government. We first discuss the theoretical and empirical framework that informs this research and then present our data, methods, and results. Finally, we discuss the implications of our results and directions for future research.

IDENTIFYING THE CAUSES AND CONSEQUENCES OF PUBLIC VIEWS OF GOVERNMENT

Trust in government has received the greatest attention among scholars studying public assessments of the national government, and the research of these scholars provides a starting point for what follows. We rely in part on a theoretical conception of trust developed by Barber (1983), who examines the meaning of trust across a range of institutions. Barber identifies trust in the broadest sense as confidence in one's expectations of the world and as a basic fact of social life. Trust serves to decrease the complexity and unknowns of social life allowing for "expectations of persistence, regularity, order, and stability in the everyday and routine moral world" (Barber 1983, 11).

Within the broad understanding of trust, Barber identifies two more specific components of trust. The first is the expectation of competence. When we allow a doctor to perform a complex medical procedure or take the advice of a tax consultant on reducing tax liability, we do so with the expectation that these individuals are competent in their areas of expertise. In the political domain, citizens may be either trusted or mistrusted in their capacity for choice of elected officials or support for public policies, depending upon evaluations of citizen competence for making decisions in these areas. Public officials may be trusted or mistrusted in developing and implementing public policy, depending on expectations of knowledge and expertise of the public officials involved in the process.

Barber's second component of trust involves expectations of fiduciary obligation and responsibility. The notion of fiduciary commitment is based on the belief that some individuals "in our social relationships have moral obligations and the responsibility to demonstrate a special concern for other's interests above their own" (Barber 1983, 14). In policy making, fiduciary responsibility is reflected in the expectation that public officials will legislate for the benefit of citizens and make decisions that serve the public interest rather than for personal or partisan gain. Fiduciary responsibility goes beyond technical competence, including the expectation that individuals in positions of public trust will act in the interests of those they represent in situations where technical competence or other aspects of the behavior of policy makers may not be publicly known.

Levi (1998) offers a theoretical treatment that emphasizes competence and fairness as requirements for establishing and maintaining trust in government. The fiduciary obligation identified by Barber, however, is also a part of Levi's conception of trust. Specifically, Levi (1998, 88) argues that, for the most part, "citizens are willing to go along with a policy they do not prefer as long as it is made according to a process they deem legitimate, and [conversely] they are less willing to comply with a policy they like if the process was problematic." Further, if citizens are to believe a process is fair and legitimate, there must be "the perception that all relevant interests have been considered, that the game is not rigged" (Levi 1998, 90). In other words, citizens expect policy makers to set aside partisan or personal interests and make decisions in a public-spirited manner, which is precisely what a fiduciary relationship implies.

Barber and Levi's theoretical treatments of trust in government further identify similar factors that are expected to influence public perceptions of trust in government. If elected officials are incompetent and do not behave in ways that serve the public interest, public trust in government is likely to decline. These factors are also consistent with Hibbing and Theiss-Morse's (2001) explanation for changes in public satisfaction with government. Hibbing and Theiss-Morse distinguish between "policy-outcome" and "policy-output" views of understanding public satisfaction with government. A policy-outcome explanation focuses on the conditions of the nation as the basis for citizen satisfaction with government; prosperity, peace, and other desirable conditions are associated with satisfaction with government. A policy-output explanation, in contrast, focuses on the match between citizens' policy desires and the perception of government policy decisions. In this view, liberals are more likely to be satisfied (and conservatives less satisfied) when they perceive that government policies reflect a liberal agenda.

In addition to policy-outcome and policy-output explanations, Hibbing and Theiss-Morse provide evidence that it is important to consider citizens' views of policy process as well. They find that citizens think that ordinary people like themselves should play a role similar to that of elected officials and bureaucrats in political decision making. However, citizens actually perceive the process of decision making as one in which elected officials and bureaucrats play a greater role than average citizens, and this has consequences. Citizens who see a larger discrepancy between their actual and desired role express greater dissatisfaction with government. Tyler (1990, 1994) and Craig (1993, 1996) similarly focus on citizens' views of the process of policy making in their examinations of trust in government. Tyler and Craig find that citizens are less trusting when they perceive policy makers to be unresponsive to the public or when they do not believe that government fairly represents all interests. Consistent with Barber and Levi's emphasis on fairness and the importance of government acting in the public interest, each of these findings reflects the importance of public concern about the extent to which policy makers can be relied on to fulfill their fiduciary responsibilities.

The current research examines the dimensions of public views of government from a time series perspective. Specifically, we develop time-series measures designed to assess public views of trust and confidence in elected officials and the institutions of government and expectations concerning the extent to which elected officials fulfill their fiduciary responsibilities. We look to indicators of the state of the economy, perceptions of the economy, important events, and evaluations of the important issues facing the nation as factors representing policy outcomes such as prosperity, and we consider the causal influence that these factors have on public evaluations of government. We also consider the consequences that evaluations of the national government may have on public support for governmental action and views of whether the nation is heading in the right direction. There has been less empirical examination of the consequences of trust in government, despite the theoretical importance of trust as a prerequisite for governmental action. We include a measure of public support for action across a range of domestic issue areas, Stimson's (1991) policy liberalism, as an indicator of public support for governmental action.

DATA AND MEASURES

In the area of public views of government, we are fortunate to have many of the same questions asked over time. For views such as trust in government, however, there is no single question asked at intervals that are frequent enough to conduct analysis over a relatively long period of time. Beginning in 1964, the National Election Studies, for example, provide a measure of trust in government at two-year intervals at best. In the 1970s, national survey houses such as the *New York Times*, the *Washington Post*, ABC, CBS, and Roper began to ask questions to assess public levels of trust in government. It is not until the 1980s, however, that these questions are asked frequently enough to allow for the analyses that follow.

For several of our time series, we rely on a technique developed by Stimson (1991) that allows for the creation of a single time-series measure on the basis of distinct questions that measure the same underlying concept.[1] Based on the availability of questions that serve as indi-

1 Stimson's method for deriving a single time-series measure relies on covariance or common movement among different time-series measures. Covariance is evidenced by similar changes in the marginal distribution of responses to distinct survey items. At least two administrations of a survey item are required to identify a change in opinion, and common movement among partially overlapping series of questions is factored into a single overall series that reflects the shared variance of the component series.

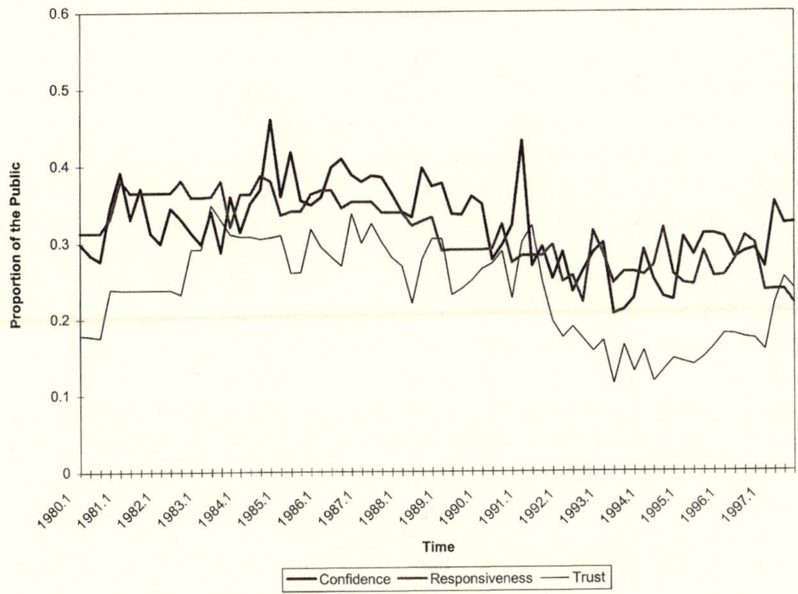

Figure 4.1. Government Trust, Responsiveness, and Confidence, 1980:1 to 1997:4.

cators of distinct evaluations of national government, these quarterly measures range from 1980 to 1997. The one exception is Stimson's measure of policy liberalism, which is available through 1996. Each measure is coded on a zero-to-one scale. For the measures of evaluations of government, higher values reflect more positive assessments of government. Figure 4.1 presents a graph of the measures of trust, responsiveness, and confidence, which we introduce first.

Trust in Government. The measure of trust in government is based on the data from six different questions that have been asked in more than one quarter of the years from 1980 to 1997. The single longest series for this measure is based on the question "How much of the time do you think you can trust the government in Washington to do what is right—just about always, most of the time, or only some of the time?" The other five questions comprising the data for the measure of trust are almost identical to this question.

Responsiveness. The measure of public perceptions of responsiveness on the part of government and public officials is based on data from twelve distinct questions. The single longest series in this measure is based on the percentage of the public saying that government is run for the benefit of all the people when asked "Would you say that government is pretty much run by a few interests looking out for themselves or that it is run for the benefit of all the people?" The second longest series in the measure is based on agreement or disagreement with the statement "I don't think that public officials care much about what people like me think." For this question, of course, disagreement is coded as reflecting a more positive assessment of responsiveness. The remaining items comprising the data for the measure of responsiveness similarly focus on perceptions of the extent to which government and public officials pay attention to citizens.

This measure of responsiveness most closely captures Barber's conception of fiduciary obligation on the part of those in government. If citizens do not think that elected officials care about or pay attention to what citizens think or that government is run for the benefit of all the people, they are less likely to feel that policy makers are setting aside personal or partisan interests when they make decisions about public policy. Moreover, setting aside such interests is a key component of a fiduciary relationship.

Confidence. We assess public perceptions of confidence in policy makers and the institutions of government on the basis of twenty-five distinct survey items. Most of the items inquire about confidence in Congress, the executive or White House, and the Supreme Court.[2] There are two questions among the data for this series that are available most frequently. These questions are: "As far as the people in charge of running Congress are concerned, would you say you have a great deal of confidence, only some confidence, or hardly any confidence in them?" and

2 Given different findings with respect to whether trust is driven by evaluations of Congress or the president (see, e.g., Citrin and Green 1986 and Feldman 1983), we also developed separate time-series measures of confidence for the executive, Congress, and the Supreme Court. The data for these measures are necessarily sparser than the data for the combined measure, however, and on both theoretical and empirical grounds, we find the combined measure more appropriate. The measures of trust and responsiveness do not specify a particular institution, and citizens do not thus necessarily focus on a particular institution when making these evaluations. Rather, different institutions may be more salient at different times. Given the general focus of the measures of trust and responsiveness, we are most interested in capturing a similarly general assessment of confidence across the three national institutions in a single measure. In addition, other examinations at both the aggregate and individual level find that there is a common element to perceptions of different national institutions (Lipset and Schneider 1987; Brehm and Rahn 1997).

"As far as the people running the White House are concerned, would you say you have a great deal of confidence, only some confidence, or hardly any confidence at all in them?" The remaining items ask similar questions about confidence in government, with the exception of two items that ask about the level of corruption among the people in government and one question about the extent to which government wastes the taxpayer's money.

This measure of confidence in the people and institutions of national government reflects a combination of assessments of technical competence and fulfillment of fiduciary responsibilities on the part of government officials. The measure of confidence clearly differs from the measure of responsiveness, however, in that expressions of confidence are more clearly related to perceptions of competence. Citizens may view policy makers as responsive to their wishes, but responsive officials will not necessarily be viewed as competent. Conversely, the expectation of competence is likely a prerequisite to the expression of confidence. How can one express confidence in the ability of the people running Congress, the executive, or the Supreme Court unless there is the belief that these individuals are competent to do their jobs? In other words, competence is a necessary component of confidence. Evaluations of responsiveness, however, do not necessarily rely on perceptions of competence, but rest on the expectation that officials will behave in a public-spirited manner and not let personal or partisan interests override the public interest.

Direction of the Country. We also include in our analyses a measure that does not directly assess citizens' views of government but focuses rather on perceptions of "things in this country" generally. The question "Do you feel things in this country are generally going in the right direction, or do you feel things have gotten pretty seriously off on the wrong track?" comprises the longest component series for this measure. The other questions that provide the data for this series are very similar in wording. Whereas our measures of trust, responsiveness, and confidence make explicit reference to the national government and public officials, the measure of direction of the country does not.

Presidential Approval. The most familiar time-series measure in our analyses is that of presidential approval. This measure is based on the question "Do you approve or disapprove of the way President [as appropriate for date] is handling his job as president?" As the most identifiable figure in the U.S. political system, the president provides a focal point for citizens' evaluations, and previous studies have linked presidential approval to trust in government (e.g., Citrin and Green 1986).

To create a quarterly measure of approval from 1980 to 1997, we rely on data from the Gallup and Wirthlin polling organizations. Once again we employ Stimson's technique for creating a single time series based on the common variance in the data from these two survey organizations.

Policy Liberalism. The measure of policy liberalism was developed by Stimson (1991). This measure reflects common variance in changes in public support for government spending and activity across a range of domestic policy areas, including health, education, welfare, aid to cities, and the environment. Higher values reflect greater support for government spending and activity.

Economic Expectations. The measure of economic expectations is based on the question "Looking ahead, which would you say is more likely—that in the country as a whole we'll have continuous good times during the next five years or so, or that we'll have periods of widespread unemployment or depression, or what?" This question is asked at regular intervals as part of the Survey of Consumer Finances and Survey of Consumer Attitudes and Behavior conducted by the University of Michigan's Survey Research Center. Higher values on this measure reflect more positive assessments of the national economic future.

Other Measures. Finally, we include two measures of public views of the most important problem facing the nation and several variables that are familiar to time-series treatments of presidential approval that we also expect to have causal influence on public evaluations of the national government more broadly. The data for the measures of the most important problem facing the nation are based on responses to the open-ended question, "What do you think is the most important problem facing this country today?" We coded references to foreign policy, defense, and international affairs as indicators of public focus on international problems as the most important problem facing the nation. References to the national debt, national deficit, and excessive government spending are coded as indicators of public focus on the national debt and government spending as the most important problem facing the nation. We include measures of quarterly change in unemployment and inflation as indicators of actual economic conditions in the nation. We include a series that denotes significant events that are likely to influence public evaluations of the president (and perhaps evaluations of government more broadly) and a series that marks the first quarter in a president's term in office. The measures of the most important problem facing the nation, change in unemployment, and change in inflation serve as indicators of the policy outcome dimension identified by Hibbing and Theiss-Morse (2001).

A Visual Examination of Trust, Responsiveness, and Confidence

Before presenting our statistical methods and results, we conduct a brief visual examination of the measures presented in Figure 4.1 and discuss descriptive statistics for these measures. In the years from 1980 to 1997, trust ranged from a high of about 35% in the second quarter of 1983 to a low of approximately 11% in the second quarter of 1994. The average level of trust in government over these years was 24%. Perceptions of responsiveness ranged from a high of almost 39% in the third quarter of 1984 to a low of about 22% in the third quarter of 1992 and again in the fourth quarter of 1997. On average, 31% of the public expressed positive perceptions of responsiveness on the part of government in the period from 1980 to 1997. Evaluations of confidence in national government ranged from a high of 46% in the fourth quarter of 1984 to a low of 21% in the second quarter of 1993. The average level of confidence over these years was approximately 32%.

The graph and descriptive statistics reveal that each of these measures reached high points in 1983 and 1984 and low points in the years from 1992 to 1997. The high points in these evaluations coincide with President Reagan's first term in office and are consistent with the view that President Reagan helped to improve public perceptions of government, at least until revelations concerning the Iran-Contra affair became public during his second term in office (Citrin and Green 1986; Miller and Borrelli 1991). Low points in these measures reflect a period of scholarly attention to increasingly negative citizen views of government and a time of change and preoccupation with scandal in national politics. The nation elected an incumbent Democratic president for only the second time since Franklin Roosevelt and the Republican Party took control of the House of Representatives for the first time in forty years. President Clinton and his administration faced allegations of wrongdoing on a series of charges, and House Speaker Newt Gingrich was fined by the House Ethics Committee. Our time series end just before allegations concerning Monica Lewinsky became public. Visual examination of Figure 4.1 suggests similar changes across the measures of trust, responsiveness, and confidence, but it is not a simple matter to assess the nature of the relationship among these variables on the basis of the visual evidence. For this, we look to time-series statistical techniques.

METHODS AND EMPIRICAL RESULTS

The literature on trust in government and other dimensions of public evaluations of government provides a rich theoretical and empirical framework. However, this body of research does produce some ambiguous expectations with respect to the direction of causal relationships. Consider the relationship between trust in government and perceived responsiveness. Miller, Goldenberg, and Erbring (1979) maintain that trust causes responsiveness but not the reverse. In contrast, Tyler (1994) and Tyler and Degoey (1996) suggest that causality runs from responsiveness to trust. Craig (1993) acknowledges the complexity of the causal question, but ultimately concludes, along with others (Feldman 1983; Madsen 1987; Brehm and Rahn 1997), that perceived responsiveness leads to trust. Just as trust and responsiveness may engage in reciprocal causation (each causing the other), trust and confidence or responsiveness and confidence may also be reciprocally related. In the context of this type of conflicting theory, Freeman, Williams, and Lin (1989) propose vector autoregression (VAR) as an appropriate statistical technique. Specifically, a VAR model is appropriate because it will help us sort out the direction of causality among our measures of public evaluations of government and other variables in the model.[3]

We estimate a seven-variable VAR model that can be thought of as seven regression equations that are estimated simultaneously. Each equation contains the same independent or causal variables, and each of the seven principal series in our analysis is also the dependent variable in one of the equations. These seven series include trust in government, perceived responsiveness, confidence in government, satisfaction with the track of the country, policy liberalism, presidential approval, and economic expectations. In addition to these seven series, our VAR model includes the two measures of the most important problem facing the nation, an events series, and change in unemployment and inflation. These variables were described in the section labeled "Other Measures" and are assumed to be causally prior to the seven series that serve as both independent and dependent variables. Thus, our VAR model treats these additional variables solely as independent variables.

The VAR model enables us to establish the direction of causality among the variables in our analysis through the use of Granger causality tests. The concept of Granger causality is based on "the idea that a variable *X* 'causes' another variable *Y*, if by incorporating the past

3 For a more technical discussion of how VAR models accomplish this, see Freeman, Williams, and Lin (1989).

history of *X* one can improve a prediction of *Y* over a prediction based solely on the history of *Y* alone" (Freeman 1983). In the bivariate case, variable *X* is said to "Granger cause" variable *Y* if *Y* is better predicted by lagged values of both *X* and *Y* than by lagged values of *Y* alone. The concept of Granger causality is easily extended to multivariate scenarios and is typically assessed through *F*-tests of blocks of coefficients. Each *F*-test provides an assessment of whether each variable among a set of variables is causally prior to the dependent variable in an equation.

The results of our *F*-tests are reported in Table 4.1. The left column of Table 4.1 lists the dependent variable for each of the seven equations in our model. The middle column shows the independent variables tested in each equation. Lastly, the right column contains "*p*-values" associated with the proposed causal variable in each equation. These *p*-values are interpreted as the probability of no causal effect, with a *p*-value of .05 or less providing strong evidence that a proposed causal variable does indeed exert causal influence. For example, based on the results of the first row in Table 4.1, the probability that confidence does not cause trust is only five out of one hundred or 5%. Statistically speaking, we can thus be relatively certain that confidence causes trust. Such results are commonly said to be statistically significant.

TRUST, RESPONSIVENESS, AND CONFIDENCE

Table 4.1 permits numerous insights regarding the causal relationships among our variables. Of particular interest to this study are the causal relationships among the dimensions of public views of government. For instance, does trust in government cause perceived responsiveness or does responsiveness influence trust? Consider first the hypothesis that trust causes responsiveness. For this hypothesis to be supported, the *p*-value associated with trust in the responsiveness equation should be .05 or less. As can be seen in the second row of Table 4.1, this is indeed the case. The magnitude of this causal effect can be evaluated by examining the trust coefficient in the second column of Table 4.2. The trust coefficient in this equation is .21, which indicates that each 1% increase in trust causes approximately .02% increase in perceived responsiveness. As discussed above, however, trust and responsiveness may in fact cause each other. Our VAR model allows us to test this possibility of reciprocal causation. The *p*-value associated with responsiveness in the trust equation is .17, which is greater than .05. Thus, we find no evidence of reciprocal causation.

The results in Table 4.1 further reveal that confidence in government has a direct causal influence on trust in government. When public

Table 4.1. *F-Tests of Blocks of Coefficients*

Equation	Block of Coefficients	p-value
Trust	Trust	.00
	Responsiveness	.17
	Confidence	.05
	Track of Country	.98
	Policy Liberalism	.40
	Presidential Approval	.64
	Economic Expectations	.24
Responsiveness	Trust	.05
	Responsiveness	.01
	Confidence	.19
	Track of Country	.78
	Policy Liberalism	.07
	Presidential Approval	.25
	Economic Expectations	.86
Confidence	Trust	.68
	Responsiveness	.21
	Confidence	.02
	Track of Country	.13
	Policy Liberalism	.64
	Presidential Approval	.75
	Economic Expectations	.04
Track of Country	Trust	.98
	Responsiveness	.64
	Confidence	.26
	Track of Country	.43
	Policy Liberalism	.81
	Presidential Approval	.26
	Economic Expectations	.04
Policy Liberalism	Trust	.02
	Responsiveness	.90
	Confidence	.40
	Track of Country	.29
	Policy Liberalism	.00
	Presidential Approval	.24
	Economic Expectations	.27
Presidential Approval	Trust	.68
	Responsiveness	.24
	Confidence	.06
	Track of Country	.40
	Policy Liberalism	.98
	Presidential Approval	.00
	Economic Expectations	.05

Equation	Block of Coefficients	p-value
Economic Expectations	Trust	.87
	Responsiveness	.52
	Confidence	.79
	Track of Country	.23
	Policy Liberalism	.95
	Presidential Approval	.05
	Economic Expectations	.00

perceptions of confidence in the institutions of national government are more positive, evaluations of trust in government are also more positive. There is no evidence of reciprocal causation between confidence and trust, as causality appears to run only from the former to the latter. Nor does perceived government responsiveness exert any causal influence on confidence. One variable that does drive confidence in government is economic expectations. When perceptions of the nation's economic future are brighter, the public is likely to express greater confidence in the national government. Conversely, expectations of economic turmoil are likely to result in lower levels of confidence.

Shown in the third column of Table 4.2, the variable representing the percentage of the public identifying international concerns as the most important problem facing the nation also exerts a causal influence on confidence. Specifically, as the proportion of the public saying that an international concern is the most important problem facing the nation increases, so too does confidence in government. This finding comports well with Mueller's (1970) notion of a "rally around the flag" effect. Although Mueller's rallying effect was specifically referring to rallying around the president, our results suggest that heightened public focus on international concerns increases confidence in the government as a whole.

Presidential Approval

The column under presidential approval in Table 4.2 reveals that our analysis also provides evidence for a "rallying" effect around the president himself. Specifically, the coefficient for our events series is .08. This means, for instance, that during the first quarter of the Gulf War, President Bush's approval rating increased by about 8% (after taking into account the influence of the other variables in the model). The

Table 4.2. *VAR Results*

	Endogenous Variable						
	Trust in Government	Perceived Responsiveness	Confidence in Government	Track of Country	Policy Liberalism	Presidential Approval	Economic Expectations
$Trust_{t-1}$	.61*	.21*	.07	.01	.11*	–.10	–.05
	(.13)	(.10)	(.17)	(.25)	(.05)	(.24)	(.31)
$Responsiveness_{t-1}$	.24	.40*	.28	.15	–.01	–.38	–.27
	(.18)	(.14)	(.22)	(.33)	(.07)	(.32)	(.41)
$Confidence_{\ t-1}$	.24*	.12	.35*	.25	–.04	.40	.07
	(.12)	(.09)	(.14)	(.22)	(.04)	(.21)	(.27)
Track of $Country_{t-1}$	.01	.03	–.23	.18	–.05	–.18	.33
	(.12)	(.09)	(.15)	(.22)	(.04)	(.21)	(.28)
Policy $Liberalism_{t-1}$	.12	–.21	.08	–.06	.86*	–.01	.02
	(.14)	(.11)	(.18)	(.27)	(.05)	(.26)	(.34)
Presidential $Approval_{t-1}$	–.04	–.07	.03	.17	.04	.78*	–.39*
	(.08)	(.06)	(.10)	(.15)	(.03)	(.15)	(.19)
Economic $Expectations_{t-1}$	–.06	.01	.13*	.20*	.02	.18*	.63*
	(.05)	(.04)	(.06)	(.09)	(.02)	(.09)	(.12)
Change in $Unemployment_t$	–.10	.06	.31	–.08	.10	.01	–.82*
	(.17)	(.14)	(.22)	(.32)	(.06)	(.31)	(.41)
Change in $Inflation_t$	–.52	.14	1.34	–.33	–.47	.02	–1.65
	(.75)	(.59)	(.93)	(1.39)	(.28)	(1.35)	(1.76)
MIP $International_t$	.03	.11	.36*	.47*	.01	.36	.04
	(.11)	(.09)	(.14)	(.21)	(.04)	(.20)	(.26)

	Endogenous Variable						
	Trust in Government	Perceived Responsiveness	Confidence in Government	Track of Country	Policy Liberalism	Presidential Approval	Economic Expectations
MIP $Deficit_t$	.07	–.14	.01	–.23	–.02	–.37	–.22
	(.12)	(.09)	(.15)	(.22)	(.04)	(.22)	(.28)
$Events_t$	.00	–.01	.01	.03	–.01	.08*	.02
	(.01)	(.01)	(.02)	(.03)	(.01)	(.02)	(.03)
New $Administration_t$	.00	–.01	.02	.08*	.00	.12*	.01
	(.02)	(.01)	(.03)	(.04)	(.01)	(.04)	(.05)
Constant	–.06	.25*	–.02	–.02	.06	.06	.50*
	(.10)	(.08)	(.13)	(.20)	(.04)	(.19)	(.25)
Adjusted R^2	.77	.70	.51	.64	.92	.69	.71
Standard Error of Estimate	.03	.03	.04	.06	.01	.05	.07
Ljung-Box Q Test	26.38,	14.34,	33.08,	31.80,	23.87,	24.78,	28.64,
	$p = .44$	$p = .96$	$p = .16$	$p = .20$	$p = .58$	$p = .53$	$p = .33$
LM Test for ARCH	0.68,	0.51,	0.40,	0.27,	0.65,	0.39,	0.63,
	$p = .81$	$p = .93$	$p = .98$	$p = .99$	$p = .84$	$p = .98$	$p = .85$
N	67	67	67	67	67	67	67

Note: * $p < .05$. Standard errors are in parentheses. Data are quarterly from 1980:1 to 1996:4. For ease of comparison, all variables are scaled on a 0–1 range. The statistically insignificant Ljung-Box and Lagrange Multiplier test statistics indicate a failure to detect the presence of any serial correlation or autoregressive conditional heteroskedasticity in the residuals.

coefficients for the two most important problem series do not quite reach the threshold of statistical significance discussed earlier, although they are both extremely close. As a result, we call attention to these two variables to make a substantive and rather interesting observation. The coefficients for these two variables, though nearly identical in magnitude, are oppositely signed. Periods of international crisis, it seems, give the president's approval rating a boost. The same cannot be said for domestic problems. When the proportion of the public identifying the deficit or government spending as the most important problem increases, approval declines. Finally, the coefficient for the variable marking the first quarter of each new administration reveals a positive effect on approval, reflecting the "honeymoon" period at the outset of a new presidential administration.

Journalists and scholars alike have written extensively about the connections between presidential approval and the performance of the nation's economy. Do actual economic conditions affect approval or does approval respond only to the public's perceptions of the country's economic conditions? MacKuen, Erikson, and Stimson (1992) supply evidence to support the latter supposition. When controlling for economic expectations, they find that measures of actual economic conditions, such as change in unemployment and inflation, have no direct effect on approval. Rather, their influence on approval is mediated by the public's economic perceptions. Economic perceptions alone, they argue, directly influence presidential approval. Our results provide support for this portion of their analysis. We find that neither change in unemployment nor change in inflation has any direct effect on approval. Our results do indicate that change in unemployment has a direct effect on the public's economic expectations. Moreover, we find too that economic expectations exert a direct causal influence on approval.

However, consistent with Freeman et al. (1998), our results contradict the conclusion of unidirectional causality reached by MacKuen et al. (1992) regarding the relationship between economic expectations and approval. MacKuen and colleagues report that economic expectations cause approval but not the reverse. In contrast, Freeman et al. find that approval may drive economic expectations and that, in some cases, there is reciprocal causation between the two. We concur. The results of our model indicate that, as expected, approval is caused by economic expectations. However, our results also indicate that approval has a reciprocal causal impact on economic expectations.

Direction of the Country

Another equation in our VAR model investigates the determinants of public satisfaction with the direction or track in which the country is headed. Is satisfaction with the direction of the country influenced by public views of trust, perceived responsiveness, or confidence in government? Our results indicate that it is not. As shown in Table 4.1, none of these evaluations has any direct causal impact on satisfaction with the direction of the nation. Only one of our principal series, economic expectations, has a causal influence on satisfaction. When perceptions of the nation's economic conditions are more favorable, satisfaction with the direction of the country also rises.

In addition to economic expectations, two of our other variables affect public views that the nation is headed in the right direction. One of these is the series identifying international concerns as the most important problem facing the nation. When public focus on international concerns is greater, the perception that the country is headed in the right direction is also greater. In other words, public satisfaction with the direction of the country increases when major problems are seen as nondomestic in nature. The coefficient for the variable marking the beginning of a new presidential administration is also positive, indicating a more optimistic view of the direction of the nation at the outset of each new administration. This is likely a reflection of the satisfaction of the nation's electoral preferences. Following the expression of electoral preferences in a presidential election, there is an increased sense among the electorate that the country is headed in the right direction. Indeed, Kornberg and Clarke (1992) suggest that elections may serve to renew the public's faith in the political system.

Policy Liberalism

In developing the concept of domestic policy liberalism, Stimson (1991) proposes that public views about the extent to which the government should spend money or do more in various areas of public policy change as a function of experiences with the consequences of previously enacted policies and in response to the cues provided by opinion leaders. We agree that these factors are likely to affect public opinion on policy liberalism. We propose further, however, that public views of government are likely to be important determinants of public support for governmental activity.

The results of our analysis provide some support for this position. As shown in Table 4.1 and the policy liberalism column of Table 4.2, trust in government has a direct and positive causal effect on policy liberalism. Moreover, the causal relationship appears to be unidirectional, such that trust causes greater support for policy liberalism but not the reverse. This finding has important implications for understanding the determinants of public support for a more active national government. Rising trust in government leads to increased public support for spending in domestic policy areas such as education, welfare, and the environment. Conversely, when trust declines, public support for government activity in these areas is also likely to decline.

DISCUSSION

We have identified and discussed the direction of causality among a number of variables. We now turn to the most significant findings in this research and some of the issues that remain to be addressed. In examining the relationships among trust, responsiveness, and confidence and their causes and consequences, we find that evaluations of trust in the national government drive perceptions of responsiveness. Trust and responsiveness are not reciprocally related, and the only variable that directly influences trust in government is confidence. When confidence in the people running the institutions of national government is greater, so too are evaluations of trust in government. Evaluations of confidence, in turn, are driven by economic expectations and focus on international concerns as the most important problem facing the nation.

The model employed in this study also permits another look at the relationship between presidential approval and the economy. Our results provide further confirmation that the effects of the objective economy on approval are mediated by economic expectations. Our results also provide additional evidence of a reciprocal causal relationship between approval and economic expectations. Furthermore, we find that satisfaction with the direction in which the country is headed is largely a function of public perceptions of the national economy and views of the most important problem facing the nation.

Perhaps the most important finding of our study is the causal connection between trust in government and policy liberalism. Domestic policy liberalism is, at least in part, a direct function of the public's trust in the federal government. Evaluations of confidence have an indirect causal effect on support for liberal domestic policies, via the influence of confidence on trust. And to the extent that election outcomes are driven by the public's liberal or conservative policy preferences (Stimson, MacKuen, and Erikson 1995), trust in government plays a role in election outcomes and the public policy outputs that follow. Our results suggest that declining levels of trust in government should be of particular concern to Democratic candidates. Since they are more likely to support the types of domestic programs included in Stimson's measure of policy liberalism, Democratic candidates may find declining levels of trust to be quite consequential. The midterm elections of 1994 provide a dramatic example of the influence of declining trust on election outcomes. In the 1994 elections, Republicans gained control of both houses of Congress for the first time in 40 years. This result, which stunned the pundits and the mass media, was no accident in our view. As discussed, public trust in government had reached a new nadir in the summer of 1994. One clear implication of our results is that voters' unhappiness with government was a major reason for the loss of over 50 Democratic seats, a repudiation not seen since the elections of 1946.

The results of our analyses are consistent with theoretical views such as those of Barber (1983) and Levi (1998) that place competence at the center of understanding public perceptions of trust in government. In particular, we find that outcomes in terms of the state of the economy and the important issues facing the nation influence public perceptions of confidence in the people running the institutions of national government, which subsequently affect public perceptions of trust and responsiveness in government. Moreover, trust and responsiveness are not themselves caused by outcomes such as actual economic indicators or views of the economy. When confidence is removed from the model, there is no direct effect of either perceptions of the economy or changes in unemployment or inflation on either trust or responsiveness. This clearly indicates that trust and responsiveness have distinct determinants from confidence. The fact that confidence is driven by measures of policy outcomes such as economic expectations and views of the most important problem facing the nation is consistent with the view that perceptions of competence are influenced by assessments of governmental performance in terms of delivering desirable policy outcomes. When economic times are good and the public is less focused on problems within the nation, citizens express greater confidence in the people running the institutions of government. The finding that trust and responsiveness are not similarly directly influenced by these measures of policy outcomes poses a question for future research.

Finally, our results are also consistent with theoretical expectations concerning the consequences of public views of trust in government. In terms of allowing policy makers to commit resources to attain societal goals, we find that declining levels of public trust in government are associated with decreased public willingness to support government spending and activity across a range of domestic policy areas. Thus, our research illuminates both the causes and consequences of public evaluations of trust in the national government. Policy makers may influence public perceptions of confidence in government by delivering desirable outcomes such as prosperity and fewer problems in the arena of domestic policy. More positive evaluations of confidence in government lead to greater expressions of trust in government, and a more trusting public is inclined to view government as more responsive to public desires and is more willing to support increased activity in a range of domestic policy areas.

The causes and consequences of public trust in government have occupied researchers for quite some time. At stake is the question of how seriously we need to view these sentiments. Are they reactions to current conditions, something that fresh faces and an improved economy will remedy? Or do they represent opinions of more consequence? Our analysis supports both these interpretations. Confidence in government institutions and the people running these institutions drives both general trust and perceived responsiveness. And these assessments are to a large extent driven by economic expectations and evaluations of the most important problem facing the nation, supporting our notion that confidence judgments primarily reflect the competence dimension of trust. But trust in government is importantly implicated in the public's policy preferences, which play a large role in shaping electoral outcomes and public policy outputs. These feelings, therefore, are of considerable consequence in shaping the context of American politics.

Part II

With Which Governmental Institutions Do Americans Tend to Be Dissatisfied?

To say Americans dislike (or like) government is misleading because of the breadth of the term government. In actuality, at any given time people tend to be much more favorably disposed toward some features of government than others. In other words, it is not simply government they dislike; it is certain aspects of government. Part II contains four essays that focus on the patterns of public approval for different *institutions* of government. Such an approach makes particular sense in the case of the United States because of the power and distinctiveness of our political institutions. The wide variation in institutional organization, purpose, and arrangement makes it possible to gain valuable information by observing people's differing attitudes toward individual institutions. If it appears as though people tend to approve of one type or style of institution more than another, we will be provided with a useful clue as to what it is about government that Americans dislike. So, the four papers in this section look across institutions rather than across time but are still concerned with the same basic question that motivated the research reported in Part I.

For example, Lilliard Richardson, David Houston, and Chris Hadjiharalambous note that "variation in citizens' assessments of political leadership across political institutions is by no means a coincidence." They believe that people have different expectations of the three branches of government, and that these expectations naturally color the relative popularity of the leaders of those institutions. Using a detailed battery of explanatory variables and data from the General Social Surveys of the late 1980s and early 1990s on "confidence in the people running . . . ," they find the following: Leaders of the executive branch, most notably the president, are evaluated primarily on partisan and performance terms. If a respondent shares the same partisan affiliation as the president and if that respondent sees economic conditions as generally favorable, it is likely that confidence in the president will be expressed. To go to the other extreme, confidence in the leaders of the judicial branch is completely unrelated to partisan and economic performance concerns. And confidence in the leaders of the legislative branch is somewhere in the middle, influenced a bit by partisan and economic concerns but not nearly to the extent as with the president.

As distinctive as American political institutions are, the Constitution connects them, and the connection between Congress and the president is especially intimate. Thus, we should not be too surprised that early research on public attitudes toward government concluded that opinion of Congress was formed in the "shadow" of opinion of the president (Davidson, Kovenock, and O'Leary, 1966). In this volume, Jeffrey Bernstein provides a more detailed investigation of the connection between approval of the president and approval of Congress. He is especially concerned with the extent to which this connection persists under conditions of divided government. Bernstein's most surprising finding perhaps is that approval of Congress is positively related to approval of the president even when the president is of the opposite political party from that controlling Congress. In other words, approval of George Bush in 1990 seems to have increased the chances of that same individual also approving of the (then) Democratically controlled Congress. This suggests that people's approval of Congress and the president is not always passed through a partisan lens, and it inclines Bernstein toward a "general cynicism" rather than "partisan control" model.

But separation of powers is only the beginning. The founders also divided power between and among levels of government and much can be learned about public attitudes toward government by comparing approval of the federal government and state governments. Popular rhetoric leads to the conclusion that the public is much more likely to look favorably upon state government than upon the federal government. After all, bringing the government closer to the people is a popular goal, and state government *is* closer to the people. But Eric Uslaner offers some needed cautionary words about the ability of "devolution" to make government popular again. Using survey data collected by the *Washington Post*, the Kaiser Family Foundation, and Harvard University, he finds that most people who dislike one level of government also dislike the other. In fact, only 17% of the respondents fit with the conventional wisdom expectation of disliking the federal government and liking their state government. Although there is clearly an ideological component to attitudes, with conservatives being more likely to distrust Washington, it turns out that conservatives are no more likely to trust the pertinent state capital. Uslaner sensibly interprets his findings as indicating that in the people's minds, "Washington isn't the problem; government is the problem."

Marc Hetherington and John Nugent are similarly skeptical about the ability of devolution to improve the public mood toward government. They begin by demonstrating that throughout history, state governments have hardly been the objects of positive feelings, and then turn to data on the actual performance of individual state governments as well as to NES data. Their basic finding is that "greater faith and confidence in subnational governance is not a function of the capability of respondents' state governments or the responsiveness of those governments to citizen input." Instead it seems as though the main reason some individuals would like power shifted to state government is merely the belief that the federal government is flawed. Though it may be natural for people to become more excited about option "B" as soon as they conclude that option "A" is a failure, Hetherington and Nugent point out that this situation creates a real danger that satisfaction with option "B" (state government) "may dry up quickly in the face of even minor indications of state incapacity."

5

Public Confidence in the Leaders of American Governmental Institutions

LILLIARD E. RICHARDSON, JR., DAVID J. HOUSTON, AND CHRIS SISSIE HADJIHARALAMBOUS

> With public sentiment nothing can fail; without it, nothing can succeed. Consequently, he who molds public sentiment goes deeper than he who enacts statutes or pronounces decisions.
>
> —Abraham Lincoln, Lincoln–Douglas debate, July 31, 1858

Public trust in political leadership is a crucial element of representative governance. In Lockean terms, people "consent" to enter into a social contract and "accept the bonds of government" because they expect those entrusted with power not to act in a self-serving manner, but to act in ways that promote the general well-being. As Miller (1974a) suggests, democracy is only possible "when the relationship between leaders and the public is based on mutual understanding and reciprocal trust rather than the use of coercive and arbitrary authority" (989). Trust is important because it serves as the "creator of collective power"(Gamson 1968, 42), enabling government officials to make decisions and commit resources without having to resort to coercion or obtain the specific approval of citizens for every decision. Furthermore, in the absence of trust, government officials do not have any leeway as they pursue long-term national interests. Promises for better days ahead ring hollow in the ears of citizens who have come to doubt the competence and integrity of their government officials.

In view of this it is hardly surprising that political observers have been quite alarmed by the collapse of public confidence in the leaders of all three branches of American government during the post-1960s era (e.g., Lipset and Schneider 1987; Greider 1992; Craig 1996; Tolchin 1996). In 1966, Louis Harris and Associates found that four in ten Americans had "a great deal of confidence" in the people running the executive branch (41%) and Congress (42%). Three decades later in 1996, barely one in ten expressed "a great deal of confidence" in the people running the executive branch (12%) and Congress (10%). A similar picture emerges when one looks at citizens' confidence in judicial leadership, though the drop has not been quite so dramatic (45% to 31%) (Harris Poll 1996).

One of the central premises of this research is that this variation in citizens' assessments of political leadership across political institutions is by no means a coincidence. The majority of the literature on the decline of political trust has focused on "government," ignoring variations in trust across different political institutions. We hypothesize that assessments of different institutional leaders vary because people have different expectations of the three branches of government. These expectations develop from socialization about what Congress, the executive, and the Supreme Court should be like. Civics textbooks, for instance, condition citizens to expect members of the legislative branch to be responsive to the needs of their constituents because Congress was designed by the Founding Fathers to be "the people's branch" (Fenno 1978). Because the media portray the president as the government's central actor (Iyengar and Kinder 1987), it should come as no surprise that people come to expect the White House to act responsibly and provide quick solutions to problems that the nation faces. Finally, from early childhood, citizens come to expect the Court to act as the guardian of citizens' civil liberties and to make sure that the laws are applied consistently (Casey 1974; Caldeira and Gibson 1992).

A second premise is that not all Americans hold identical views of legislative, executive, and judicial leadership. Personal experiences and characteristics condition citizen attitudes toward government leaders. For example, citizens may hold the executive branch responsible for the performance of the economy, but they may be more reluctant to hold congressional leaders or especially judicial leaders accountable for the state of the economy. The same general model may be inadequate for explaining attitudes toward the leadership of each institution.

In the next section we outline some expectations with respect to the effects that various personal characteristics and experiences should have upon attitudes toward legislative, executive, and judicial leadership. Then we turn to a description of the data and methods used in our analysis. We then describe patterns observed during the 1986 to 1994 period. It is important to look at a large time span for two reasons: First, public disenchantment has not grown uniformly over time (Orren 1997). Second, a longer period of time allows us to examine partisan changes in the presidency. In the last section, we discuss the implications of our findings.

EXPLAINING PUBLIC ATTITUDES IN INSTITUTIONAL LEADERSHIP: BACK TO THE USUAL SUSPECTS

Although the focus of the following analysis is on attitudes regarding confidence in the leaders of national institutions of government, the general literature on confidence and/or trust in government will serve as the basis for building a model. The analysis addresses the question: Is this same general model adequate for explaining attitudes toward the leaders of each of these institutions? Two categories of determinants that comprise the model of confidence in government leaders tested below are: sociodemographic and attitudinal.

Sociodemographic Determinants

Race. Race is the demographic variable that has most consistently been found to have a statistically significant relationship with trust in government. Whites have been found to be more likely to trust the political system and its leaders than nonwhites, even when controlling for the effects of other social characteristics (Citrin, McClosky, Shanks, and Sniderman 1975; Abramson 1983; Beck, Rainey, and Traut 1990). Distrust has been associated with nonwhites' disaffection with federal taxation and spending, quality of local services, and financial misfortune. Because the majority of political leaders are white, minorities may also be suspicious that these leaders do not have the best interest of minorities in mind. Therefore, we expect black Americans to be less confident in legislative and executive leaders than whites.

This relationship between race and confidence may be more complex for the judicial leaders. Gibson and Caldeira (1992) found that blacks who came of political age during the social activism of the Warren Court exhibited positive affect toward the courts that younger and older age cohorts did not. We would not expect, however, this positive affect to characterize African American attitudes toward the court today. Instead, the Rehnquist Court of the late 1980s and 1990s allowed a retrenchment on civil-rights issues, such as busing and affirmative action, and leaned more toward the value of social order in assessing police powers. Therefore, we expect that minorities will have less confidence in the court's leaders than whites.

Sex. We expect that men will have more confidence in leaders of all three branches of national government than women. First, women may exhibit less confidence because the majority of leaders in American political institutions are men. To the degree that symbolic representation matters, the demographic make-up of government may lead women to feel that they will not be understood nor treated fairly by political leaders. Second, women may feel disadvantaged by the present political system as exemplified by the persistence of a "glass ceiling" in government and the American workplace (Lewis 1993; Naff 1994).

Education. We expect that individuals with higher levels of education have more confidence in government leaders because they possess a greater understanding of political institutions and processes. Instead, empirical research generally has reported a negative relationship between education and approval of Congress (Davidson, Kovenock and O'Leary 1968; Patterson, Ripley and Quinlan 1992; Ripley, Patterson, Maurer and Quinlan 1992). These findings are explained by pointing out that educated people are more likely to be aware of missteps by members of Congress or partisan bickering in Washington and as a result are more critical of congressional members (Hibbing and Theiss-Morse 1995).

In comparison to assessments of Congress, less research has focused directly on the relationship between education and attitudes toward executive leaders. We expect, however, that education is likely to have a positive effect on confidence of executive leaders. More knowledge of the executive branch is likely to translate into greater familiarity and confidence with these leaders. The more unified and centralized decision-making process in executive institutions may be less troubling to the better educated than the partisan nature of deliberations in Congress.

Finally, we expect those with higher levels of education to have more confidence in leaders of the Supreme Court. Previous research has found a positive correlation between education and support for the Court (Caldeira and Gibson 1992). This effect can be explained by a greater awareness of the legal language used in the announcements of judicial decisions and the importance of the rule of law for settling societal disputes. "Simply put, to know courts is to love them, because to know them is to be exposed to a series of legitimizing messages focused on the symbols of justice, judicial objectivity, and impartiality" (Gibson, Caldeira and Baird 1998).

Income. Past research has failed to produce consistent support for a significant relationship between one's own economic experiences and attitudes toward government. The well-documented decline in trust seems to be prevalent both among Americans who have fared relatively well financially and those who have not (Miller and Borrelli 1991; Craig 1996). However, individuals who see themselves as financially well off are more likely to be supportive of government and its leaders (Miller 1983; Citrin and Green 1986; Lipset and Schneider 1987). Because of the importance of money in campaigns for elected officials, higher income individuals may feel as though they have greater access to these leaders. Thus, we expect income to have a positive effect on confidence in legislative and executive leaders.

The relationship between income and confidence in judicial leaders is more complex. On one hand, the Court protects property rights, which typically are more important to those with higher incomes. On the other, the Courts provide access to individuals fighting against social injustice, regardless of personal wealth. Therefore, we expect no significant relationship to emerge between income and assessments of judicial leadership. This expectation is corroborated by a lack of significant relationship between occupational prestige and support for the Court reported by Gibson and Caldeira (1992).

Age. Because an individual's identification with political institutions and community increases over time (Wright 1976), it is hypothesized that age will be positively related to an individual's level of confidence in government leaders. Lipset and Schneider (1987) describe the expected nature of this relationship: "as a rule, older people tend to identify more strongly with institutions simply because they have been tied to them for a longer period of time" (101). While this social connectedness explanation is logically appealing, Lipset and Schneider find the relationship between age and confidence to be inconsistent. An alternative hypothesis between age and confidence posits a negative relationship. As people get older they witness more examples of the fallibility of our leaders (e.g., Watergate, House banking scandal, Clinton impeachment). They may become less idealistic and more likely to lose confidence in the system in general and/or those involved in the political arena specifically. Given this uncertainty there is little reason to expect age to have different effects on confidence across institutions.

Union Membership and Church Attendance. According to pluralist orthodoxy, participation in voluntary associations promotes social integration, decreases feelings of inefficacy and distrust toward political institutions, and otherwise "plays a major role in democratic political culture" (Almond and Verba 1963, 320). As Wright (1976) points out in his study of alienation in the United States, these associations need not be expressly political in nature, nor need they serve politically instrumental goals. "The major 'integrative' effects are due to the 'communitarian' functions that they perform: they promote social contacts, provide sources of identity, and generally lessen the 'dissociation' endemic to modern industrial life" (Wright 1976, 147). Further, Robert Putnam, after cleverly weaving together analysis of over twenty years of development in Italian regional governments with declining bowling league rates, suggests that "generally speaking, the more we connect with other people, the more we trust them" (1995b, 665). Therefore, we expect such association/connection to be positively related to an individual's confidence in political leaders. More specifically, it is hypothesized that union members are more likely to express high levels of confidence in government leaders than nonunion members, and also that the more an individual attends church, the more likely they are to express higher levels of confidence in government leaders.

We also expect union membership and church attendance to have a more significant impact in evaluations of Congress when comparing across institutions. Attending meetings of voluntary associations makes people more tolerant of diversity in points of view and more comfortable with processes designed to iron out such differences in an effort to build consensus. Those who attend such meetings are more likely to appreciate deliberation in defining the group's goals and means to achieve those goals. As such, we expect those union members and those who attend church more frequently to be more comfortable with the partisan bickering that is often so evident in coverage of events in the U.S. Congress.

Attitudinal Factors

Personal Disposition. A popular theory among social scientists has been that mistrust of each other is a major reason Americans have lost confidence in the federal government and virtually every other major national institution. "An environment in which a majority of Americans believe that most people can't be trusted breeds attitudes that hold all politicians as corrupt, venal, and self-serving, and government action as doomed to fail" (Morin and Balz 1996, A6–A7). We expect individuals who have positive dispositions to exhibit more confidence in government leaders. No variation across institutions is expected with respect to the effects of this trait.

Personal Finances. Assessments of government leaders have been linked to the impact that government policies have on the nation's or an individual's economic situation. Previous research suggests a strong connection between support for leaders and perceptions of national economic performance and, to a lesser extent, personal economic conditions (Davidson, Kovenock and O'Leary 1968; Kenski 1977; Monroe 1978; Kiewiet 1981; Edwards and Wayne 1994). If conditions are good, this will translate into confidence in the job that political leaders are doing.

Thus, Nye (1997) relates low levels of trust to the explanation that "people may be properly unhappy with poor social outcomes even though the quality of government outputs does not change" (8). It is hypothesized that individuals with positive attitudes about their own financial situation are more likely to have higher levels of confidence in leaders of government. Furthermore, given that in the mind of most people the Court is not responsible for economic policy making, we expect personal finances to be particularly relevant in evaluations of legislative and executive leadership. After all, members of Congress and the president regularly take credit when economic performance is strong and blame others when things go sour. Thus, we do not expect to find a significant relationship between people's perceptions of their personal finances and attitudes toward those who sit on the Supreme Court.

Partisanship. Starting with the publication of *The American Voter* (1960), several studies have pointed to party identification functioning as a screening device or a filter in individuals' perceptions of political objects. Identifiers with the "in" party have been found to exhibit higher levels of confidence in political leadership than the "outs" because of the perception that the national government shares one's values (Miller 1974a; Wright 1976; Citrin and Green 1986; Hibbing and Theiss-Morse 1995). Thus, it is hypothesized that Democrats will be more likely to express confidence in executive leadership when the White House is occupied by a fellow Democrat than when the White House is occupied by a Republican. Furthermore, Democrats will be more likely to express confidence in the leadership provided by members of Congress when there are Democratic majorities in the two chambers than when Republicans control one of the two chambers. Given the absence of evidence for a significant relationship between partisan identification and attitudes toward the Court (Caldeira and Gibson 1992), we do not expect partisan loyalties to affect confidence in those who sit on the bench.

Extremism. Finally, we expect individuals with extreme political ideologies to exhibit less confidence in leaders of government institutions. Because of the need for compromise and bipartisanship necessary to produce policy, extremists will think that elected officials have either gone in the wrong direction or do not go far enough. Similarly, the tradition of relying on precedence and the rule of law will produce Court decisions that frustrate extremists. This hypothesis is supported by Caldeira and Gibson (1992): "[d]ogmatism also exerts a direct effect on support: the less dogmatic among our sample tend to lend the Court greater support" (653).

DATA AND METHODS

To test the identified hypotheses, data were taken from the General Social Survey, 1986–1994.[1] This data set contains responses to questions that probe an individual's confidence in the people running the following institutions of government: Congress, the executive branch, and the Supreme Court. Level of confidence is measured separately for leaders in each of the three branches of government. Each question has three possible responses: a great deal of confidence, only some confidence, or hardly any confidence at all. To simplify the analysis presented, we collapse the variable into two categories: a great deal of confidence and less confidence (i.e., only some or hardly any). For this reason, the models reported are estimated with logistical regression analysis.

For the sociodemographic variables, two dichotomous variables represent whether an individual is black or male. Household income is measured on a twelve-point scale, and age is a continuous variable. Education is operationalized with a five-point scale that represents the highest degree an individual has earned. Church attendance and union membership are introduced into the model to tap social connectedness to the community. Church attendance is a nine-point scale that ranges from never attends church to attends church several times a week. Union membership is a dummy variable to represent whether the respondent or his/her spouse is a member of a union.

An individual's personal disposition is measured here in two ways. First, a dichotomous variable is employed to represent individuals who say that they are very happy or pretty happy with how "things are these days." Second, personal trust is measured as another dichotomous variable to indicate whether an individual feels that "most people can be trusted." To measure individual attitudes about personal finances, two dummy variables were created from the extreme responses to the following question: "During the last few years, has your financial situation been getting better, getting worse, or has it stayed the same?" Thus, two separate dummy variables (financially better and financially worse) measure whether an individual's financial situation has improved or has gotten worse.

Dummy variables for Democratic and Republican party identification were created from a seven-point partisanship scale by combining the two

1 The General Social Survey was not conducted in 1992 so our study includes only eight years of data.

categories of responses that indicate an identification with either party.[2] To measure ideological extremism, the extremely liberal and extremely conservative categories of a seven-point ideology scale were combined into another dichotomous variable.

FINDINGS

The results of the logistic regression analysis are discussed in the following. We summarize our findings by looking at confidence in the leaders of each institution separately. In this way we can see whether the determinants of confidence differ across the three government institutions.

Confidence in Legislative Leaders

The models explaining confidence in legislative leaders are presented in Table 5.1. It is readily apparent that these models do not significantly advance our understanding of confidence in legislative leaders. This can be seen by an examination of the model chi-square statistics that reach a high level of statistical significance (i.e., 0.01) in only three years. This is likely due to the skewed distribution of the responses: less than 20% of respondents in each year express a great deal of confidence in leaders of Congress. Thus, there is little variation between people to be explained.

What is clear in these models, however, is that older Americans tend to be less confident in congressional leaders than others. This is contrary to the social connectedness argument but is consistent with the argument that older individuals will have more experience witnessing leaders engaged in behavior that is disappointing to the electorate. Beyond age, confidence in legislative leaders may be a function of partisanship, income, and education. It appears that Democrats are more confident given that Congress was controlled by the Democratic Party throughout the time period studied. This may indirectly explain the effect that income has on confidence as people with higher incomes tend to affiliate with the Republican Party. This is exemplified by the strong negative relationship between income and confidence in 1993 and 1994 when Congress and the White House were both controlled by the Democrats. As we hypothesized earlier, the more educated are less confident in congressional leaders, an effect that is likely due to their greater awareness of the partisan bickering that tends to characterize legislative debates.

2 Separate analyses were conducted by adding independent leaners in with party identifiers. There were no appreciable differences in the results obtained by using either operationalization of party identification.

Table 5.1. *Logit Results for Confidence in Legislative Leaders*

	1986	1987	1988	1989	1990	1991	1993	1994
Black	−0.35	−0.36*	−0.23	−0.74*	0.03	0.42	−0.43	0.60**
Male	0.21	0.07	0.13	0.18	−0.12	0.14	−0.00	0.43**
Income	−0.09***	−0.03	−0.02	−0.01	−0.01	0.01	−0.16***	−0.09**
Age	−0.01**	−0.01	−0.03***	−0.01**	−0.01	−0.01**	−0.01	0.01
Degree	−0.06	−0.03	−0.23**	−0.12	−0.04	−0.05	−0.27*	−0.22**
Church Attend	0.03	0.05	0.06	0.08**	0.01	0.05	0.05	0.03
Union Member	0.23	0.17	0.37	−0.02	−0.21	−0.19	0.27	−0.07
Happy	0.17	0.52**	0.64	0.55	−0.00	−0.07	0.03	−0.03
Trust	−0.11	0.13	0.19	0.25	0.35	−0.13	−0.27	0.06
Finances Better	−0.06	−0.05	0.19	−0.03	0.29	−0.33	0.13	0.19
Finances Worse	−0.46**	−0.21	−0.09	−0.51*	0.05	−0.36	0.22	−0.09
Democrat	0.12	0.41**	0.47*	0.29	−0.03	0.08	0.81**	0.34
Republican	−0.05	0.12	0.44*	0.03	0.24	0.35	0.20	−0.13
Extremist	−0.23	0.52*	−0.48	0.24	−0.52	−0.22	−0.07	−0.26
Intercept	−0.52	−1.85***	−1.38	−1.78***	−1.58**	−1.02**	−0.96	−2.21***
N	1,284	1,511	881	906	768	887	925	1,731
−2 Log 1	1,085.31	1,322.51	719.66	786.84	652.35	828.09	413.14	862.12
χ^2	21.16*	23.42*	38.38***	23.11*	9.97	18.21	31.13***	40.76***

Note: * $p < 0.10$. ** $p < 0.05$. *** $p < 0.01$.

Confidence in Executive Leaders

Table 5.2 reports the results of the models for confidence in leaders of the executive branch. These models do a much better job of explaining the variation in confidence than the congressional models. The most obvious pattern in these models is the strong effect of partisanship on confidence. Republicans are consistently positive when a Republican occupies the White House but offer negative assessments of the Clinton Administration during 1993 and 1994. To a lesser degree, Democrats offer a negative assessment of Republican administrations but turn positive during the Clinton years. It is clear that by "leaders of the executive branch" individuals are largely focusing on the president as the key executive official.

As hypothesized, "pocketbook voting" clearly affects confidence in leaders of the executive branch. As the chief policy official in an administration, the president is rewarded with confidence when economic conditions are strong and is targeted for blame when the economy struggles. This phenomenon is most prominent in the form of negative assessments of the economy as represented by the financially worse variable. The president pays a heavier price for a poor economy than Congress. Furthermore, confidence in the president is more affected by a perception of worsening financial conditions and not improving ones. This finding is consistent with the long-held belief that negative economic assessments play a more important role in shaping public opinion than do positive assessments (Key 1966; Mueller 1973; Bloom and Price 1975).

Church attendance and trust are additional factors that are correlated with confidence in executive leaders. Individuals who attend church regularly are more likely to exhibit confidence. This finding supports the social connectedness hypothesis. Similarly, trusting people offer positive assessments of executive leaders.

Confidence in Supreme Court Leaders

Table 5.3 reports the results of the logistic regressions on confidence in leaders of the Supreme Court. The models reported here provide several lessons for understanding the sources of confidence in these leaders. Three factors stand out in explaining more positive assessments of judicial leaders, as hypothesized. Those citizens who are generally more trusting are quite likely to express confidence. Likewise, more highly educated citizens, who are more likely to be aware of the courts and knowledgeable about judicial procedure, express more confidence. Men also have higher levels of confidence than do women.

Table 5.2. *Logit Results for Confidence in Executive Branch Leaders*

	1986	1987	1988	1989	1990	1991	1993	1994
Black	–0.39	–0.24	0.10	–0.68*	–0.43	–0.06	–0.21	0.01
Male	0.17	0.35**	0.39**	–0.03	–0.03	0.10	–0.03	0.12
Income	–0.05*	–0.05*	0.01	–0.01	0.08*	0.03	–0.14***	–0.03
Age	0.00	–0.00	–0.01**	–0.00	–0.00	–0.00	–0.01	0.02***
Degree	0.04	–0.04	0.00	–0.09	0.02	0.03	0.14	–0.01
Church Attend	0.07**	0.07**	0.10***	0.08**	0.07**	–0.01	–0.01	0.01
Union Member	–0.03	–0.27	–0.53*	–0.20	–0.36	0.21	–0.31	–0.69***
Happy	0.19	0.21	–0.12	–0.12	0.21	0.51*	0.31	0.03
Trust	–0.01	0.36**	0.25	0.32*	0.39**	–0.09	0.43*	0.27
Finances Better	0.40**	0.03	–0.05	0.07	–0.16	–0.33*	0.52*	0.26
Finances Worse	–0.72***	–0.43**	0.15	–0.67**	0.11	–0.44**	0.57**	–0.19
Democrat	–0.05	–0.42**	–0.31	–0.31	–0.15	–0.34	0.25	0.63***
Republican	0.63***	0.74***	0.89***	0.34	0.44**	0.64***	–0.64**	–0.79***
Extremist	–0.21	0.28	0.38	0.15	–0.33	–0.92**	0.61	–0.28
Intercept	–1.65***	–1.51***	–1.85***	–1.26**	–2.52***	–1.68***	–0.98	–2.73***
N	1,280	1,514	876	898	769	889	920	1,739
–2 Log 1	1,244.27	1,342.71	748.53	863.68	810.38	980.97	618.52	1,148.77
χ^2	66.67***	95.17***	56.74***	38.91***	38.19***	47.95***	38.89***	75.98***

Note: * $p < 0.10$. ** $p < 0.05$. *** $p < 0.01$.

Table 5.3. *Logit Results for Confidence in Judicial Leaders*

	1986	1987	1988	1989	1990	1991	1993	1994
Black	–0.26	–0.44***	–0.15	–0.42	–0.40	–0.31	–0.49*	–0.36*
Male	0.49***	0.30***	0.23	0.29**	–0.12	0.10***	0.24	0.31***
Income	–0.06**	0.00	–0.02	–0.03	0.01	–0.03	–0.03	–0.01
Age	–0.01***	–0.01**	–0.01***	–0.01*	–0.01	–0.01**	–0.00	–0.01
Degree	0.25***	0.19***	0.16**	0.10	0.22***	0.16**	–0.10	0.19***
Church Attend	0.00	–0.02	–0.07**	0.04	–0.02	0.02	–0.02	–0.00
Union Member	–0.02	–0.21	–0.16	–0.06	–0.16	–0.19	–0.49**	–0.23
Happy	0.50**	–0.02	0.11	0.21	0.14	0.09	–0.07	0.24
Trust	0.17	0.30**	0.39**	0.58***	0.30*	0.33**	0.38**	0.44***
Finances Better	0.13	0.17	0.05	0.05	0.05	0.13	0.17	0.06
Finances Worse	–0.03	–0.07	–0.21	–0.32	0.19	–0.34*	–0.32	–0.10
Democrat	0.23	0.16	0.32*	0.00	0.04	0.26	–0.17	0.46***
Republican	0.22	0.22	0.59***	0.05	0.30	0.47***	–0.05	0.19
Extremist	–0.74**	–0.13	–0.32	0.08	–0.50	–0.75**	–0.84*	–1.07***
Intercept	–0.75**	–0.70**	–0.35	–0.80	–0.92*	–0.59	–0.25	–1.40***
N	1,270	1,503	865	894	762	877	907	1,715
–2 Log l	1,485.38	1,890.24	1,079.70	1,127.91	964.95	1,117.43	1,088.77	2,030.74
χ^2	79.53***	81.76***	52.55***	41.73***	32.78***	53.72***	44.97***	96.52***

Note: * $p < 0.10$. ** $p < 0.05$. *** $p < 0.01$.

In contrast, three factors have a negative effect on confidence in judicial officials. As we expected, blacks are less likely to exhibit high levels of confidence than whites. Given the propolice stance of the Court and a decline in its support for affirmative-action programs in recent years, many African Americans have less confidence in these leaders. Additionally, ideological extremists are not pleased with the Court. As hypothesized, extremists appear to be dissatisfied with the incremental nature of judicial decision making throughout this period. More surprising is the negative relationship between age and a high level of confidence. Older individuals seem to grow more disenchanted with all leaders of government and do not distinguish between institutions in their negative assessments.

CONCLUSION

Typically explanations of citizen confidence refer to attitudes toward "government" in the abstract. Such a broad treatment of support for government leaders characterizes confidence as a phenomenon that is the same across all institutions of government. However, given that leaders of the three branches of the national government have different responsibilities and play different roles, we argue that the nature of confidence requires different explanations. The fact that citizens express different levels of confidence suggests that citizens do draw distinctions across the institutions.

The general explanations of confidence that scholars have identified in the past do not have the same effect across all three institutions. Indeed, only age is consistent in its effect on confidence in all three institutions. But even this variable is less helpful for explaining confidence in executive leaders than in the other models. Instead, confidence is characterized by different qualities for each of the branches.

Although the models explaining confidence in congressional leaders did not perform particularly well, it seems that confidence here is a function of age, education, and some partisan effects. It seems that familiarity breeds contempt in congressional leaders. In contrast, confidence in executive leaders is almost entirely explained by partisan assessments, reactions to the state of the economy, and to a lesser degree social connectedness. So clearly executive leaders are seen as partisan leaders who have a strong influence on economic conditions. Finally, confidence in the judicial leaders is not a function of either partisanship or economic concerns. Instead, it is influenced by one's understanding of judicial processes and one's personal disposition. To know the court is to love its leaders. Furthermore, assessments of the court seem to reflect one's position in relation to the perceived status quo in society. This can be seen as men tend to have more confidence in judicial leaders than women, and blacks tend to have less than whites. Ideological extremists, who by definition are committed to changing the status quo, are similarly disillusioned with judicial leaders.

These findings offer additional evidence that citizens evaluate leaders in different ways. Instead of discussing confidence in leaders of the "government," it is necessary for us to explain confidence in the leaders of each branch separately. Thus, confidence is a more sophisticated phenomenon than scholars of political behavior often suggest. Factors that cause individuals to lose confidence in the leaders of one branch of government do not necessarily result in a similar loss of confidence in leaders of another.

In one way this finding is reassuring. Different bases for forming public opinion about leaders bode well for democratic governance. When events or crises threaten public confidence in one branch of government (e.g., Watergate, Clinton impeachment), leadership in the other branches is not directly tainted. Thus, a key mechanism for the protection of democratic governance resides in the complex nature of public opinion.

In another way, it is the severe loss of confidence in the leaders of two branches of government (i.e., legislative and executive) and to a lesser extent the third (i.e., Supreme Court) that is especially troubling. If people are forming opinions in different ways, this suggests that the causes for this decline in confidence cannot be identified with specific events or factors. Instead, a large number of factors contributes to this simultaneous loss of confidence in the leaders of government. Because of the complex nature of public opinion, rectifying this condition will be even more difficult than many have thought.

6

Linking Presidential and Congressional Approval During Unified and Divided Governments

JEFFREY L. BERNSTEIN

My central focus in this chapter is on how citizen support for the executive affects support for Congress, with a particular emphasis on the dynamics of this relationship under divided and unified governments. The notion that support for one political institution should affect support for another is not new. This chapter, however, explores this point further by examining the extent to which the relationship between support for the executive and for Congress changes under divided and unified government. I develop and test two competing models, a *partisan-control* model and a *general-cynicism* model, which attempt to explain the relationship. Furthermore, I pay particular attention to examining whether the two models differently explain the attitudes of different citizens, stratified by strength of partisanship and levels of political knowledge and cynicism.

I begin this chapter with a brief discussion of the importance of understanding public support for the political system. Following this, I review some of the literature on this topic, paying particular attention to individual-level studies of support for specific institutions. I then discuss the two theories I test and elaborate my expectations for when and how each of these theories will apply. The next section develops and operationalizes the empirical model, while the following section presents the data analysis. I conclude by discussing the implications of these findings.

WHY SUPPORT FOR THE POLITICAL SYSTEM MATTERS

Does it matter what Americans believe about their political system? I believe it does for a number of critical reasons. First, feelings of political discontent that lead someone to view politics cynically might lead them to seek out less information. It is not a stretch to suggest this person might become less efficacious as a result, which may then lead to further discontent and another round through this vicious cycle. Understanding politics is not easy under the best of circumstances; for someone disengaged from the system, however, it becomes a Herculean task indeed. This concern becomes especially acute when we consider its long-term implications. We know that political values get passed from parent to child and from teacher to student (Jennings and Niemi 1974). It is easy to imagine those who oppose the political system influencing future generations to believe the worst about the American political system, regardless of the personal experiences of these future generations.

In addition, support for the broader political system can affect support for its more specific policies. We can expect, for example, that a citizen who has little confidence or trust in Congress is going to be less likely to support the policies Congress produces. If citizens believe that members of Congress cannot be trusted to do the right thing, or that they are overly influenced by "special interests," they are unlikely to accept that the laws passed by Congress represent sincere efforts to solve national problems. A potential implication of this is that citizens might comply less with the laws that Congress passes (Tyler 1990).

Moreover, we must also consider the electoral implications of citizen discontent. We might expect discontented citizens to make it a habit to vote against incumbents, regardless of party or past performance. This ensures a constant turnover of membership in legislative bodies, which to many is positive. However, we must temper our joy at this prospect with the concern that a constantly rotating body may lack the stability to address some of the complicated, long-term problems that confront all legislatures. Moreover, top people would become less likely to seek elective office, realizing that they would be working for a boss (the disaffected public) that would be impossible to please. This would have tremendous implications for the health of any legislative body.

Taken together, these points indicate that public support for the political system is important to consider for both its micro- and macro-level effects. When discontent is high, it begins a cycle that can continue in future generations. It can lead to less compliance with the laws and can have deleterious effects on the political institutions in the political system. Any attention given to this subject is thus not misplaced.

A BRIEF REVIEW OF THE LITERATURE

While a critical aspect of any democracy, support for the political system has been a comparatively under-researched area. Early work in this area dealt with support for democratic principles in the United States (Prothro and Grigg 1960), especially the principle of freedom of speech (McClosky 1964). Other work has concentrated more broadly on the link between support for the government and explanatory factors including the policies it passes (Citrin 1974; Miller 1974a), the option its political parties present (Dionne 1991), or the characteristics of the people in its government (Ehrenhalt 1991).

However much we may have learned from these different studies, they still leave us bemoaning the lack of comprehensive theories of support for political systems. Hibbing and Theiss-Morse (1995) correctly note that our understanding of support for the political system has been surprisingly devoid of significant, unifying theory. They argue that aside from David Easton's work (1965a, 1965b) on "diffuse" and "specific" support, there is little to guide us theoretically in exploring public attitudes toward the political system. Hibbing and Theiss-Morse argue that studies of overall support for the political system must begin by studying support for its institutions, the most visible components.

The notion that we should study institutions is not new. One approach many have taken previously is to study the *aggregate* levels of support enjoyed by the different institutions, linking these levels of support to various contextual variables at any point in time. Thus, for example, we see studies on aggregate levels of support for the Supreme Court (Caldeira 1986; Tanenhaus and Murphy 1981), the presidency (Kernell 1978; Mueller 1973), and Congress (Durr, Gilmour, and Wolbrecht 1997; Parker 1977, 1981; Patterson and Caldeira 1990). These studies, usually done as a form of time-series analysis, are important for understanding the dynamics of support.

Despite the many benefits of these studies, they leave us wondering the extent to which these aggregate level findings apply to *individuals*. This area has been home to some provocative recent work, especially in the legislative subfield. Recent studies have shown that individual-level congressional disapproval arises from disapproval of democratic processes that are perceived to have resulted in inefficiency, interest group influence, and professionalization (Hibbing and Theiss-Morse 1995). Others have argued that dissatisfaction with Congress stems from a discrepancy between citizens' expectations and perceptions for congressional performance (Kimball and Patterson 1997). Still other work has explored the role of the media in producing emotional reactions toward and cognitive evaluations of Congress (Hibbing and Theiss-Morse 1998). Given the central importance of understanding how citizens feel about their political system, this individual-level work is of prime importance.

One particularly under-researched area has been the link between support for one political institution and another. At the aggregate level, the literature demonstrates that support for one political institution commonly leads to support for the others (Davidson, Kovenock, and O'Leary 1966). At the individual level, however, the research is more scant. One recent publication in the legislative field concluded that support for Congress is positively affected by support for the president (Kimball and Patterson 1997). In most other studies, however, this variable has not been included in the model (e.g., Hibbing and Theiss-Morse 1995; Patterson and Barr 1995; Patterson, Ripley, and Quinlan 1992).

I argue that the link between support for the different institutions is a topic of significant importance for the study of public support for the political institutions. By understanding how individuals link their evaluations of the two institutions, we can understand the extent to which they are influenced by partisan considerations or by more diffuse system-level evaluations. Specifically, we can see whether the partisan control of the different institutions affects how people evaluate them, or whether the evaluations are determined by a general sense of cynicism or rose-colored perspective toward politics absent the context in which the evaluation occurs. This has implications for understanding not only how people view the different institutions, but also for more general concerns about how people form their political opinions. I now turn to a more elaborated discussion of different theories for how people link these respective institutional evaluations.

THEORIES LINKING SUPPORT FOR CONGRESS AND THE PRESIDENT

Hibbing and Theiss-Morse are exactly correct in arguing that studying support for the political system requires studying support for individual political institutions. In this chapter, I follow this logic and make two additional points. First, as argued previously, we need to understand more about the link between support for the different institutions. Second, and closely related to the first point, we need to understand how the links between support for the different institutions vary under different political circumstances and for different people.

This first point is not new; the literature review in the preceding section discusses the (limited) extent to which this has been done in previous research. It is my second point, however, that lies at the heart of this paper. The link between support for the legislature and support for the executive cannot be presumed constant across all years, all people, and all institutional settings. For example, under divided government, one might suspect that support for the executive *negatively* affects support for Congress and vice versa. Under unified government, we might expect the relationship to be positive.

This general prediction, however, is likely to be realized the most among citizens who are the most knowledgeable, and who pay the most attention to politics.[1] We might expect the politically astute survey respondent to know which parties control the different branches and to reflect more partisanship in offering a response to the standard institutional-support question. The less aware and astute respondents, however, would be less likely to know which institutions are controlled by which party, and correspondingly be less likely to use this information as a cue in making the support judgment. Their judgment might be based more on general dispositions toward politics and the political system. Thus, even given the same stimulus, different respondents respond differently based upon their knowledge and interest.

This discussion suggests two different theories for linking support for the different institutions. In the first theory, the *partisan-control* theory, the expectation is that control of the different branches of government should play a decisive role in this linkage. Thus, in 1990, when the Republicans controlled the White House and the Democrats controlled Congress, we would expect support for President Bush to correlate negatively with support for Congress. However, by 1993, when the Democrats had control of both the White House and Congress, we would expect to see a positive correlation between support for the two branches. As its name implies, the theory predicts that partisan control of each branch is the driving force in evaluations of support for that branch.

On the other hand, the *general-cynicism* theory predicts that partisan control of the branches is not expected to be a major predictor of the relationship between support for the president and support for Congress. Rather, the driving force in support for the institutions is the respondent's overall level of political cynicism. Citizens who have a generally cynical orientation toward the political system would be most likely to have unfavorable feelings toward both branches, while those with noncynical attitudes would be more likely to favor both. This theory posits that these overall orientations outweigh more time-specific matters of institutional control.

Of course, laying out these two theories does not imply that only one of them can accurately explain the relationship of interest here. What is more likely is that each theory works best under certain conditions, varying across respondents and time periods. For example, we might expect the most cynical respondents to be blinded by their cynicism and

1 While the concepts of political knowledge and attention to politics correlate at roughly .44, they represent distinct constructs for the study of individual-level political attitude development. For some provocative work on the relationship between the two, see Howard (1998).

therefore hate everything remotely connected to government. Likewise, we might expect those with total support for the political system to have their support for one branch imply support for the other. Those in the middle of the cynicism continuum might be less likely to behave according to the general-cynicism model and more likely to follow the partisan-control model and depend on partisanship to orient their beliefs.

We might also expect to see knowledge and attention paid to politics play roles as intermediaries. Behaving according to the partisan-control theory requires a degree of knowledge on the part of citizens; in addition to being able to recall which party controls which branch, they must also make a considered judgment that their interests are not served by divided government.[2] Citizens with the greatest levels of knowledge might therefore be expected to use the partisan-control theory more than the general-cynicism theory. This prediction, however, must be tempered by the empirical observation that cynicism correlates positively with political knowledge; in this case, familiarity breeds contempt. Thus, predictions about which types of people follow which theory must be made cautiously.

In addition to questioning the applicability of each of these theories across individuals, we can also think about which theory fits better *across time periods*. We might expect, for example, that during highly charged partisan times (such as during the budget showdown of 1995), attitudes toward the executive would be negatively correlated with attitudes toward the Congress. However, in times of relative partisan harmony, we would expect a small correlation, if any, between support for one branch and the other. With partisanship absent as a cognitive cue during these times of harmony, we expect that more diffuse feelings toward the political system (as reflected in the general-cynicism model) should carry the day. Having moved to a longitudinal perspective, however, we must immediately move back to the individual level and consider that even under these different levels of partisan strife, citizens of different levels of knowledge would respond to partisan stimuli in different ways.

I now turn to a test of both the partisan-control and the general-cynicism models, attempting to explain the link between approval of the executive and approval of Congress. In the following section, I describe the data that will be used in the empirical analysis. I also highlight the variables that I will use in the model, detailing hypotheses for each variable and discussing how each will be operationalized.

2 See Fiorina (1996) for the argument that divided government does serve the interests of many and is in fact preferred by some voters.

Data and Methods

The data used in this analysis are taken from the National Election Studies, both from the 1990 Post-Election Study (for the analysis under conditions of divided government) and from the 1992 Post-Election Study and the 1993 Pilot Study (for unified government). Given the short time in which the United States had unified government (between the election of Bill Clinton in 1992 and the midterm election of 1994), we are limited in the amount of data we can exploit that examines attitudes toward the political institutions under unified government. The 1993 Pilot Study was the only NES study in the field during this brief period. The Pilot Study returns to many of the respondents from the 1992 Post-Election Study; responses from this panel of respondents are used as data in this chapter. I indicate when describing the variables whether they came from the 1992 Post-Election Study or from the 1993 Pilot Study.

In the multivariate analysis that follows, the dependent variable is the respondent's approval/disapproval of Congress, measured on a scale from 1 (strong disapproval) to 4 (strong approval).[3] The independent variable of primary interest is approval or disapproval of the way the president (George Bush or Bill Clinton) is handling his job as president. This is measured on a similar four-point scale.[4]

The expectation for this variable's behavior is straightforward. Under the partisan-control theory, we would expect a negative coefficient for this variable under divided government and a positive coefficient under unified government. This would indicate that under divided government, approval of one branch leads to disapproval of the other, while under unified government, approval of one branch causes approval of the other, and vice versa. Were the general-cynicism model to hold, we would expect to see a positive coefficient here, indicating that those who

3 It is certainly possible to turn this model around and to measure the effect that approval of Congress has on approval of the executive. Furthermore, it is also possible to measure the effect approval that each has on the other in one comprehensive simultaneous equations model. I choose in this analysis to restrict my attention to congressional approval. The presidential approval scores are far more contextual in that they are influenced more by who holds the office at the time the question is asked. Given my more general interest in *institutional* support, I prefer to use congressional approval as the dependent variable here. In future work, I will explore treating this as a simultaneous system of equations.

4 In all analyses, the feeling thermometer rating of the president was substituted for the four-point presidential approval variable and behaved in exactly the same way. Thus, the four-point scale is used throughout for the sake of consistency with the congressional measure.

opposed the president would likely oppose Congress, regardless of the partisan control of the individual branches.

Of course, other factors besides approval of the executive affect approval of Congress. Thus, other independent variables will be added to the model in an attempt to control for factors that could affect congressional approval. One additional variable is one's approval of one's own representative measured in the same way as approval of Congress or of the executive. We know from previous research that Congress is less popular than its individual members (Fenno 1975; Parker and Davidson 1979), and that the popularity of the institution and the popularity of individual members affect each other (Cook 1979; Born 1990; Patterson and Barr 1995). Thus, approval or disapproval of one's own member of the House is included in the model. I expect that approval of one's own member should increase approval of Congress as a whole.

Political partisanship is also included in the model, measured using the standard NES seven-point scale (1 = strong Republican, 7 = strong Democrat). I have two basic expectations for this variable. First, we should see a generally high positive coefficient for this variable, as it stands to reason that Democrats would be more approving of the Democratic Congress than Republicans would. Second, and more significantly, the inclusion of this variable may help to identify a class of voters (the strong partisans) most likely to follow the partisan-control model. Thus, by stratifying the sample based upon *strength* of partisanship, we should be able to test nicely the levels to which the partisan-control theory explains institutional approval among different types of respondents.

Cynicism is also included in the model, with similar expectations to that of the partisanship variable. Cynicism is measured using a scale of six items dealing with political trust, efficacy, and general attitudes toward the political system and its members (see the Appendix for the specific measurement of this variable). Each question is scored from 0–2, where 0 equals lack of cynicism and 2 equals high cynicism. Cynicism scores are taken not from the 1993 Pilot Study for the unified government analysis but rather come from the 1992 Post-Election Study. It stands to reason that a first expectation for the cynicism variable is that more cynical respondents will be less approving of Congress than those less cynical.

However, the cynicism variable should be meaningful in ways that go beyond its direct effect on congressional approval. As with party identification, we can identify a class of respondents, based on their responses to the cynicism-scale items, who are most likely to have attitudes consistent with the general-cynicism theory. Thus, the most cynical respondents should show a positive correlation between approval of the executive and legislature, *regardless of partisan control of the institutions*. The least-cynical respondents would be less likely to exhibit this pattern; they are likely to have attitudes based upon the partisan-control theory, ceteris paribus.

Two other variables expected to influence attitudes toward Congress are attention paid to politics and political knowledge. Attention paid to politics is measured by respondents' answers to a question about how often they follow government and public affairs. Responses are coded on a four-point scale, where 1 equals "hardly at all" and 4 equals "most of the time." I can justify theoretically either a positive or negative coefficient. Including this variable in the model should help determine whether those who pay attention to politics have a positive or negative view of Congress.[5]

Political knowledge is included in the model as well. As with attention paid to politics, the direct effects of this variable are not altogether obvious theoretically. However, the likely effects of this variable will be mostly secondary (as they also would be with paying attention to politics). We might expect those who are most knowledgeable and pay the most attention to politics to react using the partisan-control model of institutional evaluation as it requires the most knowledge and political sophistication to apply. Those who are less knowledgeable and pay less attention to politics are less likely to show this effect; they may use overall predispositions such as cynicism to evaluate the institutions.

Knowledge is measured using the ANES battery of questions asking respondents to answer fact-based questions about politics and public affairs. For the 1990 data, knowledge is the sum of how many people the respondent could correctly identify (the people were Dan Quayle, George Mitchell, William Rehnquist, Mikhail Gorbachev, Margaret Thatcher, Nelson Mandela, and Tom Foley). Scores for 1990 ranged from 0–7, where 7 indicated the most knowledgeable respondents. For the 1993 data, the measure was the sum of six items, including people (Quayle, Rehnquist, Foley, and Boris Yeltsin) and facts (who determines a law's constitutionality, and who nominates federal

5 Education, the closest analog to this variable included in the Hibbing and Theiss-Morse model, shows extremely minimal effects, in a positive direction ($t = 0.1$). This is when the referent is the *members* of Congress, which is the implied referent when the question asks about "Congress," as the questions used here do (Hibbing and Theiss-Morse 1995). When the subject matter turns to support for the *institution* of Congress, education not surprisingly becomes a strong positive predictor of support ($t = 3.1$).

judges). The questions for the 1993 data were actually asked of respondents in 1992.[6]

Three additional variables are added to the model as well. First, I use the standard ANES question about a respondent's personal financial situation (again, asked in 1992). Respondents are asked whether they are better or worse off financially than they were a year ago; their answers are stacked from much worse (a 1 on the variable) all the way up to much better (a score of 5). We would expect that the higher the score on this variable, the higher the approval of Congress. Those who are worse off may be more cynical or at least may be less likely to lavish praise on politicians and the political system. There is, of course, a likelihood that the cynicism variable will conflate much explanatory power of this variable; the correlation between the two is reasonably high ($r = .17$).

Finally, I include race and gender in the model. Race is measured where 0 equals white and 1 equals African American; the expectation is that African Americans will be more supportive of the (Democratically controlled) Congress.[7] For gender, 0 equals female and 1 equals male. The expectation is that this variable will have a negative coefficient; women ought to be more supportive of Congress than men, as the Democratic Congress would produce more "woman-friendly" legislation than would a Republican Congress.

Data Analysis

The first step in empirically evaluating the theories proposed here is to run models of congressional approval for both 1990 and 1993, under divided and unified government, respectively. If the partisan-control theory is correct, then presidential approval should show a statistically significant negative sign in 1990, when government was divided, and a positive sign in 1993, when partisan control is unified. This would mean

6 The inclusion of knowledge in the model takes the place of education, a more common variable in models of this type. Knowledge gets more directly at the concept used here; were education included, it largely would be a surrogate for political knowledge. In the empirical models, the two terms correlate at .49, indicating that including both would inflate the standard errors, an unnecessary occurrence.

7 It would, of course, be nice to explore the racial component of congressional approval in more than this simple dichotomous way. The ANES variable for race does include two other groups (American Indians and Asian or Pacific Islanders); however, the number of cases in these categories proves too small for reasonable data analysis. Thus, these cases are dropped when the empirical models are examined.

that approval of a Democratic Congress is negatively affected by approval of a Republican president and positively affected by approval of a Democratic president. If the general-cynicism theory is correct, then the presidential-approval variable should show a smaller effect and the cynicism variable should have a statistically significant negative coefficient in each model.

Table 6.1 presents regression models of support for Congress using the independent variables described.[8] The immediate result to notice from the table is that presidential approval has a positive coefficient in both models, running counter to the expectations of the partisan-control theory. It appears that support for both Presidents Bush and Clinton leads to increased support for the Democratic Congress. Counter to expectations, the variable is statistically significant in the first model only. However, before overplaying the card of statistical significance, we should note the different *N*s in each model. Given 844 respondents in 1990 and 130 in 1993, the standard errors in the fourth column of the table are much larger than the corresponding standard errors in the second column. Thus, we must compare the *size* of the coefficients rather than their t-statistics.[9]

With this caveat, the models begin to make more sense. Now we see the presidential approval variable having a *smaller* impact on congressional approval under Bush as compared to under Clinton. Thus, a one-step increase (on a scale of four) in popularity for Bush leads to a .13 step increase in Congress' approval, while a one-step increase in popularity for Clinton leads to a .15 increase in Congress' approval. The key fact to note, however, is that the sign is positive in both models. This result is a first endorsement of the general-cynicism theory over the partisan-control theory.

I begin with the 1990 results. In this model, most of the variables are in the predicted direction, and most achieve statistical significance. Approval of one's own representative has a positive effect on approval of Congress; each one-step increase in approval of one's own representative moves congressional approval up by almost one-sixth of a point.

8 Using regression with only four potential values for the dependent variable can be risky. However, the model was run as well using a multinomial probit technique; no meaningfully different results were seen. Thus, for ease of analysis, the regression results are presented in the paper.

9 The 1993 model has fewer respondents since it was a Pilot Study rather than a regular American National Election Study. Given the importance of asking respondents the approval questions *while government was under unified control*, there is no choice but to use this smaller sample.

Table 6.1. *Models of Legislative Approval, Divided and Unified Governments*

	1990 (Divided Government)		1993 (Unified Government)	
Variable	Coefficient	Std. Error	Coefficient	Std. Error
Constant	2.133		2.759	
Presidential Approval	0.134*	0.035	0.152	0.108
Approval—Own Representative	0.161*	0.039	0.037	0.099
Party Identification	0.083*	0.018	0.019	0.053
Cynicism	–0.068*	0.014	–0.043	0.037
Political Knowledge	–0.144*	0.027	–0.191*	0.068
Attention Paid to Politics	–0.108*	0.040	–0.164	0.131
Personal Financial Status	–0.002	0.030	0.006	0.091
Gender	–0.029	0.069	0.023	0.196
Race	0.131	0.110	–0.077	0.339
	N = 844		N = 130	
	F (9,834) = 17.35		F (9,120) = 2.93	
	Prob > F = 0.0000		Prob > F = 0.0036	
	R-squared = 0.158		R-squared = 0.180	

Note: * $p < .05$.

Party identification is also significant, as we might expect; since the higher values here correspond to Democrat identification, the model shows that Democrats approve of Congress more than Republicans. Finally, we see statistically significant negative coefficients associated with political cynicism, political knowledge, and attention paid to politics. Thus, we conclude that people who are politically cynical, politically knowledgeable, and politically attentive are likely to disapprove of Congress.

Three of the variables included in the model show null results. Evaluation of a person's financial status (as compared to the last year) has virtually no impact on evaluations of Congress. Gender and race also show statistically insignificant results. Women are more likely to approve of Congress, as are African Americans. The signs of these coefficients are in the expected direction, although both fall far short of statistical significance. Despite this, the size of the coefficient on race is actually quite large (African Americans move .13 more in a positive direction on the scale); the standard error, however, is quite high, given the low number of African Americans in the sample.

When we compare these results to those from the 1993 data, we see some similarities and some differences. Among the similarities, cynicism, political knowledge, and attention paid to politics all have negative signs and coefficients of approximately equal size to that of the 1990 model. While the inflated standard errors mean that only political knowledge is statistically significant, the similar behavior of these variables leads us to believe that their impact on congressional approval remains roughly constant across the data presented here. Another similarity in the different models is the insignificant coefficients attached to personal economic assessments, race, and gender. Even without the inflated standard errors, none of these variables would be statistically significant, and none of the coefficients approach substantive significance.

In terms of other differences, we see that the coefficients for approval of one's own representative and for party identification have the correct sign but fall short of statistical significance. Even if we compare these coefficients to the standard error of the 1990 data, they fall far short of statistical significance. It appears that these variables explain less about congressional approval in 1993 than they did in 1990.

Further Examination of 1990 Data

The next task is to begin to unpack the coefficients linking presidential and congressional approval. In the 1990 model, we see an unexpectedly positive and significant coefficient. The relationship must be linked with additional variables in order to see under what circumstances the relationship between the two changes and under what circumstances it remains the same. For the analysis I present in this chapter, I will present correlation coefficients between the two approval variables under a variety of circumstances. This technique will allow me to present the crux of my findings in a simple, straightforward way. The correlation coefficients will thus be easy to compare with one another in the tables.

A logical first step is to present correlation coefficients between approval of Congress and approval of the president for respondents with different strengths of party identification. If we are to see any support for the partisan-control model, it will most likely be found among the strong partisans. They are the ones for whom we would expect a negative correlation between approval of the president and approval of Congress. Among the weaker partisans and independents, the partisan-control model would lead us to expect a null relationship. Table 6.2 presents the results of this analysis, where party identification is "folded over," grouping strong partisans (of both parties), weak partisans, and independents (including leaners).

The results presented in Table 6.2 provide no support for the partisan-control theory. We see that the strongest partisans are those for whom the correlation between presidential and congressional approval

Table 6.2. *Correlation Between Congressional and Presidential Approval, Controlling for Strength of Partisanship, 1990*

Strength of Partisanship	Correlation
Strong Partisans (Democrats and Republicans), n = 365	0.046
Weak Partisans (Democrats and Republicans), n = 428	0.190
Independents (Includes Democrat and Republican Leaners and Pure Independents), n = 404	0.224

is the weakest (almost zero). The weak partisans show a somewhat stronger positive correlation, while the independents, for whom we would expect no relation, show the strongest correlation. In short, even the strongest partisans do not behave in such a way as to support the partisan-control model.[10]

Next, I evaluate the general-cynicism model in more detail. According to this model, the link between congressional and executive approval should be strongest among the most-cynical people (whose cynicism should lead them to hate all institutions). This correlation is expected to be positive and significant. For people at lower levels of political cynicism, we would expect to see less of a relationship between the two approval ratings. These data are presented in Table 6.3. In this table, the cynicism scale used in Table 6.1 (and described in further detail in the appendix) is collapsed into a four-point scale. To construct this scale, respondents who scored 0–6 (least cynical) on the original scale were scored a 1, those who scored 7–9 were scored a 2, those who scored 10 or 11 were scored a 3, and those who received a cynically perfect 12 were scored a 4.

These data do not support the theories discussed thus far. Those who are the most cynical, whom we might expect to have the highest correlation between the two institutional evaluations, actually show the lowest correlation. What is more, this coefficient is negative! The most cynical respondents, whom our hypothesis suggested would have the greatest correlation between legislative and executive approval, actually have a slightly negative link between the two. This surprising result

10 It is possible to use these data to argue that the partisan-control model actually does work. The strongest partisans had the weakest coefficient showing that they were the least likely to use evaluations of one branch to color positively their evaluations of the other during times of divided government. This, however, is a rather tepid endorsement of the model. The more realistic interpretation is that even the strongest partisans were only minimally swayed by party control of the institutions in linking their evaluations of the two branches.

Table 6.3. *Correlation Between Congressional and Presidential Approval, Controlling for Cynicism, 1990*

Level of Cynicism	Correlation
Lowest Cynicism (0–6 on Original Cynicism Scale), n = 235	0.155
Moderate Low Cynicism (7–9 on Original Cynicism Scale), n = 337	0.078
Moderate High Cynicism (10–11 on Original Cynicism Scale), n = 328	0.157
Highest Cynicism (12 on Original Cynicism Scale), n = 243	–0.065

suggests that it is not a respondent's general level of political cynicism alone that guides how they link the two institutions.

As a next step in making sense of the 1990 data, I now turn to one final variable by which to stratify the correlations. The variable we look at here is political knowledge, which is a composite of correct identifications the respondent made to a variety of domestic and international political figures.[11] In Table 6.1, political knowledge took on values ranging from 0–7; in this analysis, political knowledge is trichotomous. A score of 0–1 on the original knowledge variable is scored as low knowledge, a score of 2–3 is moderate knowledge, and a score from 4–7 is treated as high knowledge. The results of this analysis are presented in Table 6.4.

Table 6.4 shows some interesting results. We see that the least-knowledgeable respondents show the highest correlation between the evaluations of the two institutions, indicating that they are the least guided by which party controls the two. The least-knowledgeable voters, as we might expect, are guided the most by their overall levels of cynicism. This conforms to expectations we had for this group. Among the most-knowledgeable respondents, however, things are different. We would have expected this group to know that different parties control the two branches; therefore, we would expect a negative correlation for the evaluations among these knowledgeable voters. In fact, we see a correlation that is almost zero. Among the most-knowledgeable voters, there appears to be no link between the two evaluations. This surprising result calls for a bit more analysis.

A final step in this process is to use political knowledge as a control and determine the extent to which both party identification and cynicism affect correlations between approval of the legislature and executive.

11 While political knowledge is the variable used here, the results are quite similar when attention paid to politics is substituted.

Table 6.4. *Correlation Between Congressional and Presidential Approval, Controlling for Political Knowledge, 1990*

Level of Political Knowledge	Correlation
Low Knowledge (0–1 on Political Knowledge Scale), n = 280	0.349
Moderate Knowledge (2–3 on Political Knowledge Scale), n = 674	0.128
High Knowledge (4–7 on Political Knowledge Scale), n = 254	0.026

Given the theoretical link between political knowledge and partisanship (the most knowledgeable respondents are the most partisan), and between political knowledge and cynicism (the most knowledgeable respondents are the most cynical), we must consider whether political knowledge acts as an intermediary in both the partisan-control and general-cynicism theories. Table 6.5 presents the correlations between approval ratings, controlling for strength of partisanship and political knowledge. I expect that as knowledge increases the correlation between approval of President Bush and the Congress will drop, perhaps even hitting the negative numbers for the stronger partisans. If this were the case, we would see an inkling of support for the partisan-control theory.

A glance at Table 6.5 confirms that this is somewhat the case. Among strong partisans, those with low knowledge score a high correlation between support for Congress and for President Bush. As we move to the moderate- and then high-knowledge categories, this correlation moves to almost zero, and then becomes (slightly) negative. Among weak partisans and independents, we see a similar effect, although the correlations never become negative. We are left with two conclusions. First, it appears that knowledge trumps partisanship overall. When examining the table, we see that the greatest effect on the correlations comes not from strength of partisanship but rather from levels of political knowledge. Second, we see that the partisan-control theory works *for respondents who are strong partisans with a high level of knowledge*. For the eighty-seven people in the lower left of the table, the partisan-control theory does a decent job explaining their behavior (note, though, that the negative coefficient in that cell is quite small). For the other 93% of the respondents, the theory is found wanting.

Finally, as a test of the general-cynicism model, see Table 6.6. The table is similar to Table 6.5, except that it substitutes levels of cynicism for strength of partisanship. We would expect that with increasing levels of knowledge, the least cynical respondents would move from positive to negative correlations. Their evaluations would not be colored by habitual dislike of the system; we would instead expect that as knowledge

Table 6.5. *Correlation Between Congressional and Presidential Approval, Controlling for Strength of Partisanship and Political Knowledge, 1990*

	Strength of Political Partisanship		
Level of Political Knowledge	Strong Partisan	Weak Partisan	Independent
Low Knowledge	0.443	0.289	0.638
	(86)	(87)	(100)
Moderate Knowledge	0.018	0.221	0.199
	(192)	(256)	(222)
High Knowledge	−0.045	0.104	0.080
	(87)	(85)	(82)

Note: Numbers in parentheses represent number of respondents fitting each cell.

Table 6.6. *Correlation Between Congressional and Presidential Approval, Controlling for Cynicism and Political Knowledge, 1990*

	Level of cynicism			
Level of Political Knowledge	Low Cynicism	Moderately Low Cynicism	Moderately High Cynicism	High Cynicism
Low Knowledge	0.439	0.216	0.358	0.213
	(54)	(72)	(76)	(52)
Moderate Knowledge	0.162	0.099	0.108	−0.102
	(119)	(192)	(176)	(156)
High Knowledge	−0.137	−0.083	0.207	−0.144
	(62)	(73)	(76)	(35)

Note: Numbers in parentheses represent number of respondents fitting each cell.

increases, these respondents would reach a more partisan-based conclusion about each institution. This appears to be the case. Among the most cynical, who approach the evaluation of Congress and the executive from a more negative frame, we would expect to see largely positive correlations regardless of knowledge level. These people, approaching the questions with disdain for all things political, would likely view the branches through the same negative frame.

The table, however, reveals a somewhat surprising pattern for these respondents. Even the most-cynical respondents are somewhat swayed by increasing knowledge to consider what I presume to be partisan concerns in rating the two institutions. The effect is not overwhelming, but it does appear among the most highly cynical. It should be noted, of course, that those with moderately high levels of cynicism do not show such a pattern. The general conclusion to which we are drawn is that respondents are greatly influenced in linking their evaluations of Congress and the executive by their overall political predispositions, i.e., cynicism. We do see some tentative support for the partisan-control theory, although this is largely confined to the most knowledgeable respondents.

For purposes of this chapter, it would be ideal if we were able to do this same type of analysis for the 1993 case (under unified government). However, analysis at any level of depth proves impossible, as the small number of usable cases in the 1993 Pilot Study would mean extremely low numbers of cases for any cells in a table like Tables 6.5 or 6.6. As desirable as it would be to compare the results we see under unified and divided government, the gods of the temple of empiricism have not provided enough data with which to do this.

CONCLUSIONS AND IMPLICATIONS

This paper has tested two competing models of how citizens link their evaluations of the executive and the legislature. After examining the data, I conclude that the general-cynicism model is the stronger model. Most citizens rate the two institutions while wearing a set of blinders, thinking the worst of the political system and the institutions that comprise it. It is an important result to note that regardless of which party controls the branches, large numbers of respondents appear to be swayed the most by their overall cynicism. When we tentatively conclude that citizens don't even pay attention to which party controls the branches (and often do not even know this information), it has a sobering effect on any hope that most citizens are paying close attention to what goes on in politics.[12]

There is, however, a class of respondents who do seem to follow the partisan-control theory and consider the partisan makeup of each institution in linking their evaluations. Those who follow this model tend to be the most knowledgeable and the most partisan of the respondents. We can say with confidence that only a small percentage (perhaps 7%) of respondents fit this model. However, they are out there. Moreover, as these are the most knowledgeable and likely the most interested, we can presume that they are disproportionately represented among the opinion leaders in the mass public. Their impact is probably larger than their numbers would indicate.

A few questions remain unanswered from this analysis. First, the limited time the United States has had unified government in the last

12 This is, of course, not to blame them for their inattention or cast aspersions on their lack of knowledge. It is just to say that most respondents simply have different concerns that fill their time and attention beyond politics.

twenty years makes it difficult to determine the extent to which the findings presented here are generalizable to all time periods or whether they just apply under divided government. The paucity of data from this time period restricts my ability to push the data further. The next time unified government occurs, we must take advantage of the opportunity to obtain more data on how citizens evaluate the political institutions.

One other unresolved issue is the extent to which the current harmony or disharmony of the time affects the link between these two evaluations. The data used here do not permit an answer to this question, but that does not change the importance of this issue. Does the partisan-control theory fit better during times of partisan division? It would stand to reason that when political discourse is framed in a "Democrats vs. Republicans" mode, the partisan control of the institutions matters more in evaluating their performances. We might even expect knowledge of institutional control to filter down to more citizens, enabling more to behave according to the partisan-control model. Future work would do well to address this issue.

Finally, more work needs to be done on the subject of political knowledge and attention paid to politics. The strong performance of the political-knowledge variable in this paper ought to lead us to think more about how we can incorporate this construct into future theories of political support and disaffection. We need to move beyond a general statement such as "familiarity breeds contempt" to answer more specific questions about this. Does the knowledge variable work differently under unified vs. divided government or during times of partisan strife vs. times of partisan harmony? We know very little about knowledge or its effect on political support; this hole needs to be filled by future work.

Support or disaffection that citizens feel for the political institutions is a key element of support for the broader system. By studying how citizens link their judgments of one institution with another, this paper has continued the process of understanding how citizens view the different institutions in their political system. Whether our concern is with microlevel attitude formation or macrolevel concerns about institutional performance, an understanding of the broader concept of support for the political system is vital.

APPENDIX

Construction of Political-Cynicism Scale

The political-cynicism scale is constructed from six items used in the National Election Studies. The items are each coded from 0–2, where 0 equals the noncynical response and 2 equals the most-cynical response.

Each question used in constructing the scale is listed below, along with the point values attached to each possible response.

"How much of the time do you think you can trust the government in Washington to do what is right—just about always, most of the time, or only some of the time?"

Just about always—0
Most of the time—1
Some of the time—2
None of the time (respondent volunteers)—2

"Do you think that people in government waste a lot of the money we pay in taxes, waste some of it, or don't waste very much of it?"

Not very much—0
Some—1
A lot—2

"Would you say that government is pretty much run by a few big interests looking out for themselves or that it is run for the benefit of all the people?"

For the benefit of all—0
Few big interests—2

"Do you think quite a few of the people running government are crooked, not very many are, or do you think hardly any of them are crooked?"

Hardly any—0
Not many—1
Quite a few—2

"Public officials don't care much what people like me think."

Disagree strongly or disagree somewhat—0
Neither agree nor disagree—1
Agree somewhat or agree strongly—2

"People like me don't have any say about what the government does."

Disagree strongly or disagree somewhat—0
Neither agree nor disagree—1
Agree somewhat or agree strongly—2

7

Is Washington Really the Problem?[1]

ERIC M. USLANER

In the 1950s and the 1960s almost 80% of Americans trusted the government in Washington all or most of the time. By the 1990s just 20–30% of Americans still had confidence in their government.

For some people the reason for the drop was straightforward: The federal government had gotten too big. Politicians tried to buy voters off through new government programs, which made them popular in their districts but bloated the overall budget. Americans don't like big government, which for some is a virtual synonym for unresponsive government. The bigger government got, the more disillusioned the public became.

If the problem of declining trust is simple, so is the solution. Give more power and responsibility to the states. Conservative theorists have long argued that centralized government is inimical to both liberty and representation. Hayek (1960, 263) argues:

> While it has always been characteristic of those favoring an increase in governmental powers to support maximum concentration of these powers, those mainly concerned with individual liberty have generally advocated decentralization. . . . action by local authorities generally offers the next-best solution where private initiative cannot be relied upon to provide certain services and where some sort of collective action is therefore needed.

1 I am grateful for the support of the General Research Board of the Graduate School, University of Maryland—College Park for a Distinguished Faculty Fellowship in 1997–8 and for other research support over the years, and to the Everett McKinley Dirksen Center for Congressional Leadership. I am also indebted to Richard Morin of the *Washington Post* and Mario Broussard (formerly of the *Post*) for making the Trust in Government survey available to me and for explaining their scale construction and coding. James Gimpel, John Hibbing, and Elizabeth Theiss-Morse made many valuable comments on earlier drafts. Some of the data used herein come from the Inter-University Consortium for Political and Social Research, which is not responsible for my interpretations.

Conservative politicians echo the arguments of theorists and advocate devolution of power to the states. The big, bloated federal government has assumed too much power, so it is hardly surprising that people don't trust it.[2] State governments are closer to the people and should be more responsive to public opinion (Peterson 1984)—and more trusted by the public. Conservatives believe that "governments directly accountable to voters will choose to spend less than a central government where the voters' will is filtered through interest groups" (Peterson 1984, 217–18). Republican Presidents Richard Nixon and Ronald Reagan made "new federalisms" key parts of their domestic agenda. These programs returned jurisdiction over wide ranges of policy to the states (Peterson 1984). The Republicans' Contract with America, which formed the basis for the party's 1994 takeover of the Congress, also promised to send many programs back to the states. Liberals are not so enamored with state governments. They see Washington as more likely to protect the interests of minorities and the poor and to have both the means and the will to regulate the environment and business more generally.

Against this thesis is an alternative that I shall show is more plausible: People either like government—both in Washington and in their states—or they don't. The choice between the nation's capital and the state capital is bogus. Conservatives (and Republicans) are not more partial to states than to Washington. Indeed, the conflict over trust in government is *not* primarily ideological. It reflects a more general distrust of government.

DATA AND METHODS

I shall test these competing claims using the *Washington Post*–Kaiser Family Foundation–Harvard University survey in late 1995, which contains a comprehensive set of questions on trust in government (Henry J. Kaiser Family Foundation 1996). The *Post* survey is a national poll of 1514 respondents. It asked people the standard trust in (the federal) government question, as well as a similar query on trust in state government. Even more critically, it also asked whether respondents trust the federal or their state government "to do a better job in running things."

I shall examine two different measures of confidence in government. The first asks people to choose whether they prefer Washington or their state governments. Here I expect to find that ideology matters a lot.

2 In both the *Washington Post* survey described later and the 1992 American National Election Study, there are moderate correlations between trust in government and the belief that the federal government is too powerful and that it wastes taxes.

The second consists of separate measures of trust in the federal and state governments. When people are not forced to choose between levels, they should not give ideological responses. Instead more general institutional preferences, faith in the larger society, confidence in the perceived responsiveness of officials to citizens, and the responsibility of the government for economic outcomes should play larger roles in more general attitudes toward trust in government (see the more extended discussion that follows). I expect that the same forces that drive trust in the federal government should shape confidence in state administrations, so I shall estimate identical models for trust in Washington and confidence in state government.

Finally, I estimate regression models for trust in state government for Democratic and Republican party identifiers.[3] My principal rationale for doing so is to examine whether partisan identifiers are more likely to feel positively about a government controlled by their own party. Republicans should be most supportive of their state government if they live in GOP-controlled states and Democrats should have higher trust in state governments dominated by their party.

THE MODELS FOR TRUST IN GOVERNMENT

Approval of the people in power and appraisals of the responsiveness of the political system should both shape levels of trust in government. But most critical to my model is ideological self-identification. Conservatives should have less faith in the federal government and more confidence in state government, if the argument for devolution made by many Republicans holds.

When people are forced to choose between levels, ideology should be the most important factor driving their preferences. Conservatives should also be more likely to approve of state governments and to disapprove of Washington. In addition to the traditional liberal–conservative scale, I also employ two other measures of ideology that seem particularly well suited to testing support for different levels of government: whether people see the federal government as a threat to their daily lives, and how often they listen to conservative talk-show host Rush Limbaugh (Blendon et al. 1997).[4] People who see the federal government as a threat

3 Partisan leaners are included with identifiers.

4 I do not employ the threat scale as a predictor for trust in the federal government or the state government because the questions appear to be different ways of expressing the same idea. The threat scale and trust in the federal government are moderately correlated ($r = -.242$, gamma $= -.393$), but I am not sure what theoretical leverage one gains by saying that people who view the federal government as a threat do not trust it.

or who listen to Limbaugh regularly are more likely to favor devolution of power to the states. On the other hand, blacks are more likely to favor granting more power to Washington, since many southern states were slow to abolish segregationist laws in the 1950s and 1960s and the contemporary movement to restrict affirmative action has stressed states' rights.

Beyond ideology, both preference for the federal or state government and confidence in government more generally should depend upon approval of specific institutions of government and feelings that public officials are responsive. Other factors that might matter include faith in people more generally, how well things are going for both the individual and the country, exposure to information, and age.

Both preference for Washington and confidence in the federal government should reflect support for specific institutions of government. People who approve of the president and Congress should be more favorable to the federal government (Citrin and Luks, this volume; Feldman 1983; Luks and Citrin 1997). An ideological account suggests that positive evaluations of these institutions might lead to *less* confidence in state governments. My alternative thesis argues the contrary: A positive view of federal institutions should be associated with approval of all levels of government.

Support for government in general—and especially for the federal government—may be rooted in how responsive people think leaders are (cf. Brehm and Rahn 1997). Beyond faith in the political system is trust in other people. As Brehm and Rahn (1997, 1008) argue, generalized trust in others "allows people to move out of familiar relationships in which trust is based on knowledge accumulated from long experience with particular people. If outcomes in a democracy are inherently uncertain, such global trust may be necessary in order for people to support democratic arrangements" (cf. Cole 1973; but for contrary results see Newton, 1998, Orren 1997, Uslaner 1998).

I also include in all models measures of how well people think that they are doing and how the country is faring. When things are going well, people give government the credit (Brehm and Rahn 1997; Lipset and Schneider 1987). They are most likely to assign responsibility to the federal government. How well you are doing should be less important for any type of trust in government than how the country is faring (Kinder and Kiewiet 1979). People who say that government actions have a strong impact on the economy may be more critical of government performance and thus have less faith in political institutions. When people see a government success story—a narrowing income gap between the rich and the poor—they are likely to be more supportive of government, especially of Washington.

We know that more highly educated and involved people are *more critical* of the Congress (Hibbing and Theiss-Morse 1995).[5] Do these findings apply to the political system more generally? I employ a battery of measures that test the hypothesis that the best informed people should have less confidence in government. One is education, which Hibbing and Theiss-Morse also use. Consistent with Hibbing and Theiss-Morse, I expect that people with more education should be more critical of both the federal *and* state governments. But, when forced to choose, they should be more supportive of state governments. People with less education—or who believe that politics and government are too complicated to understand—may simply know less about state government than people with greater understanding. And fear of the unknown may lead them to favor what they follow most: the federal government. Most people get their news about politics from television, and television news follows national politics more than state affairs. So the more people watch television, the more they should favor Washington (for an alternative view, see Hetherington and Nugent, this volume).

Another indicator of knowledge is how long you have lived in a community. People who move from one neighborhood to another have weaker roots and are less likely to participate in politics (Squire et al. 1987). They are more likely to view governmental institutions from the outside—and, thus, they may be more critical of government. Additionally, the *Post* survey team developed a political knowledge scale.[6] Finally, I employ a question about whether people get their impressions of government from friends and family (rather than from personal experience or television). Many people form their impressions of House members from talking with their friends and family. These evaluations are overwhelmingly positive (Jacobson 1992). Might the same dynamic work more generally?

Later I argue that Democratic (Republican) people who live in Democratic (Republican) states should be more favorably disposed toward their state governments. A state government of your own party should

5 This result may reflect another dynamic: The more highly educated are more likely to have postmaterialist values, which in turn lead to greater skepticism about traditional institutions (Inglehart 1997).

6 The scale is an additive measure of correct answers to questions about which party has the most members in the House and the Senate, whether there is a limit to the number of terms a president can serve, the length of a Senate term, whether one party is more conservative than the other and which party is more conservative, who was president when the Watergate scandal took place, and the names of the Majority Leader of the Senate, the Vice President, the Speaker of the House, and the Chief Justice of the Supreme Court.

make decisions that you like better—and, hence, you should be more likely to trust state government. For each state (except Nebraska, which has a nonpartisan legislature) I developed a measure of partisan representation in a state by taking the proportion of seats the Democrats hold in each house of the legislature and adding it to a dummy variable for partisanship control of the governorship. The resulting index, divided by three, is a 0–1 scale ranging from complete Republican to total Democratic dominance.[7] I include it in the estimates for state and federal government trust. If the conservative argument is correct, people who live in states dominated by Democrats should be less favorably disposed to state (and perhaps the federal) government, while people from Republican states should be more favorable. Finally, there is a long-standing trend for people to lose faith in government as they age. Trust in government, unlike trust in people (Uslaner 1998), is the province of the young.

WHO TRUSTS AND WHEN?

Most people (71% to 29%) have greater confidence in their state governments than in Washington.[8] The forced-choice question may lead us to the false conclusion that Americans like one level of government but not the other. Quite the contrary. The majority of respondents (76%) are consistent in their faith—or lack of it—in government. No confidence in either level is expressed by 58%, 18% in both. Just 7% of respondents like the government in Washington but not in their state, while 17% express solidarity only with their state administration.

So what do the models tell us about the forces that drive public support for different levels of government? The model for which level of government one prefers *is* largely driven by ideology.

IN WASHINGTON WE TRUST?

Preferences for Washington or one's state are, as expected, largely driven by ideology. I present the estimates for which level of government people

7 Independents, including the Governor of Maine, were scored .5. The index ranges from .132 for Idaho to .939 for the District of Columbia (treated as a state by measuring representation of its city council). I collected the data from *Politics in America 1996* (Duncan and Lawrence 1995).

8 Eleven percent of respondents volunteered that they trusted neither or both levels of government. I assigned missing values to these respondents.

Table 7.1. *Regression Estimates for Preference for State or Federal Government*

	Coefficient	Std. Error	t Ratio
Political Ideology	–.100****	.017	–5.741
Government Threat Scale	–.059****	.010	–6.048
Listen to Rush Limbaugh	–.028**	.015	–1.828
Confidence in Congress	.064****	.017	3.729
Personal Finances Better	.055**	.028	1.979
Hours Watch TV per Day	.010***	.004	2.421
Politics and Government Too Complicated	.034***	.013	2.717
Age	.003****	.001	3.434
Education	–.023***	.010	–2.446
Income	.014	.010	1.421
Black	.264****	.045	5.816
Constant	.547	.121	4.531

Note: * $p < .10$. ** $p < .05$. *** $p < .01$. **** $p < .0001$. $R^2 = .156$. S.E.E. = .410. F = 15.116.

trust more in Table 7.1.[9] Positive signs on the coefficients indicate preferences for the federal government.

The three most powerful predictors of which level people trust are all linked to ideology: the government threat scale, race, and political ideology. Blacks are almost 30% more likely to prefer the federal government to their state, while conservatives and people who see government as threatening are each 20% more supportive of their state than are liberals and those who are not afraid of centralized power. Listeners to Rush Limbaugh's talk show are 8% more likely to favor state government. Perhaps the program converts listeners to Limbaugh's anti-Washington message. Equally (or more) likely, people who listen to Limbaugh already share his views on the federal government.[10]

9 The summary statistics in Table 7.3 provide support for using SUR estimates. The intercorrelation among residuals for the trust in federal and state government equations is .388, strongly indicating that the two equations are not independent. There is less support for a strong relationship between the two measures of trust and preference for one level of government or the other, with correlations of residuals of .073 and –.148. Both are significant, however.

10 A regression predicting frequency of listening to the Rush Limbaugh show finds ideology and the government threat scale as two of the three strongest predictors (together with income).

Preferences for different levels of government reflect people's world view. A black who never listens to Rush Limbaugh, does not see Washington as a threat, and identifies as a liberal has a .72 probability of preferring Washington. A white conservative who says that Washington is a threat and who regularly listens to Limbaugh has just a .31 probability of preferring the federal government.

There is limited evidence that evaluations of the state of the economy have any effect on which level of government people like. Only your own economic situation—and not the national economy—affects your preferences. Even here the impact is weak: People who say their finances are getting better like Washington more, but simple family income is not significant.

There is more support for the idea that information matters. People who pay a lot of attention to television are more likely to get news about national affairs and people who say that politics and government are too complicated should understand national affairs better than the often unheralded world of state politics. So heavy television viewers and people who say that politics is too complicated prefer the more familiar world of Washington. And so do people with less education—and the young as well. Young people are also less likely to pay attention to state politics, which may seem more remote to their world. The more exposure you have to state government, the more likely you will be to prefer it. With limited information about either level, people will favor the more familiar one.

Other variables matter as well, but not so much. People who like Congress also prefer the federal government. It seems reasonable to argue that this might also reflect ideology. The Republicans took control of the House of Representatives in 1995 for the first time in four decades and approval of Congress is stronger for Republicans and conservatives than it is for Democrats and liberals. But there is less ideology to this linkage than one might first think. First, if there is an ideological connection, it should be for conservatives to favor smaller government closer to the people. There is no clear ideological link between support for Congress and which level of government one prefers. Second, the connection between approval of Congress and trust in the federal government is hardly new. It is one of the most time-tested variables in trust in government research (Citrin 1974; Feldman 1983).

Ideology matters most for which level of government people prefer. But it plays a decidedly secondary role in the more general measures of confidence in the federal or especially the state governments (see Table 7.2). Conservatives *are* more likely to distrust Washington, but they are

Table 7.2. *Regression Estimates for Trust in Levels of Government*

	Trust in Federal Government			Trust in State Government		
	Coefficient	SE	t Ratio	Coefficient	SE	t Ratio
Political Ideology	–.064***	.022	–2.871	–.013	.026	–.491
Confidence in Clinton Administration	.082****	.020	4.078	.050**	.023	2.174
Confidence in Congress	.202****	.022	9.227	.161****	.025	6.406
Blame Clinton or GOP for Shutdown	–.030	.040	–.744	–.034	.046	–.739
Officials Don't Care What People Think	–.070****	.019	–3.803	–.041**	.021	1.956
Trust in People	.062**	.037	1.659	.104***	.043	2.445
Personal Finances Better	.050*	.035	1.457	.026	.040	.664
Income Gap Narrower than Twenty Years Ago	.038*	.025	1.535	–.002	.028	–.060
Government Responsible for Economy	–.111***	.035	–3.148	–.142****	.040	–3.535
Political Knowledge Scale	–.013**	.007	–1.784	.009	.008	1.048
Years Lived in Community	.001	.001	1.139	–.001	.001	–.549
Get Impression of Government from Friends	.107*	.065	1.642	–.025	.074	–.336
Partisan Representation in State	.207**	.098	2.107	.203	.112	1.816
Age	–.004****	.001	–3.466	–.005****	.001	–3.961
Education	–.033***	.012	–2.649	–.035***	.014	–2.438
Constant	3.341****	.153	21.881	3.289****	.175	18.861

Note: * $p < .10$. ** $p < .05$. *** $p < .01$. **** $p < .0001$. Federal Government: $R^2 = .210$. S.E.E. = .511. F = 15.778. State Government: $R^2 = .110$. S.E.E. = .587. F = 7.901.

no more supportive of state government than are liberals. The regression coefficient for ideology in the equation for trust in state is not significant.[11]

Trust in both Washington and state governments is largely driven by more general confidence in political institutions. People who like governmental institutions like government. Confidence in the Clinton administration and in Congress were the most important determinants of trust in government. What may be surprising is that approval of the president and the Congress are almost as important for trust in state government as they are for faith in Washington. The regression coefficients are larger for both measures for trust in the federal government—by 64% for presidential approval and by 25% for congressional favorability. People who believe that public officials don't care what people think are alienated from both levels of government. Anger at unresponsive politicians is more important for confidence in the federal government than for the states—perhaps reflecting the view that state officials are more in touch with people's wishes. I also included a variable measuring whom people blame for the government shutdown in 1995. I expected that if there were either an institutional or an ideological effect of the shutdown on confidence, we would see that people who blamed the Republicans would be more favorable to Washington. But there was no effect on either level of government.

Personal finances and the size of the income gap between rich and poor each play a minor role for trust in the federal government. Neither is significant in the equation for state government. But when people see the government as responsible for the economy, they are more critical of *both* levels of government. Ironically, the impact is slightly stronger for trust in the state government than for faith in Washington. These results confirm Chubb's (1988) finding of a strong spillover from national economic conditions to evaluations of state politics.[12]

Familiarity doesn't always breed contempt. The more knowledgeable have less faith in Washington, but are no more likely to have more (or less) confidence in their state government. Length of residence in a community does not affect trust in either level of government. People who learn about the federal government from their friends and family have a slightly more positive view of Washington but not of their states. There are few signs that close ties to government either raise or lower trust. The sole exception comes from education. As Hibbing and Theiss-Morse (1995) find, the more highly educated are less supportive of governmental institutions. Young people have considerably more

11 Listening to Rush Limbaugh was not significant for either trust measure, nor was race (so I excluded both from the model).

12 Chubb examined voting returns for state legislatures for incumbent parties.

confidence in government than their elders. Finally, people living in states dominated by Democratic office-holders are more trusting in both state and federal institutions. Trust in people does have a spillover effect on trust in government. Its effect is much stronger for state government than for Washington, perhaps because the federal government seems more remote from daily life than the states.

There are two lessons in the estimates for trust in federal and state government. First, neither is largely driven by ideology. There are only modest correlations between trust in the federal government and support for reductions in *federal* spending on the environment (gamma = –.244) and on foreign aid (gamma = –.305) and minuscule correlations with cutting defense, Medicare, and welfare (gamma = –.106, –.158, and –.125, respectively). There is virtually no relationship between trust in state government and attitudes toward federal spending, regardless of the program.[13] If ideology were a key determinant of support for state governments, then we should expect stronger relationships for programs that could be transferred to the states (welfare and perhaps the environment and Medicare). But we don't.

There is a similar dynamic in more open-ended questions about *why* people do not like Washington, and why they do have favorable impressions of states. Conservatives are far more likely than liberals to say that they distrust Washington because the federal government wastes taxes, interferes too much in people's lives, and spends money on the wrong things (gamma = –.314, –.285, and –.262, respectively). But they are no more likely than liberals to dislike Washington because it does not reflect their values (gamma = –.076). There are no significant differences among liberals, moderates, and conservatives across a wide range of possible reasons for *liking* state government. *Liberals* are very slightly more likely to believe that states spend money wisely, are more responsive to the public, and are less dominated by special interests than the federal government is (gamma =.046, .054, and .034, respectively). Conservatives are just a little bit more likely to say that states waste less in tax money, solve problems quickly, and better reflect people's values (gamma = –.115, –.106, and –.007, respectively).

The argument that Washington is really the problem gets little support from this analysis. Ideology plays no role at all in trust in state government. When we force a choice between levels of government, there is a strong role for the left–right spectrum. When we simply ask people how much they trust either level of government, these core values become far less important. People do prefer state government to Washington. The

13 The gammas are –.119 for the environment, –.084 for foreign aid, –.022 for defense, .046 for Medicare, and .002 for welfare.

mean trust scores are 2.38 for the former and 2.25 on a four-point scale; 21% of people give higher scores to their state governments, while just 8% are more supportive of Washington. Yet, higher trust for state government is *not* driven by ideology. Liberals are just as supportive of state governments as conservatives.[14] Liberals, like conservatives, prefer state institutions to Washington.

Second, most people do not discriminate between Washington and their state governments; 71% give identical trust scores on the four-point scale to the two levels of government. When people are asked whether federal government activity has made things better or worse across several policy areas, people who thought the government had a deleterious effect were less trusting of the federal government (though often weakly so). People who believe that federal programs made violent crime worse, created more single-parent families, increased the gap between the rich and the middle class, and made the air dirtier were less likely to trust the government in Washington. But they were also less likely to have faith in their state governments.[15]

Not surprisingly, what drives confidence in one level of government also leads to faith in the other. The correlation between support for Washington and support for the states, as measured by the predicted values from the regression estimates, is .902. Support for either level of government is not the same thing as a forced choice. The correlation between the preference measure and confidence in Washington is .408; the correlation with trust in state government is just .266.

THE PARTISAN CONNECTION

Do Republicans and Democrats think differently about issues of federalism? No. Both Democrats and Republicans who believe that federal action makes things worse on air pollution, the income gap between rich and poor, single-parent families, and violent crime are less trusting of the federal government—and the correlations are of similar magnitude. Both Republicans and Democrats who believe that the federal government has made things worse on these policy areas are less trusting of their *state* governments as well.[16]

14 The mean scores are 2.37 for liberals, 2.38 for moderates, and 2.40 for conservatives ($F = .17$, $p < .85$, two-tailed). The correlation between ideology and trust in state government is .015.

15 The gammas for federal and state government are: violent crime (–.418 and –.289), single parent families (–.274 and –.202), the income gap (–.306 and –.285), and the environment (–.213 and –.132).

16 While the correlations are not quite as consistent across parties for trust in the state government, they display no coherent pattern.

I estimate separate regression equations for trust in state government for GOP and Democratic identifiers. I present the models in Table 7.3; they contain almost exactly the same variables as the estimates in Table 7.2.[17]

Based upon the results so far, I expect that Republicans and Democrats would base their trust in state government on similar logics. Mostly they do. Support for Congress has big spillover effects for both Democrats and Republicans. Decreasing income gaps also make both groups of identifiers supportive of state institutions. People who see the government as responsible for the economy are more critical of state governments (especially among Republicans). Young people who identify with both parties have higher levels of trust.

Yet, there are some differences. Interpersonal trust matters more for Republicans than Democrats (though the reason is unclear). Community ties, as measured by the length of residence, is more important for Democrats. Knowledge leads Republicans to become more disaffected than it does for Democrats (cf. Uslaner 1997). The impact of the political knowledge scale is only significant for Republicans, and the coefficient on education is 44% higher for Republicans.

Approval of President Clinton only matters for Democrats. More critically, the partisan composition of state governments is only significant for Democrats. Recall the logic of decentralization advocated by conservatives: Washington is too distant and out-of-touch. National politicians believe that they can expand their base by providing additional federal programs. Leaders at lower levels of government are closer to the people and will thus better reflect the public's preferences. Some voters will be liberals, and they may elect Democrats to office and be happy with what they have chosen. The Democratic model in Table 7.3 supports this: Democrats who live in states dominated by Democratic office-holders are more likely to trust state government. Some voters will be conservatives and will elect Republicans to office. In turn, they should be happier with their institutions. But they are not. GOP identifiers living in states with lots of Republican office-holders have no more faith in state government than their counterparts in states led by Democrats.

Context matters for Democrats. Democratic identifiers are more likely to base their decisions to trust government on policy grounds if they live in Democratic states than if they reside in states dominated by Republicans. Democrats who believe that federal policies have led to decreases in single-parent families, violent crime, and the income gap like govern-

17 I deleted blaming Clinton or the GOP Congress for the government shutdown because of collinearity.

Table 7.3. *Regression Analysis of Trust in State Government by Party Identification*

	Democrats			Republicans		
	Coefficient	SE	t Ratio	Coefficient	SE	t Ratio
Political ideology	.021	.035	.583	–.032	.035	–.919
Confidence in Clinton Administration	.066**	.030	2.204	.009	.030	.286
Confidence in Congress	.196****	.037	5.308	.179****	.029	6.198
Officials Don't Care What People Think	.043	.030	1.448	.014	.026	.543
Interpersonal Trust	.128**	.062	2.068	.179****	.051	3.505
Personal Finances Better	.022	.055	.397	–.132	.049	–2.713
Government Responsible for Economy	–.101**	.059	–1.717	–.150***	.050	–3.027
Income Gap Narrower than Twenty Years Ago	.076**	.042	1.808	.080**	.035	2.287
Years Lived in Community	.003**	.002	2.039	–.001	.001	–.589
Political Knowledge Scale	.016	.013	1.275	–.014*	.011	–1.283
Get Impression of Government from Friends	–.171	.122	–1.398	.103	.085	1.211
Partisan Representation in State	.343**	.154	2.238	.012	.142	.083
Age	–.006***	.002	–3.446	–.005***	.002	–2.802
Education	–.041**	.020	–2.096	–.059***	.018	–3.330
Constant	3.107****	.237	13.094	3.495	.215	16.293
R^2			.131			.177
Adjusted R^2			.108			.154
S.E.E.			.610			.540
N			535			520

Note: * $p < .10$. ** $p < .05$. *** $p < .01$. **** $p < .0001$.

ment more (data not shown). Their policy views have a bigger impact on their views of Washington than on the states. Republican confidence in both federal and state governments shows modest correlations with evaluations of policy performance—but it does not matter whether Republican identifiers live in states dominated by their own party or by Democrats. *If there is a partisan or ideological component to the state–federal divide, it is among Democrats.* Trust in government depends more on policy agreement and the political environment for Democrats than for Republicans.

If confidence in government were driven by an ideological aversion to big government, we should see stronger effects on policy for Republicans. Republicans (and conservatives) hold that the public has turned against Washington because the federal government has become too intrusive. Smaller units of government are said to be closer to the people, and thus more representative of a state's population. If there is, as Hayek argued, an irresistible tendency of the central government to be big government, conservatives (and Republicans) should feel most comfortable not just in smaller units, but also in states governed by their own party. After all, some electorates are liberal: Republicans disparagingly speak of the "People's Republic of Massachusetts" or, alternatively, "Taxachusetts." But states dominated by the GOP (New Hampshire, Idaho, and Utah) should be more hospitable to Republicans, who should express greater satisfaction with government there.

Yes, people who see the federal government as threatening are far more likely to distrust both the state and federal governments. But plenty of people other than Republicans or conservatives dislike government. Republicans do not like state government any more if they live in GOP dominated states than if they reside in Democratic territory.[18]

SO YOU SAY YOU WANT A DEVOLUTION?

There is plenty of reason to worry about trust in the federal government. It is down sharply from the 1950s. In the *Post* survey just 25% had confidence in the federal government. We don't know how to rebuild trust in government. Yet, there does not seem to be much payoff from looking for an alternative to Washington.

18 I created a dummy variable for state partisanship divided at the theoretical midpoint (.5) on the zero–one scale. Republican identifiers living in GOP-dominated states are no more likely to trust state government than GOP identifiers in Democratic states (with means of 2.42 and 2.40, respectively, for an $F = .17$, $p < .34$, one-tailed).

Is Washington Really the Problem?

Washington is not the problem. Government is the problem. People who do not like the federal government do not like their state governments either. The states are not the reservoir of good will among the American people. Yes, they are more popular than Washington, but not by a huge amount. Only 35% of people trust their state government, to be sure, a lot more than trust Washington, but far from a majority.

These results pose a challenge both to ideologues and to centrists. There is no support for the Republican/conservative argument that states can serve as a more popular alternative to the federal government. Neither ideology nor partisanship drives trust in state government. Ideology has modest effects on confidence in the federal government. These small effects undermine the conservative argument *and* a more centrist counterargument. Dionne (1991) and King (1997) maintain that Americans have become disenchanted with government because they see the two major parties and their associated interest groups as being too extreme. Strong ideologues—on the left as well as the right—have attacked government as being out of touch. This leaves the center as the bastion of support for government, but even the middle has lost confidence over time as the right and left attack Washington. Nevertheless, centrists should be more supportive than stronger ideologues. There is some support for this view: *Strong liberals and strong conservatives* are more critical of the federal government than are moderates (gamma of ideological strength with trust in Washington = –.213). But this relationship vanishes in multivariate analyses.

Ideology doesn't seem to be the key to trust in government, either from the right or from the center. Trust seems to depend on a positive view of institutions and their incumbents. But there is still a puzzle of what drives negative views of our national institutions. There is *not* a single anti-Washington syndrome, for people who approve of the president are *not* any more likely to like Congress (gamma = –.021).

While the president and Congress seem to constitute different political realms, the states and the federal government do not. If you do not like Washington, you are not likely to be convinced that your state is more trustworthy. People dislike their states for mostly the same reason they do not like Washington. Some do not like other people much either and transform their general malaise to a critique of government. Governmental performance is an important force in trust. But the general impression is that lots of people simply do not like government of any type for any reason. If you do not like green eggs and ham, you will not care if they are served in a house or with a mouse.[19] Shifting the locus of power will not solve the problem of trust in government.

19 If you don't get this allusion to Dr. Seuss, you don't have children.

8

Explaining Public Support for Devolution
The Role of Political Trust

MARC J. HETHERINGTON AND JOHN D. NUGENT

INTRODUCTION

For all the celebration in American political culture of decentralized government and decision making close to the people, American state governments have been widely reviled through much of our history. Recent scholarship has indicated that the leading framers of the Constitution were driven less by the particular failures of the Articles of Confederation than by their perceptions of the inability and unwillingness of state governments to address pressing social and economic problems (e.g., Rakove 1997). State governments everywhere, and particularly in the south and southwest, were long known for illiberal attitudes toward racial minorities. During the Progressive Era, state-governmental corruption prompted movements for initiatives and referenda and measures such as the Seventeenth Amendment, which took power out of the hands of often-crooked state legislatures. The implementation mechanisms of many Great Society–era programs reflected continuing distrust of the state governments by sending authority and/or federal money directly to cities, bypassing state governments that were viewed as antiquated, unrepresentative, and incapable.

Against the backdrop of this historical legacy, current high levels of popular support for the devolution of decision-making authority to state (or local) governments are, at least on their face, something of a mystery. What has changed that would convince majorities of skeptical politicians and members of the public that state governments should be the loci of policy making today? Part of the explanation lies, no doubt, in the widespread efforts of nearly all state governments over the past thirty years in terms of constitutional revision, legislative reapportionment and professionalization, strengthening executive authority, and increasing fiscal capacity (Van Horn 1989; Bowman and Kearney 1986; Reeves 1985).

By many measures, state governments today are better prepared to govern effectively than ever before.

Given the chronically low levels of political knowledge in the United States (Converse 1964; Delli Carpini and Keeter 1996; Luskin 1987), however, it seems far-fetched to believe that many Americans are acutely aware of these developments. Rather, we believe that there is another explanation for widespread popular support for devolution, and it involves increasingly negative feelings about the federal government. Scholars have amply described trends in public opinion since the late 1960s of increasing distrust in the federal government and skepticism about its ability to address problems effectively (Blendon et al. 1997; Hibbing and Theiss-Morse 1995). Scholars have disagreed about the causes of the remarkable declines in trust of the federal government and, accordingly, most of the scholarly debates have been concerned with documenting these causes.

In this paper, we adopt an approach to political trust that is somewhat unique in two senses. First, rather than treating political trust as an effect of various social, political, cultural, and/or economic factors, we view it as a cause of other attitudes (see also, Hetherington 1998, 1999). Second, we look to what we believe may be the flip side of declining trust of the federal government, namely, increasing confidence in state governments. We are interested in why it is that growing numbers of Americans today say they believe that state governments do or could spend tax dollars more wisely and formulate better public policy than the federal government. Is the current popularity of state governments the result of effective state governments, or is it the result of a rejection of the federal government, as manifested in low levels of political trust at that level?

We argue for the latter. In short, we find that distrust of the federal government increases confidence in lower levels of government. While partisanship and ideology play a somewhat larger role in helping us understand why people have more faith in state and local governments than the federal government, our results suggest that distrust of the federal government has more explanatory power than do a range of state characteristics that should be predictive of a state's ability to govern effectively. In fact, residents of states with more effective and responsive state governments are often more supportive of the federal government than those from states with less effective and responsive governments.

PUBLIC OPINION OF STATE GOVERNMENT OVER TIME

While it is difficult to get a precise sense of public sentiment about state governments before the survey era began, a good deal of circumstantial evidence suggests that citizens have generally held their state governments in low regard. The brief historical review that follows offers some context in which to understand the uniqueness of current popular support for state governments.

After winning independence from Great Britain, citizens of the several states institutionalized their strong suspicion of governmental authority in weak state executive branches and unstable legislatures (Wood 1969; Jensen 1950). By 1787, the failures of state governments to meet the challenges facing their young states was "as important an element in the movement for constitutional reform as the more conspicuous failings of [the federal] Congress" (Rakove 1997, 29). Many of the early political habits of state governments proved difficult to break under the 1787 Constitution, and political and constitutional reform moved slowly in the states. State constitutional arrangements that perhaps wisely limited executive authority also made it impossible for governors to provide leadership, and the authority given to state legislatures was often used with little restraint.

The quality of state governments and officials remained generally low in the nineteenth century, as many state governments proved unable to respond to the exigencies of the emerging industrial economy. "What little public confidence in their state governments remained after the bank scandals and the turnpike fiascos of the 1840s was completely undermined by the rapid spread of industrial capitalism in the Grant–Hayes–Arthur epoch. Party oligarchies, supported by patronage and leagued with corporate giants, bought and browbeat governors, legislators, and administrative officers as the great public utilities, essential to urban industrialism, were established. Railroads, traction companies, gas suppliers, electricity distributors needed and got state privilege and state protection" (Young 1958, 179; see also Graves 1936).

An additional indicator of unfavorable public assessments of state governments is the movement for popular election of U.S. senators that began in earnest in the 1870s (Haynes 1938). Moreover, the introduction and spread of the use of the initiative around the turn of the twentieth century indicates the popular distrust of state legislatures at the time. Beginning with South Dakota in 1898, the initiative "spread rapidly after its initial adoption and nearly all the states that now authorize it enacted the provision in the next twenty years" (Reeves 1985, 278; see also Magleby 1995). At about the same time, nearly a dozen states adopted recall provisions as a means of removing public officials, although the procedure has rarely been used against state officials (Graves 1936; Reeves 1985).

Support for governors during the presurvey era was also mixed. In a few states, the governorship was an important office invested with significant political and legal authority; in others, it was a largely symbolic post. In almost all cases, state legislatures were far more influential (Bryce 1888; see also Bowman and Kearney 1986; Wood 1969). The weakness of the governorship was particularly evident in the southern states, whose post-Reconstruction constitutions established very weak and often fragmented authority distributed among several individuals.[1]

The beginning of the survey era coincided with the advent of the New Deal, which raised the profile of state legislatures and particularly governors as they assumed new roles as executors of various New Deal programs. The public favored other levels of government. In 1936, a majority (56%) said that they favored a concentration of power in the federal government rather than in state governments (44%). In 1939, a strong plurality (41%) thought the federal government was more honest and efficient in performing its duties than local (17%) or state (12%) governments (Blendon et al., 1997; see also Bennett and Bennett 1990; Donahue 1997). Support for the federal government appears to have been ascendant, in part due to the inability of state governments to do much on their own to ease the effects of the Depression.

As postwar trust in the federal government reached its high-water mark in the mid-1960s and began its decline, public opinion regarding state government began a slow climb. Surveys in the late 1960s found that about half of the public ranked state governments either first or second in terms of the level of government they followed most closely (Jennings and Zeigler 1970). Surveys from the 1970s provide mixed impressions of public sentiments, with many finding varying levels of support for or trust in state, local, and federal governments. Even so, local government frequently garnered the most support, with support for both state governments and the federal government lagging five to ten points behind (Roeder 1994). Importantly, however, it is clear that on average, state governments were perceived in an increasingly positive light at about the same time that people were losing faith in the federal government.

Today, state governments continue to do quite well in surveys relative to federal governments, although their absolute levels of support vary according to what sorts of questions are asked. When asked which level of government they trust to do a better job in running things, six in ten (61%) choose their own state government, while only one in four (24%) choose the federal government (Blendon et al. 1997; see also Donahue 1997). Another group (Pew Research Center for the People and the Press 1998) found that people trust their state governments more than the

1 An extreme example of the longevity of this phenomenon is seen in the fact that the governor of North Carolina did not get the veto power until 1997.

federal government, although their trust in state governments was far from overwhelming. Only about one in three Americans say that they trust their own state government to do the right thing just about always (5%) or most of the time (30%).

In short, while it is clear that many citizens still have reservations about their state governments and would not want them to assume across-the-board responsibility for making public policy, current support for state governments is generally strong, particularly when viewed in the historical context of persistent distrust of state governments as outlined above.

IS TRUST IN STATE GOVERNMENTS THE RESULT OF THEIR CURRENT ABILITIES TO GOVERN?

Beginning in the late 1950s and early 1960s, most states began to reform and invigorate their governments (Bowman and Kearney 1986). Given the generally positive developments and reforms at the state level, it is a reasonable hypothesis that current popular support for state governments is the result of improved public perceptions of state performance. While we find this account plausible, scholars need to consider carefully what composes these perceptions. First, it is difficult to objectively assess the performance of state governments relative to the federal government because responsibility for so few programs has recently switched between the branches. Hence, there is a strong possibility that these perceptions are largely symbolic in nature. The behavior of elites and the use of political symbols should, therefore, come into play. The championing of devolution by many Republicans surely legitimizes the view that state and local governments are capable of effective policy making. In addition, attitudes toward the federal government likely color those toward the states. Indeed, many general conceptions of American federalism are based on the notion that Americans can and do shop around among levels of government (Beer 1993; Shattschneider 1960). In the next section, we develop the argument that state government popularity is, in part, a function of the federal government's unpopularity.

AN EXPLANATION OF POPULAR SUPPORT FOR DEVOLUTION AND STATE GOVERNMENTS

Having established that current public opinion of state governments is now generally favorable and having presented some historical data that suggest this rising tide of confidence in state governments has coincided with a loss of faith in the federal government, we propose that distrust of the federal government is among the most important considerations driving support for state governments and for the devolution of decision making from the federal level to the states. Despite the dramatic improvements in the modal quality of state governments over the past thirty years and increases in the amount of faith the public says it has in state and local governments, we believe such confidence is less a reflection of any demonstrated abilities of state and local governments as it is a reaction against the federal government.

Data

To test our hypotheses, we turn to data from the 1996 National Election Study (NES). In 1996, the NES asked a range of questions designed to gauge relative popular support for different levels of government. Most central to our analysis, the study asked respondents their general attitudes concerning which level of government they had the most faith and confidence in. Although this question does not tap trust in state governments directly or make explicit reference to transferring control of programs from the federal to the state governments, it does allow us at least a crude examination of the sources of mass support for state and local governments relative to the federal government.

Explaining Support for Devolution

To measure relative support, we turn to the following question. The NES asks, "We find that people differ in how much faith and confidence they have in various levels of government in this country. In your case, do you have more faith and confidence in national government, the government of this state, or in the local government around here?" If a respondent says the federal government, we code that respondent as 1. If the respondent says either state or local government, we code that respondent as 0.[2] This question allows us to examine why people might like to see more state and local involvement in policy making.

To explain people's opinions about which level of government they have the most faith and confidence in, we introduce a host of variables. Most central to our argument is the role of trust in the federal government. Since we believe that current mass support for state and local control reflects a loss of support for the federal government rather than

2 We should also note that the results are consistent no matter how this question is dichotomized. So, for instance, if we code it state against other, or local against other, we get the same pattern of results. Given that people are likely less inclined to make a distinction between state and local government than federal and state or federal and local, we chose this approach.

the widespread recognition of objective abilities of states and localities, trust in the federal level should powerfully affect relative confidence levels. To tap political trust, we use the NES's traditional four-item index. While scholars have debated the validity of this scale (e.g. Citrin 1974; Lodge and Tursky 1979), the index, when taken as a whole, does seem to behave in a pattern consistent with the conceptual definition of political trust (Hetherington 1998). In creating the index, we take the respondents' mean scores on the four items. To conserve data, respondents need to provide only one valid response.[3]

Our argument hinges on the performance of other variables in the model as well. We merged a range of aggregate-level variables tapping key state characteristics with the individual level data, assigning the states' characteristics to residents of these states. If people residing in states with more efficient, capable, or flexible governments are more inclined to prefer state and local control, this suggests an understanding that their particular state and local governments might be able to address political problems better than the federal government. If, on the other hand, the characteristics of a person's state government do not explain a relative preference for subnational government, then this preference may simply be due to symbolic rather than objective considerations.

Some might be concerned that our approach is somewhat asymmetric. Specifically, we use attitudinal measures regarding the federal level and objective measures regarding the state level to explain whether people have more confidence in national or subnational government. While we would prefer attitudinal measures of both, the NES does not ask respondents their perceptions about state government. Given the absence of attitudinal data, one solution would be to introduce objective measures of both state and federal government performance. Since all those surveyed are U.S. residents, however, we cannot use objective measures about the federal government in our cross-sectional model. Such measures would be constant for all observations.

We do not believe this asymmetry is particularly problematic, however. First, provided people's perceptions about state government are grounded in performance, the objective state measures that we employ here should provide the foundation for residents' perceptions of their state governments. Hence our measures should affect the dependent variable just as perceptions might. Following a similar logic, Markus (1988) finds that objective economic measures exert an even more profound effect on presidential vote choice than perceptual measures of voters' personal financial situation.

3 The results are consistent if we require that respondents answer all four items.

Second, even if perceptual data for state government performance were available, we believe our hypothesis regarding the importance of trust in the federal government would still be borne out. We do not expect that, in the present analysis, our objective measures of state performance will have a strong effect on preferences for subnational government. Lets assume for a moment that we are correct. If the perceptual data about state government were available and did have a strong effect, it would suggest that these perceptions were not highly correlated with objective performance. If not performance, the perceptions must be fueled by something else, and the number one candidate is again people's feelings about the government in Washington. Hence distaste for Washington would likely have both a direct effect on the dependent variable and an indirect effect through its effect on perceptions about state government, if we had analogous perceptual questions about state government available to us.

To assess the flexibility and effectiveness of state governments, we introduce several variables. First, it is reasonable to expect that people who reside in states in which ballot initiatives and referenda are both permitted and used will be more enthusiastic about their state governments relative to the federal government. Presumably, direct democracy provides residents a measure of direct control over public policy or at least provides them with the sense that this is the case. The experience with initiatives in California, for example, indicates that despite some notable problems and unanticipated consequences of the initiative process, residents nonetheless express overwhelming support for their continuation (Schrag 1998).

Second, people should have more confidence in state and local governments that are financially sound. If there is an informed foundation for support of the state level, people who live in states with lower per-capita state debts should be more inclined to support their state and local governments relative to the federal level than those with higher state debts. It would be reasonable for them to believe that their state would administer programs more efficiently. To tap the efficiency of a state government, we use the per-capita state debt at the end of 1995 as reported by *The Book of the States, 1996–97*.

Third, whether a person views his or her state as capable of paying for programs might also predict support for state and local government. Some suggest that state governments would not be able to pay the costs associated with large-scale devolution, which would in turn result in diminished services (Gold 1996). This should be less of a concern among people who reside in states with large tax bases, and if a state is capable of meeting fiscal challenges, people from that state should be relatively more supportive of their state and local governments than the federal government. As an indicator of fiscal capacity, we use a measure developed by the Advisory Commission on Intergovernmental Relations.

Fourth, although not as objective a foundation for support for greater local control as the previous three indicators, a state's political culture may hold explanatory power of its residents' opinions. Elazar (1966) identifies three broad state political cultures—traditionalistic, moralistic, and individualistic. People living in states in which the traditionalistic subculture is dominant tend to believe that government can play a positive role in society, but people from these states want governmental activities limited to maintaining the existing social order. This view is consistent with old-time conservatism. People living in states characterized as moralistic tend in general to support the government as a vehicle for achieving a good society. These states might be linked to a more old-style activist, liberal agenda, other things being equal. Of the state subcultures, this should be the one least consistent with support for state and local government. Finally, the individualistic culture is characterized by a pragmatic approach to governmental action. Government is viewed as an arbiter of competing private interests rather than a guarantor of power or benefits to the needy masses or the privileged elite. While a certain amount of initiative in the economic realm might be encouraged, government involvement should promote private initiative. People from these states might be most supportive of state and local control as the best alternative to putting decision-making authority in the hands of the federal government.

A range of other attitudinal and demographic controls are also potentially relevant. Republicans and conservatives alike have made devolution a centerpiece of their political rhetoric. Indeed, the principle of local control has long been a defining attribute of Republican platforms and campaign initiatives, such as the Contract With America. Given the importance of these issues on the elite level, those who are more conservative on the issues and those who are Republican party identifiers should pick up on these cues and, therefore, be less supportive of the federal government relative to state and local government (Zaller 1992). We measure partisanship on the traditional seven-point scale, and we measure ideology as respondents' mean self-placement on each of the NES's seven-point issue scales. Again, to conserve cases, respondents need provide only one valid issue response.

We also include controls for sex and race. Given that the federal government, through the actions of the Supreme Court, Congress, and the president, has historically done more to address the concerns of women and blacks, both groups should presumably identify the federal government as the level in which they have the most faith and confidence. This should be particularly true for blacks, given the painful legacy of state and local policy.

Finally, the type of political information that people receive may have an effect on the level of government in which people have the most confidence. Perhaps the more people hear about the federal government, the less they like it, particularly given the increasingly adversarial and scandal-driven news coverage of recent years (Patterson 1993). We also know that media coverage of state government and politics tends to be spotty at best (Gurwitt 1996; Cohen 1995), and there are indications that people know less about their state governments than about the federal government and its higher-profile heroes, villains, and problems. The present news arrangements suggest that the more news a person consumes, the more negative information that person will receive about the federal government, but not about state governments. Hence, heavy consumers of news should be more likely to identify state and local governments as more effective than the federal government. Since television should have stronger effects on public opinion than print media (Iyengar and Kinder 1987), we use television news consumption in our model.

The full model, cast in the logit form, is the following:

$$\begin{aligned}\Pr(\text{FEDMOST}_i) = (1 + \exp[-(\beta_0 + \beta_1\,(\text{Political Trust}_i) + \beta_2\\ (\text{Initiative and Referendum}_i) + \beta_3\,(\text{Moralistic State Culture}_i)\\ + \beta_4\,(\text{Traditionalistic State Culture}_i) + \beta_5\,(\text{State Debt}_i) + \beta_6\\ (\text{State Fiscal Capacity}_i) + \beta_7\,(\text{Partisanship}_i) + \beta_8\,(\text{Ideology}_i)\\ + \beta_9\,(\text{Female}_i) + \beta_{10}\,(\text{African} - \text{American}_i) + \beta_{11}\,(\text{Television}\\ \text{News Consumption}_i)])^{-1} \qquad (1)\end{aligned}$$

where exp is the exponentiation to the base *e*, the subscript *i* refers to the *i*th individual, and Pr(FEDMOST) is the probability that the respondent chooses the federal government as the level of government in which he or she has the most confidence. The descriptive statistics for each of the explanatory variables appear in Table 8.1.

Results

We begin by examining relevant descriptive statistics. Table 8.2 contains the proportion of people who identify either the federal or state government as the level in which they have the most faith and confidence, broken down by several of the state characteristics previously described. The results are quite striking and mostly run contrary to the notion that people support government closer to home because there are objective reasons to expect better results. People who reside in states with statutory initiatives and referenda are actually more supportive of the federal

Table 8.1. *Descriptive Statistics for Explanatory Variables*

	Mean	Standard Deviation	Minimum	Maximum
Trust in Federal Government	–0.504	0.454	–1	1
Partisanship	3.683	2.127	1	7
Mean Issue Position	–0.085	0.967	–3	3
Sex (Female)	0.551	0.497	0	1
Race (African American)	0.109	0.312	0	1
National News Consumption	3.619	2.729	0	7
State Has Initiative	0.235	0.424	0	1
Moralist State Culture	0.330	0.470	0	1
Traditionalist State Culture	0.318	0.465	0	1
State Debt	1,423.550	983.974	431	4,969
State's Fiscal Capacity	100.444	14.607	65	178

Note: Number of Cases: 1434.
Source: American National Election Study, 1996.

Table 8.2. *Proportion of People Identifying Federal and State Government as the Level They Have the Most Faith in, by State Law, Efficiency of State Government, and State Fiscal Capacity, 1996*

State Characteristic		Most Faith in Federal	Most Faith in State
Efficiency	Above Average	30	38
	Below Average	31	35
	Difference	–1	+3
Capacity	Above Average	33	35
	Below Average	28	39
	Difference	+5**	–4**
Has I&R?	Yes	35	36
	No	29	37
	Difference	+6***	–1

Note: Rows do not sum to 100% because we exclude support for local governments from the table. * $p < .05$. ** $p < .01$. *** $p < .001$. One-tailed tests.
Source: American National Election Study, 1996.

government relative to state and local government than those in states without it. They are statistically neither more nor less supportive of state governments, however.

A state's fiscal capacity, at least in a bivariate sense, also seems to make a difference in terms of people's confidence in the federal government. Again, however, the difference is contrary to what one might expect. People who live in states with above average fiscal capacities actually have somewhat more relative faith in the federal government than those who live in states with below average fiscal capacities, and those from above-average capacity states also have less confidence in their states relative to those from below-average capacity states.

Only in the case of per-capita state debt, our measure of state efficiency, is the sign consistent with what one might expect if there were an objective basis for more support for state governments. The magnitudes of the differences, however, are not statistically significant at conventional levels.

While there is not much bivariate support for the notion that a relative preference for subnational government has an objective foundation, perhaps these state characteristics fare better when proper controls are implemented. Table 8.3 contains the estimates from the model presented in Equation (1). The dependent variable is whether the respondent identifies the federal government as the level he or she has the most faith and confidence in. We estimate separate models for each of the state government characteristics alone along with the attitudinal and demographic controls, which appear in columns one through four of the table. We also estimate a full model with all state characteristics included at the same time, the results of which appear in the last column.

In terms of sign and significance, a number of findings are noteworthy. First, as expected, trust in the federal government is correctly signed and significant in each of the models. The same is true for partisanship and mean issue position. The state characteristics, however, do not fare as well. Whether a state has statutory initiatives and referenda is significantly predictive of confidence in the federal government relative to subnational governments, but it is positively signed. Consistent with the bivariate results, those from states with provisions for direct democracy are actually somewhat more supportive of the federal government than those from states without them. This finding runs contrary to the notion that support for government closer to the people implies a desire for local control. The same is true of a state's fiscal capacity. It is significant in the full model, but those from higher-capacity states are actually more supportive of the federal government relative to state and local governments than those from low-capacity states.

A state's political culture also seems to affect perceptions of the federal government, but not in the way we anticipated. Those from traditionalistic states are the most supportive of the federal government, significantly more so than those from both individualistic and moralistic states. In the full model, the results suggest that those from moralistic states are significantly less supportive of the federal level, relative to other levels, than either those from traditionalistic or individualistic state cultures.

Finally, our measure of state government efficiency has no effect on confidence in the federal government relative to other levels in either the

Table 8.3. *Whether Respondent Identifies Federal Government as the One in Which He or She Has the Most Confidence (Logistic Regression Estimates)*

	Model 1 (I&R)	Model 2 (Culture)	Model 3 (Efficiency)	Model 4 (Capacity)	Full Model
Intercept	−0.181	−0.168	−0.015	−0.612	−1.563***
	(0.191)	(0.207)	(0.206)	(0.450)	(0.506)
Trust in Federal Government	0.539***	.533***	0.531***	.524***	.544***
	(0.132)	(0.133)	(0.132)	(0.132)	(0.134)
Partisanship	−0.214***	−0.213***	−0.216***	−0.220***	−0.218***
	(0.034)	(0.035)	(0.034)	(0.035)	(0.035)
Mean Issue Position	−0.398***	−0.436***	−0.401***	−0.382***	−0.423***
	(0.074)	(0.075)	(0.074)	(0.074)	(0.076)
Sex (Female)	−0.127	−0.163	−0.121	−0.109**	−0.172
	(0.124)	(0.125)	(0.124)	(0.124)	(0.127)
Race (African American)	−0.020	−0.234	−0.087	−0.061**	−0.154
	(0.189)	(0.192)	(0.187)	(0.188)	(0.194)
National News Consumption	0.066**	0.067**	0.068**	0.066**	0.064**
	(0.023)	(0.023)	(0.023)	(0.023)	(0.023)
State Has Initiatives and Referenda	0.330*	—	—	—	0.426**
	(0.143)				(0.152)

	Model 1 (I&R)	Model 2 (Culture)	Model 3 (Efficiency)	Model 4 (Capacity)	Full Model
Moralistic State Culture	—	–0.168	—	—	–0.370*
		(0.155)			(0.166)
Traditionalistic State Culture	—	0.438**	—	—	0.485***
		(0.148)			(0.156)
State Debt	—	—	–0.000	—	–0.000
			(0.000)		(0.000)
State's Fiscal Capacity	—	—	—	0.005	0.014**
				(0.004)	(0.005)
Number of Cases	1,434	1,434	1,434	1,434	1,434
Beginning-2XLL	1,756.68	1,756.68	1,756.68	1,756.68	1,756.68
Ending-2XLL	1,589.95	1,578.821	1,593.48	1,592.92	1,561.09
pseudo R^2	.11	.12	.11	.11	.13
% Correctly Predicted	70.6	71.3	70.4	70.4	72.2

Note: * $p < .05$. ** $p < .01$. *** $p < .001$. One-tailed tests. Parameter estimates are unstandardized maximum likelihood estimates; standard errors in parentheses.
Source: 1996 American National Election Study.

separate models or the full model. Taken as a whole, these results suggest that whether people have more faith in state or local government than the federal government has very little to do with whether they might receive better services. In fact, when these measures do exert an effect, their direction is most often counter to expectation. People do not seem to perceive correctly the importance of the features of their state governments that are relevant to better performance.

The attitudinal variables also produce a couple of noteworthy results. Although we expected that a larger amount of national television news consumption would cause people to be less confident in the federal government relative to other levels, the reverse is true. Despite television's overwhelmingly negative portrayal of the national government, the more one watches, the more likely one is to identify the federal government as the most competent. This might suggest that heavy news consumption conditions viewers to think of the federal level as the proper locus of policy making. Finally, contrary to expectations, neither sex nor race has a significant effect on which level of government a person has most confidence in.

A word or two about the magnitude of the effects is also in order. The effect of trust in the federal government relative to other variables is impressive. In moving from minimum to maximum trust while holding all other variables constant at their means, the probability of identifying the federal government as the level that instills the most confidence increases by .239 points. This is only slightly smaller than the .252-point increase in probability caused by moving from strongest Republican to strongest Democrat and is larger than the .089-point increase in probability caused by moving from minimum to maximum television news consumption. Ideology has by far the largest effect. In moving from most liberal to most conservative, the probability of choosing the federal government drops by .476 point. Finally, living in a state that allows initiatives and referenda increases the probability that a respondent chooses the federal government by .090 point, and living in the state with the highest fiscal capacity improves the probability of choosing the federal government by .344 point.

We should also note that the overall fit of the model is not particularly strong, with the full model's pseudo r-square statistic only .13. Although we would like to see better goodness of fit, the low r-square is noteworthy for two reasons that support our analysis. First, some might have argued at the outset that trust in the federal government, our key explanatory variable, is the same thing as relative confidence in the federal government over subnational governments, which is our dependent variable. The results do not support this contention. If the two concepts were synonymous, the overall model fit would be significantly better. Second, responses to the dependent variable must not be particularly predictable, given that we have included all of the likely suspects on the right-hand side of the equation. This is further evidence that these preferences for subnational control are not particularly well reasoned.

CONCLUSIONS: THE NATURE OF PUBLIC TRUST IN STATE AND FEDERAL GOVERNMENTS

We have established that people who are the least trustful of the federal government are also the most likely to view state and local governments as the most capable levels of government. In addition, we have found that greater faith and confidence in subnational governance is not a function of the capability of respondents' state governments or the responsiveness of those governments to citizen input.

These findings have several important scholarly and political implications. The growing literature on trust in government has largely ignored the possibility that the public makes its assessments of governmental trustworthiness comparatively; that is, by considering which of several levels of government to which voters have elected representatives is likely to best address pressing problems. The notion that this might occur is not new. Madison noted as much in *The Federalist*, No. 46, when he wrote that "the federal and State government are in fact but different agents and trustees of the people, constituted with different powers and designed for different purposes" (Rossiter 1961, 294). A more recent formulation of this idea holds that "[l]ike the federal government, state governments also express the national will. The nation can use both levels or either level of government to make itself more of a nation: that is, to make the United States a freer, wealthier, more powerful, and indeed more virtuous human community" (Beer 1993, 21).

We argue that these theoretical statements hold a great deal of power to explain the results presented previously. While Madison and Beer were making general statements about the tendency of the sovereign people to invest trust in the governments they believe will best achieve the outcomes they desire, their expectations make even more sense when combined with what we know about relative levels of political confidence. While declining trust in the federal government is not the only reason an individual might have more confidence in his or her state or local government than the federal government, our results indicate that it is a powerful reason. Most importantly, trust in the federal government outperformed measures of state-governmental capacity and responsiveness as explanations for levels of confidence in those governments.

Based on these results, we argue that scholars should not limit their searches of the roots of government trust to the successes or failures of one level of government. Despite a great deal of imprecise talk about "the government" in this country, there are in fact nearly 87,000 governments in the United States by one estimate (Lowi and Ginsberg 1996), and any given individual is subject to the authority of at least a half-dozen of them. Americans appear to realize that their policy goals can be pursued by more than one level of government and evidently change their views concerning which is best qualified to do so, although perhaps not in a very informed manner. While trust in various governments is probably not a zero-sum game, our data seem to indicate that decreasing trust in the dominant level of government does lead to increased confidence in others.[4]

The capacity of state governments, on the other hand, seems to have little impact on public confidence in state and local governments. We began with the plausible expectations that citizens living under state governments with lower debts, greater capacities to raise revenue (and thus fund governmental programs), and opportunities to decide policy questions by initiatives and referenda would offer more positive evaluations of state governments in general. We found none of them to be supported by the evidence. Instead, we find that symbolic considerations, such as trust in the federal government, partisanship, and ideology, drive support for state and local control.[5]

Normatively, this is not the most reassuring conclusion to reach. First, in terms of Madison's and Beer's account of citizens shopping around among governments for the attainment of policy goals, it suggests that this process is not necessarily based on objective or demonstrated measures of governmental capability but rather by negative perceptions of another level of government. It also suggests, as one observer has argued (Bok 1997), that the federal government may not have lost the confidence of the American people on its merits but may have done so despite performing fairly well. Conversely, if current public satisfaction with

4 Incidentally, we do not believe the reverse is true. Trust in the dominant branch should not be damaged by increased faith in lower levels of government. Greater faith in nondominant branches only provides the opportunity to shop around for their favored level.

5 An additional source of citizen satisfaction with state governments or a desire for those governments to deal with problems in particular issue areas might be evidence that the federal government has devolved authority over a given policy area to state governments and that those governments have exercised that authority well. The major hurdle for this explanation is that very little authority has actually been devolved in recent years, despite much talk of a "devolution revolution" (Nathan 1996). Indeed, there are only two commonly cited examples of devolution: congressional repeal of the national 55-mph speed limit and welfare reform (Kincaid 1998).

state governments is based on something other than the demonstrated abilities of those governments to address problems, that satisfaction may dry up quickly in the face of even minor indications of state incapacity.

We have noted that current levels of public support for state governments are rather unique when viewed against a history of lackluster public sentiment for those governments. Given this history, we were led to believe that the popularity of subnational governments may stem from something other than their performance and capability. The analysis presented supports the proposition that popular support for subnational governments is in significant part the result of declining trust in the federal government. Future research should build upon the notion that Americans make comparative assessments of the various levels of government under which they live.

Part III

Do Actions on the Part of Politicians Cause Americans to Be Dissatisfied with Government?

In the first two parts of this volume it became apparent that much about public attitudes toward government could be learned by paying attention to how those attitudes change over the years as well as to how attitudes change when the focus is shifted from one political institution to another. But so many different types of specific political activities take place within any given time period or even any given political institution that some scholars may wish to analyze the actual specific activities themselves. This, in fact, is the strategy followed by the authors of the three chapters that constitute Part III. Perhaps, given its size and openness, it is not surprising that all three chapters touch mostly on activities in Congress. Where better to observe large numbers of politicians engaged in a variety of readily observable activities? But the uniting mission of these papers is to discover, regardless of the particular era or institution, whether or not certain political activities can be said to foster popular distrust. If the answer is yes, consideration could be given to the possibility of taking steps to limit activities that cast government in a bad light.

The first such political action connected to a negative public mood, however, is probably one that cannot be reformed away unless we wish to limit First Amendment rights by reenacting some form of a sedition act. Amy Fried and Douglas Harris contend that public dissatisfaction is given a substantial boost by the "anti-government rhetoric of politicians." They note that as recently as the 1960s the speeches of the political elite promoted the legitimacy of the political system and that participation and citizen trust were high; but soon thereafter both the political left and right were actively attacking that same system. They believe the general situation has continued until elites are now able to reap significant organizational, electoral, institutional, and policy rewards from such actions. They also see political conservatives as coming to be the dominant practitioners of the "attack government" strategy. Using the struggle to enact comprehensive health-care reform during the first Clinton Administration as an example, they show how distrust of government can be a tool in policy debates. So Fried and Harris's partial answer to the question of why people are negative toward government is that politicians encourage the people to be negative because the politicians realize such an attitude will often serve their interests.

Focusing particularly on Congress, David Brady and Sean Theriault take issue with the inclination of some scholars to conclude that any institution so large, open, and responsive is bound to be unpopular. While conceding that it will be difficult for Congress to be popular, they nonetheless convincingly assert that certain actions of members of Congress unnecessarily exacerbate public unrest. They begin by pointing out that the "inevitably unpopular" argument does not square with the fact that Congress is sometimes popular. As recently as the late summer of 1998, congressional popularity was at 63%, so it *is* possible for Congress to be reasonably popular. What would assist Congress to garner more public approval? Brady and Theriault cite four practices that depress congressional approval levels. First, members of Congress will confuse and mislead the public to obtain a desired outcome, such as a pay raise for themselves. Second, members too often engage in hyperbolic rhetoric that encourages the public to think difficult solutions have quick fixes and that trivializes serious policy debate. Third, consistent with the insights of Fenno (1975) and of Fried and Harris (this volume), members of Congress are not averse to running for Congress by running against and reaping personal political gains by bashing the institution itself. And fourth, the most extreme and shrill members tend to be the ones the public sees the most, thus leaving the impression that the institution is filled with media-conscious, combative ideologues when in fact there are at least a respectable number of serious, willing-to-negotiate moderates. Drawing on recent events in Congress, including the Persian Gulf War debate, budget reconciliation, and the impeachment proceedings against President Clinton, they are able to illustrate their points. Their systematic evidence on the connection between ideological extremism and media presence is especially telling and their conclusion that a politically naive public is not the sole reason for an unpopular Congress must be taken seriously.

Carolyn Funk also believes the actions of politicians contribute greatly to public dissatisfaction with government, but the evidence she offers is completely different from that provided by Brady and Theriault. In fact, it is completely different from the type of evidence presented in virtually all of the other chapters. Funk conducted an imaginative experiment in 1998 in which participants were exposed to either cordial or acrimonious debate. The findings seem to show that experimental subjects reacted more negatively to acrimonious debate. While this may seem reasonable, it does suggest that there is hard, experimental evidence that "the behavior of political leaders . . . contributes to public dissatisfaction with government." Of course, this is not the same as concluding that if all congressional debate were cordial, Congress would be popular, but Funk's creative research is consistent with the notion that there is something politicians can do that would improve public attitudes toward government.

9

On Red Capes and Charging Bulls
How and Why Conservative Politicians and Interest Groups Promoted Public Anger

AMY FRIED AND DOUGLAS B. HARRIS

> When the bull came out did you notice that one of the banderilleros ran across his course trailing a cape and that the bull followed the cape driving at it with one horn? They run him that way always, at the start, to see which horn he favors. The matador, standing behind his shelter, watches the bull run by the trailing cape and notices whether he follows the zig-zagging cape on both his right and left sides, this showing whether he sees with both eyes and which horns he prefers to hook with. He also notices whether he runs straight or if he has a tendency to cut ground toward the man as he charges.
>
> *Death in the Afternoon*, Ernest Hemingway (1932, 65)

Even as the public's long-standing distaste toward government goes through its latest permutations (Pew Research Center for the People and the Press 1998; Broder and Balz 1999), there continue to be more than enough explanations of distrust in government. Yet the multiplicity in research on political dissatisfaction conceals a certain uniformity, and this implicit agreement masks a potentially important dynamic. All previous explanations assume that political alienation is an unfortunate consequence of other developments or dynamics. For some scholars, the underlying cause giving rise to the effect is economic, for others it is based in citizens' misunderstandings of the democratic process, and so on—but for all, political distrust is inadvertent, certainly not the fruit of a conscious effort.[1]

1 Hibbing and Theiss-Morse (1995) tie distrust to citizens' dislike of democratic processes; Putnam (1995a) and Brehm and Rahn (1997) focus on declining social capital; Patterson (1994) and Jamieson (1992) argue that media framing plays a role; Reich (1997) and Greider (1992) emphasize the shrinking of the middle class and citizens' voices in the political process; and Schneider (1997) and Germond and Witcover (1994) emphasize reactions to political scandals.

In contrast, we work with the presumption that because political leaders are advantaged by shifting public sentiment, some leaders may have wished to increase political distrust. Rather than seeing growing public alienation as an accidental by-product, it may well be that this is another example of what one of us has called "the politics of public opinion." From this point of view, public opinion and perceptions of public opinion are political resources, used strategically by elected officials and interest group leaders. "Groups and political figures refer to and attempt to modify public opinion because they want to employ this important resource. Perceptions of public opinion legitimize policy stands, provide political cover for government officials, and become a matter of political struggle" (Fried 1997, 9). These struggles involve leaders who have competing political and policy agendas, and who employ all possible assets to succeed.

While leaders try to affect opinion and perceptions of public opinion, elites are not magicians who can use incantations to manifest their desires. Furthermore, the current manifestation of distrust is part of a broader cultural disposition among Americans.[2] At various times, different groups of elites focus on groups in the population who are likely to distrust the government for their own particular reasons. Distrust clearly involves strategizing for concrete purposes but not Svengali-like powers of elites.

Instead, to push this metaphor-making, elites are more like matadors who can aggravate a peevish bull, waving a red cape to encourage the bull to charge. The banderilleros (described in this chapter's opening quotation) study how the bull reacts to the cape, thus enabling them to plan future moves, avoid danger, and gain glory. Citizens who distrust government are the metaphorical beast here. No implication about their lack of reason is meant. However, this analogy suggests that, in some environments, particular individuals can catalyze persons with ornery temperaments to react. Furthermore, strategizing political elites analyze and learn about the public, so that they can work with their allies to incite the responses that will help them.

In the 1950s and early 1960s, U.S. elites' speeches promoted the legitimacy of the political system and citizen trust and participation were high. But the political culture of that time is no more. By the mid- to late 1960s, both the political left and right actively attacked the political system itself,

2 Our view of culture is indebted to Pierre Bourdieu (1977) and emphasizes patterns of practices, including public speech. Rhetorical practices are not just signs of the new politics but also contributors to political culture. In changing typical patterns of public talk about the legitimacy of government action, elites have modified the cultural contexts of citizen action and opinion.

arguing that there were ingrained flaws threatening either equality or liberty or both. As Gary Orren points out (1997, 95), anti-government rhetoric by politicians and in the media "is now a dependable and constant feature of the contemporary political culture. At federal, state, and local levels, on the campaign stump and in their official capacity, public officials malign government in terms both abstract and specific." Although this paper analyzes how conservative politicians and interest groups promoted public anger, others do the same thing for similar strategic reasons. While conservatives discredit government's activities when it comes to regulating businesses, redistributive taxation and spending plans, and race-conscious programs, liberals argue that government frequently should not be trusted in national-security matters and has no legitimate role as an arbiter of reproductive and sexual choices. The singular message of distrust provides both an all-encompassing message and a vehicle elites can use to appeal to diverse groups.[3]

Four Benefits of Distrust

The broad cultural trend of distrust toward government, we argue, was reinforced and developed by political elites. These elite efforts were aimed toward four types of tangible political gains: (1) to develop and maintain political organizations, (2) to influence citizens' voting decisions, (3) to promote situationally beneficial views about the proper powers of U.S. institutions, and (4) to legitimize and delegitimize policies. We later show how these benefits were served in our analysis of attacks on Congress as an institution and opposition to proposed health care reforms.

Organizational Benefits. Elites can seek to promote political alienation to help them build organizations focused on public anger or to modify organizations to focus on public anger. These organizations can be used to support particular candidates and policies. Interest groups fill and maximize available niches in a political community (Gray and Lowery 1996); the emergence of public distrust provided such a niche into which groups could be built or altered to exploit.

3 While niches are carved out by groups and are important to a group's identity, competitors for the same niche can cooperate, forming coalitions. Indeed, as Gray and Lowery (1996, 196) point out, there is significant variation in niche width, "the level of specialization entailed in a niche," and this affects whether similar groups will work together. Any niche formed around political distrust is surely wide enough that many groups could develop strategies which speak to, reinforce, and develop those constituencies.

The scope of this chapter precludes us from an extensive discussion of the organizational benefits politicians can accrue by promoting public distrust. But our investigation of the institutional benefits and policy benefits of public distrust indicates that Republicans and conservatives believed that anti-government rhetoric could make them a stronger team. Distrust toward government gave conservative organizations unifying rationales and "moral frameworks" for their actions, which they used in their institutional attacks on Congress and health-care reform.

Electoral Benefits. Elites may seek to promote distrust in government in order to affect how citizens vote. If they portray themselves as more trustworthy and in opposition to those who do not deserve the public's trust, citizens may vote for them. Political parties out of power are much more likely to benefit from citizen distrust, for negative evaluations of those in power frequently lead voters to reject the majority party (Fiorina 1981). Influencing the relative participation of different groups also affects which side wins (Schattschneider 1960).

Candidates often run for Congress by running against Congress (Fenno 1978). This became a concerted effort in 1994 as conservatives who had been cultivated by GOPAC and had become part of a political "farm team" for Republicans in the 1980s used anti-Congress rhetoric to run for Congress individually and to achieve a Republican majority collectively (Fenno 1997). Anti-government sentiment was a significant impact on the 1994 vote (Ladd 1995).

Institutional Benefits. Institutional combat has supplemented elections as a sphere of elite conflict (Ginsberg and Shefter 1990). We argue that cultivating public distrust in the institutions controlled by your opponents can be a key factor in institutional combat. Throughout the 1980s, Democrats sought to assert Congress' role while implicitly seeking to weaken the presidency's claim to dominance. Republicans' support of the presidency in the 1980s reflected their control of that institution, and their attacks on Congress were explicit during this time.

Policy Benefits. In addition to desiring power, political elites wish to achieve certain policy goals (Kingdon 1993). By promoting distrust in government and associating that distrust with their political opponents' policy ideas, elites can decrease support for their adversaries' goals and help legitimize one's own policy goals. One example is provided by President Clinton's proposed health-care plan, an endeavor with which many Republicans disagreed. Johnson and Broder (1996) and Skocpol (1996) argue that health care's defeat can be explained, in part, by strategic efforts to link it to perceptions of elitism and corruption in the federal government.

CULTIVATING DISTRUST IN CONGRESS: INSTITUTIONAL, ORGANIZATIONAL, AND ELECTORAL BENEFITS

Public distrust of government generally and specific governing institutions individually is cultivated by elites seeking political advantage, as they appeal to key constituencies and the general public. Although traditionally politicians—performing the role of loyal opposition—have been reluctant to call into question the legitimacy of institutions or to cultivate public mistrust of institutions, in recent years divided government and increasingly consistent patterns of party control of institutions have changed the nature of political opposition. Conservatives and liberals have behaved like what Piper (1994) calls "situational constitutionalists," seeking to empower the institutions they control while simultaneously weakening the institutions headed by the opposing party. Democrats championed the presidency and Republicans championed the Congress until 1968. After the 1968 elections elevated Richard Nixon to the presidency and Congress continued to become more receptive to liberal views, Democrats and Republicans "reassessed" the proper role of presidential and congressional power. From the 1970s through the 1990s, Democrats became Congress boosters and Republicans (particularly after the 1980 presidential election) saw the value of a strong presidency (Piper 1991, 1994). Nearly permanent divided government in the post-1968 years heightened the incentives politicians had to assert the legitimacy and powers of their institutions and weaken the institutions directed by the opposing party.

From Loyal Opposition to Competing Governors

While divided government could produce a situation in which both parties contribute to and promote the legitimacy of the government, it can also spur competing teams of politicians to use their position to promote distrust of the opposition and its political base. Inflammatory rhetoric is employed in tandem with attempts to strip institutions controlled by rivals of their political power. Not only can this produce policy stalemate, but it can also add fuel to public disaffection with government, as elites foster distrust in order to gain institutional, electoral, and organizational benefits.

In discussing the "normal patterns of oppositions in the United States," Dahl wrote that "Oppositions seek limited *goals* that do not directly challenge the major institutions or the prevailing American system of beliefs" (1966, 34). Dahl contends that "oppositions concentrate on limited changes within the established framework of ideas and institutions. Oppositions, then, are typically opposed only to specific policies or the personnel of government." Indeed, it is often in the interest of opposition parties (particularly in two-party states) to affirm the legitimacy and promote public trust of the institutions of government as they might control them one day. Dahl's view of American oppositions assumes a heterogeneity of intraparty preferences and a perceived need on the part of the opposition party to cooperate with the majority. But as the Democratic and Republican parties became more internally cohesive and ideological in the 1980s, one key determinant of this "cooperative opposition" changed. Moreover, the prevalence of divided government in post-1968 American politics makes it difficult to identify an opposition. Instead, both parties consider themselves the governing party and attempt to strengthen their claims to majority status and their ability to govern within the institution that they control.

Divided government in post-1968 American politics caused each party to rethink its previous ideological attachments to the institutions of government. As a result, each would act to weaken the institution that it previously had championed. Democrats reasserted a congressional role in domestic and foreign policymaking, most notably though the Budget and Impoundment Control Act (1974) and the War Powers Resolution (1973). Republicans, much in accord with their ideological predispositions against government, began to turn their attention toward trimming perceived abuses of power and process in the Congress.

Although Republicans began changing their views about the role of the presidency after the Nixon election, the Carter administration followed by Republican control of the Senate from 1981 to 1986 led to some muting of the situational constitutionalism that would expect Republican support of the presidency and opposition to congressional power. After Democrats regained control of the Senate in the 1986 elections, however, the lines were clearly drawn; the presidency was a Republican institution and the Congress—now both House and Senate—was Democratic. Conservatives, Republican officials, and then the party itself (at least as measured through its platform) became presidentialists and—perhaps more overtly—strong anti-congressionalists. Starting with a number of books published with the support of the Heritage Foundation and culminating with Republican platforms and the Contract with America, the Republican rhetorical assault on Congress took shape. Conservatives and Republicans asserted presidential power, questioned the exercise of congressional prerogatives, and employed inflammatory rhetoric in order to both increase the relative power of the institution they controlled at the expense of the institution controlled by Democrats and in an effort to take over the Congress.

The edited volume *The Imperial Congress: Crisis in the Separation of Powers* (Jones and Marini 1988) provides one example of the conservative efforts to delegitimize Congress. In the forward, Newt Gingrich (xi–x) wrote:

> The 100th Congress . . . is an imperial Congress reigned over by an imperial Speaker enacting special-interest legislation. . . . Madison, Jefferson and Hamilton tried to insure against the rise of an imperial Congress . . . the present-day Congress has become the most unrepresentative and corrupt of the modern era. . . . Such an imperial Congress mocks the American precept of self-government. . . . Every citizen should be concerned about the arrogance and corruption of the present-day Congress. At stake is the liberty of the American public.

Jones and Marini agreed that contemporary congressional practices proved threatening to liberty and democracy; they wrote: "Congressional control over the permanent bureaucracy, from micromanaging programs to hiring and firing executive branch personnel, constitutes a threat to the separation of powers and ultimately to democratic rule" (1).

Where the first half of *The Imperial Congress* focused on the founders' vision of Congress' powers, the second half took aim at the practices of the contemporary Congress. Specifically, it discussed "such distortions in the traditional congressional operations as micromanagement, the hypocrisy of Congress, its lack of accountability, its thirst for power" (Jones and Marini 1988, 105–6). One chapter focused on the "banana republic–style electoral politics" (Hammond and Weyrich 1988, 224) as the source of Democratic dominance of the House. Another criticized congressional overdelegation to and micromanagement of the executive, arguing that "The worst aspect of this system is the corruption it fosters and thrives upon" (West 1988, 311). Gabriel Prosser suggested that conservatives (particularly conservative presidents) could redress the imbalance of power, if they would "DENY LEGITIMACY;" "the new president must deny legitimacy to his congressional opponents and to the systems and structures which they control" (332–3).[4]

In a similar work, *The Ruling Class: Inside the Imperial Congress*, written under the sponsorship of the Heritage Foundation's U.S. Congress Assessment Project, Eric Felten (1993) held that "Deceit, calumny and character assassination are commonplace as our representatives strive to augment their power. Washington has been poisoned with their

4 Prosser concedes, "That does not mean refusing to recognize the authority of a duly elected Congress, but taking great pains to send one consistent message to the American people concerning the president's adversaries" (333).

machinations and our political system sickened as well" (6). Within Congress: (1) the "casework scam" (97) had produced "a rigged and fraudulent system" in which "voters manage to like their own particular Member while holding the institution and the rest of its inmates in contempt" (73); (2) committee and subcommittee hearings had degenerated into "Barnumocracy" (29), as chairs and members clamored for television coverage; (3) the recently passed Americans with Disabilities Act would lead to prosecution of businesses in "trials [that] are pure Kafka" (39); and (4) there is a "staff infection on Capitol Hill" (85) so that "Congressional staff run a shadow government" (79).[5] Felten questioned Congress's fitness to tax and spend funds, saying that "Free citizens should shudder at the thought of such a paternalistic arrangement" (53–4).

Republican platforms started to reflect conservatives' anti-Congress rhetoric as well. While the 1980 and 1984 Republican party platforms included only one negative mention of the congressional process, by 1988 and 1992 criticism of the Congress and its processes became an increasingly frequent part of the Republican platform.[6] In 1988, Republicans criticized the Congress or the exercise of congressional power twenty-seven times. In that year, Republicans held that Congress was "no longer the people's branch of government" but rather "the broken branch" and claimed that the Democrats controlling Congress were "an arrogant oligarchy that has subverted the Constitution." In its dealings with the executive branch, Congress has "sabotaged the Republican program to control the federal budget" by "smuggl[ing] through pork barrel deals." It also had exhibited "excessive interference" in the area of foreign policy. Moreover, Republicans maintained that: (1) the House "Ethics Committee has become a shield for Democrats" and that Democrats "protect their cronies"; (2) Democrats "stole a congressional seat;" (3) leaders "rig adoption of substantive legislation on mere procedural votes;" and (4) leaders "viciously penalize independent Democrats who vote their conscience." Republicans also implied that Democrats had subverted "accountability, order, and truth in government" in spending decisions.

5 On this last point, Felten (1993) continues by arguing that "anyone who challenges the system is run out of town by a special prosecutor" (79).

6 In fact, there were two positive mentions of Congress in the 1980 Republican platform. In both 1980 and 1984, the one negative mention concerned the congressional budget process. Only in 1988 did the Democratic platform have a mention of congressional powers comparable to the Republican mentions. In 1988, clearly in a reaction to the Iran-Contra Affair, Democrats called for an "American foreign policy that will . . . respect our Constitution, our Congress."

The attack on Congress continued in the 1992 Republican party platform with eleven negative mentions of Congress, and one subsection of the platform entitled "Cleaning up the imperial Congress." The platform read: "The Democrats have controlled the House of Representatives for 38 years—five years longer than Castro has held Cuba. . . . Their entrenched power has produced a Congress arrogant, out of touch, hopelessly entangled in a web of PACs, perks, privileges, partisanship, paralysis, and pork." The platform continues, "The Democrats have transformed what the framers of the Constitution intended as the people's House into a pathological institution" in which "incumbents abused free mailing privileges," leaders "ri[g] rules," and Democrats "stac[k] campaign laws to benefit themselves." Charging that the Congress has encroached severely on executive authority, the platform says that "'Advise and Consent' has been replaced by 'slash and burn'" and that Congress "has permitted rogue prosecutors to spend tremendous amounts to hound some of the nation's finest public servants." And turning their attention to the budget process, which was "at the heart of the Democrats corruption of Congress," Republicans likened the process to an "old shell game" dominated by congressional "double-talk."

This anti-Congress rhetoric was taken more directly to the Congress itself by insurgent member turned leader Newt Gingrich. Through the Conservative Opportunity Society, a congressional caucus Gingrich helped found, Gingrich and other COS members used the press and public exposure within the House itself to spread—among other messages—this anti-Congress sentiment.[7] Moreover, through GOPAC, Gingrich sought to imbue potential future Republican congressional candidates with anti-government and anti-Congress thought. Through video tapes and talking points, Gingrich provided budding Republican candidates with a common language that questioned the legitimacy of the Democratic Congress and its "corrupt liberal welfare state." According to Clift and Brazaitis (1996, 238), one GOPAC flyer, entitled "Language: A Key Mechanism of Control," "offered a word list for candidates who wanted to 'speak like Newt.' It recommended sixty-four words and phrases to define Democrats, such as 'pathetic,' 'sick,' 'corrupt,' 'bizarre,' and 'traitors'."

These efforts proved particularly fruitful in the Republican campaign to achieve majority status in the House and in serving as an important part of the new Republican majority's agenda in the 104th Congress. Echoing the terminology of Gingrich and conservative intellectuals of the late 1980s and early 1990s, class of 1994 Representative Joe

7 For an examination of COS efforts in this regard, see Barry (1990, 165–8).

Scarborough told Nicol Rae (1998): "Most of us campaigned against an 'Imperial Congress' and talked about the 'affluent lifestyle' of Congress" (82). According to Fenno (1997), that "anti-institutional message of the freshman candidates was the same nearly everywhere in the country [in 1994]. It was a coordinated, wholesale, frontal attack on the institution . . . [and that institutional argument] dovetailed nicely with the institutional argument that their leader had been making for sixteen years" (34).

Republican complaints regarding Congress started in 1988. Why not 1986 or 1984 or 1980? To empower the executive in 1980 was still to empower the Carter Administration. To weaken Congress in 1984 was to weaken a Congress half of which (the Senate) was controlled by a Republican majority. After the 1986 elections when Congress was returned to unified party control, but the Congress and the president were controlled by Democrats and Republicans respectively, the battle lines were considerably clearer for situational constitutionalists. Once Republicans lost control of the Senate, they were more comfortable articulating the anti-Congress message Gingrich had been articulating throughout the 1980s. In 1988 *The Imperial Congress* was published and the Republican platform began to consider the ills of Congress. Thereafter Republicans and conservatives were more unified and resolute in their criticisms of Congress.

Confidence in Congress: Ideological Dimensions

The next question is "what effect has the conservative attack on Congress had on public confidence in the institution?" Data from the General Social Survey from 1982 to 1994 shows that after 1988 there was an increasing likelihood that conservatives—as opposed to liberals and moderates—would view Congress unfavorably. Figure 9.1 compares conservatives' distrust toward Congress to moderates' and liberals' by charting the difference between the percentage of conservatives reporting having "hardly any" confidence in Congress and the respective percentages of liberals and moderates with "hardly any" confidence.[8] From 1982 to 1986, the ideological difference switches back and forth with

8 It is important to note that an examination of the General Social Survey on this question from 1974 to 1980 reveals that conservatives generally were more likely to express "hardly any" confidence in Congress during that time as well. At some points, particularly 1977 and 1978, the differences are as large as in the late 1980s and early 1990s.

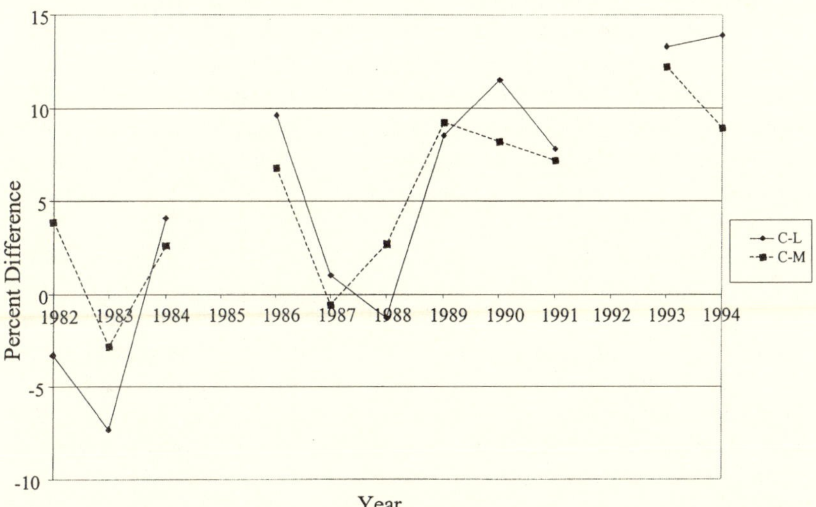

Figure 9.1. The Ideological Confidence Gap, 1982–94. *Source*: General Social Survey, 1982–94. Note: The question regarding confidence in Congress is, "I am going to name some institutions in this country. As far as the people running these institutions are concerned, would you say you have a great deal of confidence, only some confidence, or hardly any confidence in them at all?" The other question used asked respondents to self-identify as liberal or conservative; the breakdowns given by the GSS are "extremely liberal," "liberal," "slightly liberal," "moderate," "slightly conservative," "conservative," and "extremely conservative." In this figure, "moderates" are those who self-identified as "moderate" and "slightly" liberal or conservative. The values in the figure represent the difference between the percent of conservatives expressing "hardly any" confidence in Congress and the percent of liberals and moderates respectively. Values are missing for 1985 and 1992.

conservatives being more distrustful in some years and liberals being more distrustful in others. In 1987 and 1988, conservatives, moderates, and liberals express "hardly any" confidence at roughly the same rate. Soon thereafter, however, the percentage of conservatives' reporting having "hardly any" confidence in Congress diverges sharply from the views of moderates and liberals. This divergence occurred as Republicans began to step up their criticism of Congress. In 1989, 30.3% of conservatives reported having "hardly any" confidence, while only 21.8% of liberals and 21.1% of moderates did. The gap remains (and mostly widens) throughout 1994. While the 1989 conservative–liberal gap had been 8.5 and the conservative–moderate gap 9.2, by 1993 the conservative–liberal gap was 13.3 and the conservative–moderate gap was 12.2. In 1994, the conservative–liberal difference was 13.9 and the conservative–moderate gap narrowed to 8.9.[9]

Republican efforts at criticizing Congress in the late 1980s and early 1990s seem to have corresponded with an increasing importance of ideology in determining distrust of Congress. Although the percentage of liberals and moderates expressing "hardly any" confidence increases significantly from 1990 to 1993, those levels of distrust never match conservative levels. Republicans encouraged distrust of Congress in part to assert the prerogatives of the institution they controlled (the executive) and to take over the Congress as well. Thus, we should not be surprised that public confidence in Congress declined in the late 1980s and 1990s.[10] By cultivating distrust among conservatives, conservative politicians went a long way to influencing the downward trend of confidence; they were particularly successful because congressional scandals coincided[11] with their assault on the institution and moderates and liberals became increasingly distrustful as well.

POLICY AND ELECTORAL BENEFITS OF DISTRUST IN THE HEALTH CARE DEBATE OF 1993–4

Born on September 22, 1993, President Clinton's health-care reform plan was declared dead by Senate Majority Leader George Mitchell on September 26, 1994. Like other major debates over health care in the United States, the policy battle of 1993–4 involved many members of the Democratic party in support of a greater role for government and most Republicans opposed to such an expansion. Since the result was consistent with many Republicans' view about the proper place of government, the defeat constituted a policy benefit for the party. When responding to the proposal, Republican leaders hoped that their achievement would lead to electoral success, thus enabling them to remake national policy. Indeed, Clinton's failure translated into a Republican congressional

9 In 1993, 51.3% of conservatives reported having "hardly any" confidence in Congress while 38.0% of liberals and 39.1% of moderates did. In 1994, 48.3% of conservatives reported this level of distrust of Congress while 34.4% of liberals and 39.4% of moderates did. The narrowing of the conservative–moderate gap in 1994 is consistent with 1994 exit polls showing a majority of moderates supported Democrats.

10 Using a slightly different measure and different polls, Hibbing and Theiss-Morse (1995) find the decline to occur at a similar time as well.

11 This is not to imply that those scandals were all purely coincidental to the Republican attack on Congress. See, for example, John Barry's (1990) characterization of Gingrich's reasons for pursuing an ethics investigation of Speaker Wright.

majority, gained in part as Republicans built upon and helped further develop distrust of government.

These policy and electoral benefits were, to the extent possible, to be delivered to one segment of the Republican party: the conservatives. By winning the policy battle, the status of this group would be enhanced and their leadership within the party secured.[12] While the degree to which conservative Republicans anticipated and planned for health-policy efforts was not known at the time, there were public reports that some wished to use the issue strategically. For example, one memo written by Bill Kristol to congressional Republicans in December 1993 was widely reported. Passage of health care, Kristol warned, would help advocates of government programs and would undermine efforts to decrease government involvement in the economy.[13] Rather than entering into compromises, Kristol argued that Republicans would be better served by declaring that there is no health-care crisis and by refusing to support any health-care legislation.

Although proponents of reform dominated elite rhetoric in early stages, opponents later overshadowed them and their rhetoric consciously emphasized messages of distrust (Koch 1998). These messages were effective because American citizens were ambivalent about government. According to one study (Zis, Jacobs, and Shapiro 1996), Americans' views about health care are complex and involve diverse values, including individual responsibility, fear of government intervention, and interest in serving community needs. Over time, public support for the Clinton plan dwindled. While 59% supported the plan in September 1993, only 44% did in mid-June 1994 (Jacobs and Shapiro 1995).

We looked at rhetorical strategies used to defeat the Clinton plan. Congressional Republicans used terms with negative implications to describe the proposal, such as "socialized (or socialistic) medicine," and "big-government," and argued that "Gestapo-like" tactics would be used by "health care bureaucrats." Republican rhetoric also linked health-care to Whitewater, as they argued that one should not trust President Clinton on either.

12 Skocpol (1996, 133) argues, "[I]nsurgent conservatives opposed to a strong domestic role for the federal government discovered that an all-out ideological attack on Health Security offered an excellent way for them to gain ground, first within the Republican Party and then in the general electorate. Counterattacks from stakeholders and ideologues became mutually reinforcing over the course of 1994 and shifted critical resources of money and energy toward a radicalized, much more conservative Republican Party."

13 See Skocpol (1996, 146–7) for quotes from Kristol's original memo and others. Johnson and Broder (1996) discuss the Kristol memo on pp. 233–4.

The Clinton Administration ruled out a single-payer approach to health care because they wished to avoid claims that the government wished to take over the health-care system. But their approach offered no protection from this characterization. A search of the Congressional Record showed that the plan was frequently termed "government-run health care." During the 103rd Congress, this phrase was used 127 times, with 108 of those occurring in 1994. The peak number of references (42) was made in August 1994, the month in which Congress engaged in extensive debate. Another claim often leveled against the Clinton plan was that one's health care would be run by "Washington bureaucrats." This term was used in discussions of health care 208 times in 1994, with 47 in August alone. Similar phrases, such as references to "big government health care" and "health care bureaucracy" were also fairly common.

Debate about health care often employed comparisons. Whether discussing Canadian and British health care or simply characterizing the legislation, members of Congress called the plan socialized medicine, socialist, socialistic health care, or some similar variant 109 times in the 103rd Congress. Stronger terms were rare but show the range of discourse adopted. Representative Cox (R-CA), for example, said (*Congressional Record*, February 18, 1993) of the Canadian health-care system:

> We are tempted to call it "Gestapo medicine." The only surprise is that there are not guards armed with AK-47s posed in every doctor's office. The system tells the doctor where to practice, limits his ability to take care of the patients, and then grossly underpays him.

A less severe comparative strategy was to wonder if the health-care system would deliver the "efficiency of the post office and the compassion of the IRS"; this phrase was used four times.

Another way House Republicans connected health-care reform to the issue of trust involved discussion of Whitewater. According to Johnson and Broder, these links were made as part of a conscious plan to promote distrust of President Clinton, the Democrats, and their policy ideas. Lamar Smith (R-TX), a close associate of Mr. Gingrich, wrote a memo to House Republicans in March 1994 in which he urged them to make this connection and suggested various "quotes of the day" for their public statements (Johnson and Broder 1996). Whitewater references made on the House floor in March 1994 numbered fifty-seven. The number of references dropped from this peak (with eight in April, eighteen in May, and thirteen in June), while rising again, with twenty-nine in July and twenty-eight in August. While not every mention of Whitewater was accompanied by a remark about the health plan, other times the connection was quite clearly drawn. Representative Collins (R-GA), for instance, stated (*Congressional Record*, March 24, 1994), "Yes, the President has small business experience. It is called Whitewater Development." Four months later, Representative Hefley (R-Co) said of Mr. Clinton (*Congressional Record*, July 12, 1994), "He promised health care reform, but delivered an unworkable socialist health care scheme. He promised the most ethical White House in history, but has delivered the most scandal-ridden administration in memory." And in August, Congressman Doolittle (R-CA) tied together the health-care plan with a series of issues, ranging from Clinton's statements and actions on tax cuts, spending, draft status during the Vietnam War, marijuana smoking, and Whitewater (*Congressional Record*, August 11, 1994). Through these sorts of statements, proposals on health care thus were linked to questions about the size and effectiveness of government, the sense of alienation people feel from large-scale organizations (i.e., bureaucracies), and personal scandal.

At various times in the process, conservative and moderate Republicans took separate policy positions, as the moderates worked with Democrats to negotiate an acceptable compromise. However, intraparty divisions on whether some version of health-care reform would constitute a policy benefit were overcome by the unifying vision of the electoral success to be delivered by defeating health-care proposals altogether. Conservative Republicans worked with their allies in the business community to urge moderate politicians and groups to refrain from endorsing reform of any kind (Skocpol 1996; Johnson and Broder 1996). For instance, Bill McInturff, pollster for the Health Insurance Association of America and the Republican National Committee, told Johnson and Broder (1996, 428)

> My concern in May [1994] was that we had a Republican group—mostly senators—who had spent ten to twenty years of their careers trying to do the right thing, trying to find a fairly rational health care plan for this country. I said, essentially, "Hey, what do you want? Do you want a Republican majority in the Congress or do you want health care policy?" We had a group of Republicans who would have picked health care policy. Our most important problem, from the political side, was not letting those people defect and pass a health care plan I personally wouldn't have wanted and that would really have eroded our party's ability to be in the majority.

This strategy helped conservative Republicans gain a policy benefit and cement their coalition of shared interests, ideological adherents, and financial supporters.

Republican leaders believed that defeating the heath plan would deliver both short-term and long-term electoral benefits. In contemporaneous interviews with Newt Gingrich by veteran journalists Haynes

Johnson and David Broder, Mr. Gingrich indicated that he had thought about the political benefits of stopping health-care reform efforts several years before the Clinton plan was proposed, and he "anticipated that denying Democrats victory on health reform would pave the way for Republicans to win control of Congress" (Johnson and Broder 1996, xiii). Furthermore, Mr. Gingrich and his brain trust believed that passage of any new health policy would make it nearly impossible for Republicans to ever win the House of Representatives. Social Security and Medicare had provided Democrats with a potent campaign issue, and any new government guarantees of health security would tie greater numbers of Americans to the Democratic party and to the patronage of the federal government.

CONCLUSION

This chapter has shown that elites not only react to the public's distrustful mood, but also seek to shape it, frame it, and employ it. Distrust in government, like other substantive elements of public opinion, is a potential political resource that political leaders try to use to their benefit. For Republicans, the political culture of distrust and discontent was not a mere backdrop to their action, but something to develop. Indeed, by using this sentiment to appeal to their constituencies, strategic elites delivered organizational benefits, electoral benefits, institutional benefits, and policy benefits.

Both strategic and philosophical motivations animated conservative efforts to cultivate distrust. Conservatives have long-established principles and policy objectives that suggest that lower tax burdens, decreased social spending, state-level decision making, and the increased utilization of market-based rather than government-based decision-making processes are superior to their alternatives. But one need not be a liberal to be concerned about the overall decline in confidence in governing institutions. In the past, conservatives worried that criticisms from the left undermined government legitimacy[14] and the Republican strategy dis-

14 In the late 1960s and early 1970s, conservatives worried that leftist criticisms of government and other institutions (as well as revelations about covert operations) significantly undermined authority and could threaten citizens' beliefs in the legitimacy of government. For example, in the 1975 book *The Crisis of Democracy*, Crozier, Huntington, and Watanuki raised the specter of "ungovernability," which could arise from "the delegitimation of authority." Historically, conservative thinkers such as Edmund Burke hailed national traditions and institutional legacies and criticized those who would radically change existing systems.

turbed some contemporary conservatives.[15] For some, it is probably of greater concern that fostering distrust is a natural strategy of principled politicians seeking to dismantle, retrench, and devolve power in Washington. Either way, scholars should not be surprised that distrust in Congress and the government has increased when distrust is a key resource and linked to the aims of a political party on the rise.

And on the rise they were. In a triumphant denouement, conservative Republicans won their cherished political prize: majorities in the House and Senate. However, the political distrust that swept the Republicans into office turned out to be a tool they could not easily control. Like the bullfighter who no longer can turn his bull, the Republicans found political danger where there had been advantage. Indeed, Republican efforts to delegitimize government created instruments that could and would be used against them. According to Fenno (1997, 17):

> [B]y couching his attacks in the language of institutional corruption and the personal abuse of power, Gingrich deliberately manipulated and made worse an existing public cynicism and lack of confidence in the nation's most important representative institution. . . . In working to take control of the House, he had also undermined and weakened it in the public eye.

When House Democrats (using a strategy of distrust) focused on Speaker Gingrich's ethics, this undermined Republican claims that they were more deserving of the people's trust.

Furthermore, the link between Republicans and the message of distrust in government left them vulnerable when the public decided that government served some positive purposes. Following the Oklahoma City bombing in April 1995, commentators, scholars, and political leaders spoke out on behalf of government workers and the government.[16] Some months later and leading up to the budget battles of 1995 and early 1996, some Republicans joked that no one would notice the federal government shut down. Yet distrust toward government did not, after all, run that deep and the Republicans suffered a slide in the polls (Maraniss and Weisskopf 1996). While the cultural conviction of distrust was widely popular, it appears it was only strongly felt among a smaller niche. Thus it proved difficult to use this sentiment to govern, particularly outside the House and after the initial flurry of action.

15 During the 104th Congress, conservative Senator Dan Coats (R-Indiana) said, "Newt's belief that to ultimately succeed you almost had to destroy the system so that you could rebuild it . . . was kind of scary stuff" (Balz and Brownstein 1996, 121).

16 See Drew (1996) on President Clinton's rhetoric about "anti-government extremism" and the Oklahoma City bombing.

Indeed, elite strategies focused around political distrust forced Republican leaders to continue their appeals to the more ideological freshmen and public constituencies. These beliefs had provided ideological cohesion to the Republican electoral team (and continued to do so); however, this combination of beliefs and ideological newcomers limited Republican leaders. As Fenno (1997) chronicles, minimal experience in legislating was seen as a badge of honor among the new Republican members of the House, for they were not part of the corrupt Washington establishment. This lack of experience, growing out of many years in the minority and linked to an anti-government ideology, led them to eschew compromise and long-term planning. Republican leaders' rhetoric and actions in the early days of their majority status helped create a negative image and poor public opinion of their House Speaker, Mr. Gingrich, which the Democrats used in the 1996 and 1998 elections. By early 1999, the Republican Party was increasingly seen as the "impeachment party"; its public standing was in decline, as citizens associated it with attack rather than with proactive policy proposals (Broder and Balz 1999).

Public distrust, of course, has not gone away. Nor will strategic efforts to use and develop further mistrust. Indeed, the rhetoric of distrust is part of our cultural milieu. As such, this mood is not a mere background to action nor simply an effect of other dynamics, but a resource and political enabler, capable (at times) of yielding important benefits. However, while those who seek to use it hope they will gain, the cantankerous public may calm itself or otherwise not cooperate with such plans and thus may turn away from those who wish it to charge.

10

A Reassessment of Who's to Blame
A Positive Case for the Public Evaluation of Congress

DAVID W. BRADY AND SEAN M. THERIAULT

That Americans disapprove of Congress is generally as well accepted as any stylized fact in American politics. From 1974 (when Gallup first asked a congressional approval question) through 1997, congressional approval hovered around 30%. The average for 54 Gallup polls taken over the 23 years was 31%.[1] At no point did a majority of Americans approve of the way Congress did its job—approval climaxed in 1974 at 48% amid the Watergate proceedings. Such bleak numbers led Glenn Parker (1981, 33) to conclude, "Congress, like Prometheus, is inevitably doomed to suffer indignities." Sometimes, however, stylized facts turn out to be fiction. In 1998, Congress enjoyed widespread popular support, reaching a high of 63% in late September.[2] Notwithstanding Congress' current popularity, the causes and consequences of the American public's disapproval of Congress have been studied in classrooms.

The myriad opinions and explanations of low congressional approval can generally be broken down into two schools of thought. The first argues that the American public's disapproval of Congress is based on policy or conditions. Low congressional approval is an artifact of either a recessing economy or policies inconsistent with the public's preferences. Sometimes the latter is caused when Congress enacts policies that the public does not like; however, it is more likely caused when Congress does not respond to the public's demand for policy.

The second school of thought absolves Congress of its doggedly low approval in arguing that low approval stems from the Framer's institutional design. Fred Harris (1995, 92), a former member of Congress and chief defender of the institution, summarizes:

> By its nature, Congress is conflictual, and sometimes confusingly, disturbingly, unattractively so. This is another reason for its seemingly perennial

1 *The Gallup Poll Monthly*, February 1998, p. 16.
2 *Time*, September 28, 1998, p. 40.

unpopularity. We say we like democracy, yet we hate conflict. But dealing with conflict, offering a forum for it and for its resolution—these are essential elements of democratic government.

Parker (1981, 49) takes Harris' argument a step further by blaming the public: "The public often lacks the basic understanding of the legislative process that would lead to an appreciation of the significance of legislative actions." Although congressional defenders admittedly place some of the blame on members themselves, they generally conclude similarly to Harris (1995, 143): "The U.S. congressional is today, perhaps more than ever, a place of largely well-motivated, well-prepared, and high-minded professional members."

Hibbing and Theiss-Morse (1995) provide an integrated explanation for low congressional approval. Their comprehensive and systematic argument consists of elements from both schools. They argue that "large staffs, mossback politicians, and oversized benefits packages" (146) lead to congressional unpopularity. Additionally, they demonstrate how the American public unrealistically expects members to legislate without the democratic vulgarities defined as "diversity, mess, compromise, and a measured pace" (147). For them high approval scores would result from both more responsible action by members of Congress and a more informed and understanding American public.

Even though the arguments summarized above represent a number of different explanations for low congressional approval, they each, either explicitly or implicitly, contain a comment element: low approval is at least partially the fault of the American public. Each explanation suggests that a more informed, educated American citizenry would not evaluate Congress as poorly as it does.

Before giving in fully to any of these explanations, we think that it is fair to ask if the American public legitimately holds the views that it does. In other words, do populist reasons exist for the public to view Congress negatively? Or, do members explicitly perpetuate the American public's cynical evaluation? We do not claim to have a definitive answer to these questions, rather we offer several speculative arguments that place the blame of low congressional approval squarely upon the members. We argue that it is *because of* the decisions made by the political elite that the American public disapproves of Congress. We present four practices members actively engage in that lead to congressional unpopularity. Each practice is briefly mentioned in this introduction before we present the more complete argument.

First, members of Congress avoid difficult votes by engaging in questionable legislative procedures. They employ these procedures to circumvent accountability. In this section, we examine the history of the congressional pay raise. We argue that individual members of Congress sacrifice the integrity of the institution so they can receive salary increases without paying a political price.

Second, members frequently engage in hyperbolic rhetoric. The hyperbolic rhetoric takes two forms. First, they employ Perot's quick-fix rhetoric in claiming to have easy solutions to hard problems. Unfortunately, the public hears the rhetoric and is left profoundly disappointed when their expectations are not realized. Second, and inversely, divergent proposals are not debated meaningfully; rather, the consequences are overblown and exaggerated in hopes of demonizing the proponents and killing the proposals. Members not only lose credibility when the consequences are not realized, but in the process the practice demeans the institution. We discuss the rhetoric used by Democrats during the Persian Gulf War debates and Republicans during Clinton's first budget as examples of this irresponsible rhetoric.

Third, members run for Congress by running against it. A popular campaign tactic in congressional elections is to bash the institution. Challengers try to tie incumbents to the "mess in Washington," as incumbents try to persuade the voters to send them back so an experienced voice can fight against the "Washington establishment." Congressional campaigns also intensify other activities disliked by the public such as negative campaigning. In this section, we show that as the elections get closer and more people pay more attention, the American public's approval of Congress decreases.

Last, and perhaps most important, the public face of Congress distorts the internal workings of the institution. While ideological extremists bash each other on television as well as in newspapers, the moderates are left to negotiate and legislate. We show, through a series of tests, that those who are most influential in passing legislation are least likely to show up in newspapers and television talk shows. Consequently, the public witnesses a higher proportion of fighting and combative rhetoric than actually exits. Those aspects of Congress that Americans like least, according to Hibbing and Theiss-Morse, are those that they see most.

QUESTIONABLE LEGISLATIVE PROCEDURES

Hibbing and Theiss-Morse (1995, 61) argue that "the very openness of the legislative process, which might otherwise be thought to endear Congress to the people, is much more likely to have the opposite effect." They suggest that the public unfairly disapproves of Congress because they dislike the characteristics that are "endemic to what a legislature is" (60). In their analysis, they present a rather benign view of the legislative process. Here, we argue that members often subvert the normal process to obtain outcomes that might not otherwise be realized. In doing so, members of Congress make the process appear even uglier than it already is. When the public witnesses a debasement of a process it already views skeptically, can we be surprised that they disapprove? David Dreier (quoted in Evans and Oleszek 1997, 25), a reform-minded member of the House, argues, "I don't think it's mere coincidence that the growing prevalence of restrictive floor procedures has coincided with the decline in public support for Congress." We show how the politics of congressional pay raises subverted the normal process. We speculate that both the subversion and the enactment of pay raises causes an already skeptical public to express disgust at Congress.

Congressional Pay Raises

Congressional pay raises are an explosive issue. Indeed, as James Madison noted over 200 years ago, "There is a seeming impropriety in leaving any set of men, without control, to put their hand into the public coffers, to take money to put in their pockets" (quoted in *1989 Congressional Quarterly Almanac*, 58). Unfortunately for members of Congress, the Constitution reserves for them exclusively the duty to decide their pay.[3] Controversies surrounding congressional pay are nearly as old as the republic itself.

Lest the American public think this controversy of increasing pay is a recent phenomenon, the congressional history is replete with stories surrounding congressional pay raises. In 1816, members changed their pay from a per diem basis to an annual salary. During the next election, many members lost their seats amid the public's rebellion, including nine who resigned even before the election (*Congressional Quarterly*, February 4, 1989, 210). Perhaps the most audacious pay raise occurred in 1873. Just as the 42nd Congress was drawing to a close, members not only passed a 50% salary increase, but they made it retroactive for two years. Not surprising, the majority party paid dearly for this abuse of public authority. In the next election, 96 members of the Republican majority lost their seats (*1989 Congressional Quarterly Almanac*, 59).

The more recent history is also illustrious. In 1953, Congress established the Commission on Judicial and Congressional Salaries in hopes of delegating the duty of setting their pay to a commission. Two years later, upon the recommendation of the commission, Congress voted to

3 Article I, Section 6 of the Constitution mandates: "The Senators and Representatives shall receive a Compensations for their Services to be ascertained by Law, and paid out of the Treasury of the United States."

increase their salaries from $12,500 to $22,500.[4] In an attempt to keep pace with inflation, members again increased their salaries in 1964 to $30,000.[5] Three years later, they modified the old commission giving it a new name and new powers. The President's Commission on Executive, Legislative, and Judicial Salaries would meet every four years to make salary recommendations to the president. If the president included them in his budget, then they automatically became law unless either chamber passed a resolution to block them. In this way, members could increase their pay without having to risk public scorn by explicitly voting for it.

The commission was not raising their pay quickly enough, so Congress instituted additional devices. Following the inflationary early 1970s, Congress enacted a proposal that would "make members eligible for the same annual October cost-of-living increases given to other federal employees" (*1989 Congressional Quarterly Almanac*, 59). It was not until 1981, when Congress rejected four consecutive cost-of-living increases, however, that the procedure became automatic. In 1985, Congress made it even more difficult to prohibit a pay raise increase. In response to a Supreme Court decision against the use of the legislative veto, Congress required both chambers and the president to disapprove of a pay raise within thirty days of the president's submission of his budget in order to stop the automatic increase. In exploiting their newly enhanced rules, members from both chambers passed a resolution to disapprove of the 1987 increase exactly one day after the thirty-day cutoff (which resulted in an almost 20% salary increase). Critics called this the "vote no and take the dough strategy" (*Congressional Quarterly Weekly Report* 1988, 3523).

The following year, the Senate passed the Grassley Amendment that "prohibit[ed] members from receiving a pay raise proposed by the president unless both the House and Senate explicitly voted for it" (*Congressional Quarterly Weekly Report* 1988, 2695). When the House failed to pass the same measure, Senate conferees on a 5–2 vote agreed to drop it from the conference report. In 1989, the commission recommended a 51% salary increase. The Senate voted to disapprove the pay raise in hopes that the House, where the agenda is more easily manipulated, would save the day. Unfortunately for them, one day before it would have automatically taken effect, Speaker Wright, already under intense scrutiny for his alleged ethics violations, buckled under public pressure and held a vote to kill the pay raise. Before caving in to the pressure, Wright strategized for the increase by both scheduling little

4 *1989 Congressional Quarterly Almanac*, 59.

5 Harris 1995, 18.

legislative business prior to the thirty-day cutoff and trying to stiff-arm an adjournment vote as an increasing disapproval vote pended on the cutoff date.

Despite the public's rebuke early in the year, Congress was not ready to let their pay raise die. By tying the pay raise to a series of ethics provisions including a reduction in permissible honoraria, a restriction on the amount and kinds of gifts, and a prohibition on the conversion of campaign cash to personal income after retirement, members hoped that a pay increase would be more publicly palatable. These rule changes were coupled with a 10% immediate salary increase for Senators and an 8% immediate as well as a 25% future increase for Representatives. The measure passed in the waning days of the session. In 1991, the Senate brought its pay scale in line with the more progressive House scale so that their salaries were again the same at $125,000.[6]

Since 1953, members of Congress have tried numerous attempts to increase their pay without politically paying for it. They have delegated the responsibility of setting their pay to a commission. They have linked it to inflation. They have delegated it to the president. They have made increases automatic. Finally, they have hid it amongst a series of reforms.

Have any of these strategies been successful in isolating the members from a public that frowns upon congressional pay raises? No. In each case, the pay raise became public. It invited criticism—not only because of the ends (increasing congressional pay), but also because of the means (perverse legislative procedures) (Hibbing 1983). The following comment from a participant in a Hibbing and Theiss-Morse (1995, 209) focus group was not atypical, "Well, I think for starters they wouldn't be voting themselves incredible pay raises when the rest of the country is taking pay cuts or layoffs. This, I think, was a slap in the face, a direct slap in the face to every American that has a job, or wants a job and doesn't have a job." Indeed, over three-fourths of the survey respondents claimed that the pay raise contributed to their dislike of Congress (Hibbing and Theiss-Morse 1995).

Fortunately for members, the public disapproves of the institution for these pay raise debacles. Except for 1816 and 1873, it appears that members have not been individually harmed. In this sense, the strategies devised for increasing their pay without repercussions have worked. A by-product of these questionable legislative procedures is an American public who lacks trust in Congress. Fortunately for members, broken trust in an institution does not typically have adverse electoral consequences for individuals.

6 Hibbing and Theiss-Morse 1995, 69.

EASY SOLUTIONS—DIRE PREDICTIONS

Through CSPAN members of Congress can speak directly to the American public. With this privilege comes a responsibility to lead, inform, and educate. Unfortunately, the hallowed chambers of Congress sometimes bear a striking resemblance to an elementary school playground. In this section, we argue that politicians engage in hyperbolic rhetoric to the detriment of the public's approval of political institutions, generally, and of Congress, specifically. The hyperbolic rhetoric of politicians is manifested in two ways. The first is the simplification of complex public policy problems. Instead of outlining the difficulty of rigorously and systematically solving complex problems, political actors frequently simplify the problems not so much to solve them but to gain politically. When the quick-fix solutions fail, the process is demeaned, and the American public reacts negatively. Second, politicians exaggerate policy implications in hopes of not only defeating the policy but also humiliating the policy's proponents in the process.

That politicians engage in hyperbolic rhetoric cannot be disputed. In this section we offer several case studies as proof. That this leads directly to public disapproval of Congress is speculation, albeit speculation with just cause. Funk (this volume) finds that "the presence of animosity in political debate leads to negative reactions." This is consistent with the Hibbing–Theiss-Morse (1995, 18–19) argument:

> To put it simply, Americans tend to dislike virtually all of the democratic processes described above. They dislike compromise and bargaining . . . they dislike debate and publicly hashing things out, referring to such actions as haggling or bickering. . . . They want democratic decision-making processes in which everyone can voice an opinion, but they do not prefer to see or to hear the debate resulting from the expression of these inevitably diverse opinions. . . . The American people want democratic procedures, but they do not want to see them in action.

They suggest that even when Congress acts responsibly as it did in passing the first real attempt at deficit reduction in 1990, "The people were angry at the haggling, the bargaining, the delays, and the visible politicking that was involved." We submit that the hyperbolic rhetoric of politicians exacerbates these negative feelings. Should we be surprised that the American public disapproves of an institution that it hears engaging in behavior that it purports to despise?

The Persian Gulf War

Members engaged in hyperbolic rhetoric in the Persian Gulf War debate. Instead of discussing the simplicity of the problem, they proffered drastic predictions. In what *The New York Times* (January 13, 1991, 1) described as "the plainest choice between war and peace since World War II," members could not refrain from exaggerating the consequences. Members who opposed President Bush's attempt at the "practical equivalent" of a declaration of war frequently debated the resolution on its merits, discussing the finer points of economic sanctions versus military action; however, more than a couple of members could not resist the temptation to humiliate their proponents by exaggerating the consequences of military action.

Even though *The Washington Post* (January 13, 1991, A1) characterized the debate as "the most intense, solemn, and emotional debate seen in the Capitol in many years," mean-spirited debate reared its ugly face. In addition to her "Armageddon" prediction if we went to war, Senator Barbara Mikulski (quoted in *The Washington Post*, September 8, 1998, A10) predicted that our declaration would "produce terrorism that would 'wreak havoc' on the United States." Senator Carl Levin (*Congressional Record*, January 11, 1991, S303) also predicted widespread terrorism: "The aftermath will be volcanic explosion of radicalism and fundamentalism which will engulf the region with an unpredictable outcome, and a reign of terrorism which will be felt worldwide." Representative Cardiss Collins's (*Congressional Record*, January 11, 1991) remarks in the House were even more draconian, "War is not just a word. In today's world it refers to massive death, destruction, and annihilation; hardship, food and medical shortages; economic disability, and countless other forms of disaster."

In comparison to these end-of-the-world prophesies, Representative Nancy Pelosi's prediction of environmental disaster seems understated:

> Some of the consequences could be—according to the United Nations Environment Program—oil spills equal to a dozen *Exxon Valdez* spills coursing through gulf waters; oil fires raging for weeks and perhaps months; smoke and debris blocking sunlight, causing temperatures to drop and altering crop seasons which could result in widespread famine; toxic plumes ascending to the upper atmosphere and falling as acid rain; millions of fish, dolphins, sea birds and other marine life wash onto Gulf shores; chemical contamination of air, water, and vegetation; the Persian Gulf as a dead sea. [*The New York Times*, January 13, 1991, 10]

Lastly, members could not help but compare a potential Gulf War to Vietnam. Congressman Jim Traficant (*Congressional Record*, January 12, 1991, H401) made this parallel, "If Members think the gulf cannot turn into a Vietnam, let me tell Members something: Yitzhak Shamir and King Fahd are both singing 'Onward Christian Soldiers.' I assure Members that it can happen."

Hind sight, of course, is always perfect. Certainly, few military experts expected our victory in the Gulf War to be as clean and quick as it was. We do not doubt that these members believed in their dire predictions. Our argument, quite simply, is that when the American people hear these frightening predictions and then observe something different, it is not surprising that they loathe public debate and "bickering" and consequently evaluate Congress negatively.

1993 Budget Reconciliation

Democrats in Congress are not the only ones guilty of offering dire predictions. President Clinton's first budget in 1993 is a perfect representation of everything Americans do not like about democracy in action. Partisanship, bickering, multiple stages, slowness, and unseemly debate ruled the day. Republican opposition to the budget was unanimous. Their rhetoric was exaggerated at best, and irresponsible at worst. From the floor, Republican after Republican promised economic devastation if the Clinton budget was adopted. Representative Jim Bunning (quoted in *The Washington Post*, August 6, 1993, A13) argued, "It is a tax-and-spend bill, pure and simple. It won't reduce the deficit, but it will injure the country and decimate the economy. It's a job-killing bill from the word go." Representative Dick Armey's analysis (quoted in *Congressional Quarterly Weekly Report* 1993, 2122) was taken from the same page, "This plan is not a recipe for more jobs. It is a recipe for disaster . . . taxes will go up. The economy will sputter along. Dreams will be put off, and all this for the hollow promise of deficit reduction and magical theories of lower interest rates."

The Republican leaders' predictions were not any less drastic. Then–Minority Whip Newt Gingrich (quoted in *Congressional Quarterly Weekly Report* 1993, 2122–3) "predicted that the package would lead directly to a 'job-killing recession.'" The ranking Republican on the Budget Committee, John Kasich, offered, "We'll come back next year and try to help you out when this plan puts the economy in the gutter." Once again, hindsight is perfect. Nonetheless, when predictions are so clearly off-the-mark, how can we expect the American public not to disapprove of Congress?

In this section we do not offer any direct evidence that the hyperbolic rhetoric of members causes low congressional approval. Instead, we suggest that the bickering that is detested by the American people exacerbates their malevolence toward Congress. Indeed, even members of Congress criticize the absurdity of this hyperbolic rhetoric. Ironically, Congressman Ron Dellums (*Congressional Record*, January 11, 1991, H214), a former flame thrower, commented during the Gulf War debate,

"I simply want to express my frustration with the process, not designed to challenge any Member. However, if Members observe these proceedings, to use the term 'debate' is a euphemism. It really stretches the definition, because there is literally no exchange taking place here. Maybe that is a product of how we are here, but we are simply parading into the well, giving each other speeches." Given that even members are frustrated, how can we demand more from the American public?

RUNNING FOR CONGRESS BY RUNNING AGAINST IT

When Richard Fenno (1977, 914) soaked and poked over twenty years ago, he stumbled across a phenomenon that has become one of the most universally accepted and recognized congressional campaigning tactics. He found:

> The diversity of the House provides every member with plenty of collegial villains to flay before supportive constituents at home. Individual members do not take responsibility for the performance of Congress; rather each portrays himself as a fighter against its manifest shortcomings. Their willingness, at some point, to stand and defend their votes contrasts sharply with their disposition to run and hide when a defense of Congress is called for. Congress is not 'we'; it is 'they.' And members of Congress run *for* Congress by running *against* Congress. [Italics in original.]

Although a new discovery for Fenno in the late 1970s, the ability of incumbents to win reelection by blasting the institution is unquestioned today. Congress has become the popular punching bag for politicians of both political parties and every ideology. Indeed, Senator William Proxmire (quoted in Patterson and Caldeira 1990, 26) lamented from the Senate floor, "No one and I mean nobody ever defends the Congress. In more than thirty years in this branch of the Congress, and in literally tens of thousands of conversations back in my State with people of every political persuasion I have yet to hear one kind word, one whisper of praise, one word of sympathy for the Congress as a whole." If members of Congress view their place of employment so negatively, why are we surprised that the American public also expresses negative attitudes about Congress? We submit that the relationship between members of Congress and Congress is one of the strangest relationships in employment history. When was the last time Bill Gates ridiculed Microsoft to keep his job?

Fenno (1977, 914) found that the "villains" blamed by the seventeen members that he traveled with ranged from "the old chairmen" to "the inexperienced newcomers" and from "the tools of organized labor" to "the tools of big business." All the possible different characteristics of members were vilified by someone. Instead of attacking specific members through unflattering descriptions, members often focus their wrath upon the entire Washington system. An example of this strategy is when Barbara Mikulski, a twelve-year veteran of the Senate who is notoriously adept at using the rules to her advantage, "portrays Congress as an entrenched and wily enemy. Her speeches are laced with the gunpowder terms of combat: She is forever 'doing battle,' a 'scrapper' waging war along with other 'tough fighters'" (*The Washington Post*, September 8, 1998, A10).

Frequently, the Congress-bashing lines are the ones that receive the best response from a member's audience. Consider three examples. First, former member Dewey Short's (quoted in Davidson, Kovenock, and O'Leary 1966, 18) description of the House was "that supine, subservient, soporific, supercilious, pusillanimous body of nitwits." Incidentally, Short has the rare distinction of losing two congressional elections as an incumbent. Second, Representative Pat Schroeder (quoted in Harris 1995, 1) jokes, "Please don't tell my mother I'm a politician. She thinks I'm a prostitute." The third example is from Senator Don Nickles (quoted in Harris 1995, 1), "I'm going to tell you some good news: Congress is out of session." When members score such easy points by ridiculing Congress in front of the folks back home, why should we expect the folks back home to have anything other than a negative impression of Congress?

This Congress bashing rhetoric is just one activity that intensifies during congressional campaigns. In addition to criticizing Congress, competing congressional candidates also engage in personal attacks, irresponsible rhetoric, and negative campaigning. How does the public react to these activities that we know they dislike (Hibbing and Theiss-Morse 1995; Funk, this volume)?

We provide an answer by analyzing approval numbers. As congressional elections become more imminent, ignoring Congress becomes more difficult for the American public as news coverage and political ads become ubiquitous. What happens when the American mind is more focused on politics and when the political arena is intensified by elections? Using data from three different polling firms (Gallup, *New York Times*/CBS News, and *The Washington Post*/ABC News) over twenty-four years, we analyze 114 different polls to hazard a guess. The dependent variable is the percentage of poll respondents who approve "of the way the U.S. Congress is doing its job?" The independent variable of interest is the number of months before an election the poll is conducted. What happens to approval when elections near? With a simple specification of including only the independent variable of interest, we see (from column one of Table 10.1) that for each month away

Table 10.1. *Explaining the Public's Disapproval of Congress*

Coefficient	Model 1	Model 2	Model 3	Model 4	Model 5
Months before Election	0.25*	0.25*	0.29**	0.38**	0.50**
Trend		0.20	0.12	−0.08	−0.73
Gallup			−4.48**		
CBS/NYT			−2.33		
105th Congress				27.38**	31.88**
105th Congress* Months before Election				−1.35**	−1.52**
Constant	31.08	13.17	22.32	34.66**	94.45**
Observations	114	114	114	114	91
R^2	0.04	0.07	0.12	0.40	0.48
F-value	4.84	4.02	3.86	18.34	19.67

Note: * $p < .05$. ** $p < .01$.

from an election Congress' approval increases by more than a quarter of a point.

To ensure that this simple specification is not acting as a proxy for a general increase or decrease in congressional popularity overall, the second model includes a time trend. The results from this specification show that each month away from an election increases popularity by about the same amount even though there is a general trend toward a more popular Congress. The third model ensures that these results are not an artifact of aggregating different polling firm's numbers. The coefficient in this specification increases to almost one-third of a point for each month. According to these numbers, congressional approval is seven points higher just after an election than it is just before an election.

The 1998 congressional election cycle is unique due to the timing of President Clinton's testimony before the grand jury and Independent Counsel Kenneth Starr's report to Congress. For the first time since Fenno's discovery, members of Congress have a more appealing punching bag than their place of employment. Members have turned their wrath from Congress to the other end of Pennsylvania Avenue, much as they did in 1974—the previous high point in congressional approval. This switch in strategy provides us with a good test of our hypothesis. If congressional approval decreases even as members refrain from bashing it, our argument is called into question. If, however, approval increases as members focus their indignation upon another political actor, we will have further evidence supporting our hypothesis. As such, the fourth model includes a dummy variable for the 105th Congress and an interaction term to see how this new strategy systematically affects congressional approval. The results are striking! The coefficient on the length variable increases to 0.38, while the indicator variables show that approval is up twenty-seven percentage points and increasing 1.34 points per month as the 1998 midterm election nears. When we restrict our sample to those polls taken after 1988, we find even stronger relationships (column five).

Once again, we cannot say with absolute certainty that our argument is correct, only that it is highly suggestive that the American public is making a rational decision when it is confronted with the behavior of members of Congress.

Policy Is Centrist. Commentary Is Extreme

We believe that the strongest case for the people and against the political elite arises when the former are systematically and persistently presented with a skewed view of the legislative process. That is, policy is made via compromises wherein the major actors are ideologically moderate senators and representatives who reach agreements acceptable to majorities of the House and Senate. These individuals like Sam Nunn (D-GA) and Nancy Kassebaum (R-KS) are reasonable left-of-center and right-of-center senators whose policy views are well within the mainstream. Yet, in general it is not the moderates' voices that are heard discussing major policy issues; rather, the public hears the left and right. Clearly, this point is true when one thinks of shows such as *Crossfire* and *The McLaughin Group* where left and right are paid to yell at each other. If the informed public does not hear from the center but only the left and right then we could explain some of the Hibbing–Theiss-Morse thesis via an induced distortion of the legislative process. In order to test this thesis—policy is made in the center and the public hears the ideologues thus exaggerating the amount of bile in the system—we examine a couple of different dependent variables.

This reason for the public's condemnation of Congress is different from the previous three. In each of the first three, members alone engage in behavior that the American public dislikes. The display of political hollering that occurs on most political shows is caused by the member, the media, and even the public. We do not think that any one of the three is exempt from criticism; rather, the first two use each other to appeal to the third. Members use extreme rhetoric to gain the spotlight. The media offer the spotlight because they have concluded that the American public is more likely to watch a fight than it is a meaningful discussion of the issues.

Although the extremists get the coverage, the moderate's role in a legislative body is crucial. Indeed, Weingast, Gilligan, and Marshall (1989),

Weingast and Rodriguez (1995), Krehbiel (1998), and Brady and Volden (1998) argue that the median's interpretation of legislation is most important because it is her presence among the enacting coalition that makes the measure pass. The winning side in the debate must make the necessary concessions to ascertain her vote. Given the primacy of the moderates in both enacting and interpreting legislation, it would not be unreasonable to expect their faces and their quotes to show up in the media's digest of legislative affairs. After all, they are the ones who ultimately decide the fate of legislation. The conventional wisdom of who gets news coverage, however, is exactly the opposite. Stephen Hess (1986, 5) summarizes, "The consensus among journalists, senators, and scholars, then, is that the national media pay more and more attention to less and less important senators," which he defines as "the mavericks, the junior members, and the blow-dried but empty headed." It is in questioning this consensus that Hess (1986, 5) conducts a study of "which senators get covered by the national news media, and why."

After examining thirty years of data from three different media outlets (Associated Press stories, national news magazines, and the network evening news programs), Hess concludes that the conventional wisdom is incorrect. He finds, "The coverage of the national news media from 1953 through 1983 has increasingly directed attention to the definable leaders at the expense of the nonleaders, mavericks, and others" (6). These findings cast doubt upon the meaningfulness of the distinction between "outsiders" and "insiders" or "show horses" and "work horses." Rather, it suggests that the "insiders" and the "work horses" are the same as those getting media coverage.

Another comprehensive study of who gets covered comes to a very similar conclusion. After examining data from 1969 through 1986, Timothy Cook (1989, 68) finds, "Doing something out of the ordinary may once have been sufficient to win publicity, but now gaining a subcommittee chair may be a necessary precondition for nonleaders to make national news." Both of these studies share a common methodological approach. They develop rather sophisticated mentioned indices and then examine the ranks of the members. They find without exception that the leaders—not the ideologues—are at the top of the lists. They do not, however, conduct any multivariate test to see if ideological extremity matters when controlling for leadership position.

To see if ideology influences media coverage in a more subtle way, we conducted our own tests that include not only variables that operationalize the findings of Hess and Cook, but also variables to test the conventional wisdom. Our dependent variable for the first test was the number of times *The New York Times* mentioned a senator's name from January 1, 1997, to June 5, 1998. To isolate particular systematic biases, we included a variety of control variables. First, we included three indicator variables for the senators from the states that immediately surround and include New York City (Connecticut, New Jersey, and New York) so that the results are not biased by local news stories. Second, we include institutional variables: whether the senator was a Democrat, was the majority or minority leader, or was a chair or ranking member of a committee. We decompose the last variable into the most and least important committees as defined by Hess (1986). We also include the member's age and seniority in addition to a measure of his or her ideological extremity. For the last variable, we operationalize it as the distance between the member's ideology and the mean legislator's ideology, so that extreme liberals and extreme conservatives have the same score.

Table 10.2 shows the results from the multivariate regression. Certainly evidence exists to support Hess's and Cook's findings. Being party leaders increases their *New York Times* mentions by over 250. Serving as chair of a major policy committee increases mentions by almost 80. When controlling for these measures, however, age and seniority have little influence upon press coverage. The results also support the conventional wisdom. For each point away from the median that a legislator is, she receives roughly one more mention in *The New York Times* even while controlling for institutional position. Mavericks, it seems, still get a disproportionate amount of coverage.

The results described above from the multivariate regression contradict the conclusions reached by both Hess and Cook. Two possible explanations could account for this contradiction. First, the more sophisticated methodology of multivariate regression could detect an undercurrent of the media's preference for ideological members that Hess and Cook did not observe. Or, second, times might have changed. The media might now prefer to give coverage to mavericks whereas in the 1980s and before they sought comments from the leaders in the Senate. To test which of these explanations account for the difference between this study and the earlier studies, we perform a similar multivariate test on the data collected by Hess from the 98th Congress (1983–4).[7]

The data from the earlier congress does show that position remains a good predictor of media coverage. In addition to position, the

7 Hess develops a media index using mentions in the "*National Newspaper Index* for *Christian Science Monitor*, *Los Angeles Times*, *New York Times*, *Wall Street Journal*, *Washington Post*: *Television News Index* of Vanderbilt University for ABC, CBS, NBC evening news; and *Face the Nation* (CBC), *This Week with David Brinkley* (ABC), *Meet the Press* (NBC)" for 1983.

Table 10.2. *Who Gets Media Coverage? A Multivariate Regression Answer*

Coefficient	1997–8 *NYT* Mentions	Hess's Media Index (1983)
New York	318.15**	
	(42.12)	
New Jersey	88.73*	
	(40.55)	
Connecticut	61.68	
	(40.36)	
Ran for President		275.97**
		(27.38)
Democrat	−34.11**	−21.47*
	(11.83)	(10.92)
Party Leader	254.67**	182.28**
	(39.72)	(36.49)
"A" Committee Chairs	79.27**	37.95**
	(18.23)	(12.23)
"B" Committee Chairs	27.98	68.26**
	(17.36)	(16.68)
Age	−0.38	
	(0.50)	
Seniority	−0.13	
	(0.62)	
Ideology	0.98*	0.67*
	(0.50)	(0.36)
Constant	27.32	9.43
	(31.57)	(11.57)
Observations	100	100
R^2	0.62	0.65
F-value	14.44	28.73

Note: * $p < .05$. ** $p < .01$.

ideological extremity of the senators does indeed influence media coverage.[8] For each ideological point away from the median member in the Senate, a senator receives two-thirds of a mention. Given that the media coverage index for the 98th Congress has a mean of forty-nine, this effect is quite substantial. In sum, this reanalysis of Hess's data shows, perhaps, that an undercurrent of media favoritism toward extreme senators was present afterall, at least in the latter part of Hess's study.

How do these results relate to our thesis that the public should not be blamed for disapproving of Congress? In concluding their study, Hibbing

8 We include an additional variable, ran for president, that indicates if the senator announced his desire to seek his party's nomination for the presidency (these include Cranston, Glenn, Hart, and Hollings).

and Theiss-Morse (1995, 147) argue, "People do not wish to see uncertainty, conflicting options, long debate, competing interests, confusion, bargaining, and compromised, imperfect solutions. They want government to do its job quietly and efficiently, sans conflict and sans fuss. In short, we submit, they often seek a patently unrealistic form of democracy." The results from the Hess and Cook study would suggest that the media depict a realistic version of law making. Our results suggest that the public are subject to an overrepresentation of those things that they like least in the legislative process. They may be, in part, given the car wreck that they really want; however, the members and the media glorify the fight and downplay the meaningful debate. Is it surprising that the public disapproves of an institution that they see engaged in unnecessary and ideological bickering when it is this "messy debate" that they loathe the most?

CONCLUSION

In what for us is an unusually normative paper, we have attempted to redirect some of the criticism that has been placed at the feet of the Congress-disdaining American public. Scholars, journalists, and politicians have been making "if only the American public understood" arguments since the political process began opening up in the 1960s. We have suggested that the American public has in fact understood the cues, signals, and messages sent by members of Congress, the political elite, and the media. Indeed, they have understood them too well. In this chapter, we presented four arguments that restore some faith in the public's ability to reach rational evaluations of Congress.

First, the American public sees members of Congress avoiding difficult issues by placing them in perverse legislative procedures. We have shown that members have employed questionable legislative practices when it is in their interest. By doing so, the politicians escape accountability. We showed how the members of Congress have been willing to risk institutional approval to secure pay raises.

Second, the American public sees members of Congress engaged in hyperbolic, highly symbolic, and meaningless rhetoric in their debates. Politicians either promise easy solutions that are necessarily incapable of solving complex problems or engage in draconian predictions not only to defeat a proposal but to humiliate its proponents. These rhetorical practices debase the practice of debate. Consequently, the American public impugns what it sees as "bickering."

Third, the American public sees members of Congress bashing Congress. If those who make up the institution are unwilling to defend it, how can we expect the public to approve of it? Instead, each electoral cycle the public sees veteran legislators—many of whom have spent more of their life in Washington than they have in their district—running from the "Washington system." Not only do members run against Congress, but they also run negative campaigns and engage in the exact behavior that the American public loathes. We show that as elections near, the American public increasingly disapproves of Congress.

Fourth, the American public sees extremists talk, yell, and debate on television—unfortunately, they do not see moderates legislate. We have shown that when controlling for a variety of factors, ideologically extreme members are more likely to appear on television and in newspapers then their moderate counterparts. Because ideologues are more resolute in their desire to be visible and the media are predisposed to cover conflict, the American public is rarely exposed to the moderate give-and-take that results in mainstream government policy.

We understand that Congress is faced with difficulties inherent within the Constitution. It mandates that representatives be popularly elected by the represented. Consequently, 435 members in the House are elected by 435 different constituencies and 100 senators are elected by 50 different constituencies. This electoral set-up provides incentives for members of Congress to act with a keen eye toward their districts that at times can be detrimental to the nation.

In addition to the particularistic focus of members, we must recognize that the legislature is only one of three branches in the federal system established by the Constitution. This separation of powers system provides a number of veto points at which policy initiatives die. The system was designed to be slow, unresponsive, and lethargic. As such, the decisions made by members of Congress may be rational, but so too may be the evaluations made by the American public.

We also recognize that as parties have gotten stronger, the distribution of preferences in Congress has become more bimodal. This causes party leaders to be further left and further right, which bears directly upon our argument. Nevertheless, it has been our purpose to claim, even if not in the strongest sense, that the American public has legitimate reasons to hold Congress in low esteem not because of policy or the legislative process but because of the behavior of political elites.

We have not argued that the American public is absolved from all blame in perpetually poor approval ratings for political institutions, nor have we argued that members of Congress or the media should accept all the blame. Furthermore, we do not claim to have the definitive answer on why the American public disapproves of Congress. Rather, we have only suggested that a Congress-disapproving public is simply reacting to what it sees being played out by the political actors on the political stage.

11

Process Performance
Public Reaction to Legislative Policy Debate

CAROLYN L. FUNK

Public satisfaction with government is commonly thought to reflect the performance of government leaders. For the most part, however, performance has been defined in terms of policy outcomes or economic conditions. Defined in these ways, leader performance has, indeed, been shown to have an important effect on public attitudes toward the leader, government institutions, and government in general (see Citrin and Green 1986; Citrin, this volume; Fiorina 1981; Owen and Dennis, this volume). Performance evaluations are also made about the behaviors of leaders during the *process of governing*, however.

The processes of government are increasingly visible to the public at large. More information about the political process is available to a wider audience than ever before. In the last ten years, there has been an explosion of news outlets that relay the workings of government to the public. A wide array of cable and Internet sources give frequent "behind the scenes" portrayals of the political process. As with any television audience, the public is (for the most part) a spectator to the performance carried out by elected officials and their aides. It's only common sense to hypothesize that the behavior of elites engaged in the processes of governing influences public views toward government. Remarkably little is known about public reactions to these aspects of leader performance, however (see Hibbing and Theiss-Morse 1995, 1998).

The present study seeks to understand how elite behavior in carrying out the processes of governing contributes to overall support for government and its institutions. This analysis is limited to performance evaluations of the process and not outcomes. This is not to deny the importance of outcomes in explaining public satisfaction toward government. Down the road, it will be important to integrate findings on attitudes toward governmental processes with attitudes toward outcomes. As a first step in that direction, I evaluate the sources of public attitudes toward processes in isolation from outcomes.

This analysis is limited in scope in one other regard. It looks solely at reaction to the behaviors of congressional leaders in the process of legislative policy debate. Political debate is a core part of the U.S. political system. In a world thought to be filled with competing interests, deliberation and debate are critical to resolving differences. Both our judicial and legislative institutions use formalized procedures for debate as the central element of dispute-resolution. For Congress, in particular, legislative policy debate is a major element of the process of governing in the institution. Mansbridge (1980) argues that the U.S. political system is based largely on adversarial politics. In comparison to other countries, the formal structures of the United States suggest that this is a more adversarial than consensual political system (see Lijphart 1984). A better understanding of the ways citizens experience debate is likely to further our understanding of how adversarial politics affects the connection between government and mass citizens.

POLITICAL DEBATE AND SOCIAL CONFLICT

Political Debate as a Democratic Procedure: The Importance of Voice

Political debate can be seen as part of a procedure for resolving conflict over public policy issues. In legislative bodies, the contours of political debate are specified in formal rules of the institution and the final decision is made on the basis of democratic voting rules. Free and open debate guarantees every participant a voice in the decision-making process. It is the opportunity for voice that is thought to underlie positive reactions to debate. Debate is a mechanism that guarantees a voice in the process to all participants. Past research, especially on experience with the courts and the police, has shown that the opportunity to voice one's concerns and give one's interpretation of events is a key source of perceptions that fair decision-making procedures have been used (Lind and Tyler 1988; Tyler 1990).

Beliefs about procedural fairness have a number of important consequences. People separate the process by which a decision was made from the outcomes of the decision itself. Belief that a fair process was used influences satisfaction with the distributive outcome of the decision. This is particularly important when the outcomes do not match preferences. Procedural fairness increases the likelihood that the outcome will be accepted regardless of whether that outcome was preferred. As Tyler (1990) explains, a desire for fair procedures in decision making stems from the belief that fair procedures will, on average, result in fair outcomes. In a sense, fair procedures are thought to create that reservoir of good will that is critical to Easton's (1965b) notion of diffuse support for the system. Fair procedures make it more likely that even unwanted policies by government authorities will be accepted as legitimate.

Congressional policy debate has formalized rules for assuring that all legislators have an opportunity for voice. If political debate was only a matter of voice, then congressional policy debate should be seen in a fairly positive light especially because it follows fair procedures.

Recently, a number of congressional scholars have questioned whether the public responds positively to democratic procedures such as deliberation and debate. Support for Congress is thought to be lower than that of other institutions precisely because this is where the practice of democratic procedures, especially debate, is more visible to the public eye (Hibbing and Theiss-Morse 1995). There are two issues underlying conjectures of public distaste for political debate. One is that the public dislikes democratic procedures. Public distaste, in this case, may stem from the conflict inherent in debate itself. The other is that the public dislikes the way elites carry out democratic procedures. In this case, public distaste stems from the practice of debate as it is commonly carried out by elites.

Political Debate as Social Conflict

The mere presence of debate communicates some degree of social conflict on the issue. After all, if there were no disagreement there would be no need for the debate. Conflict is generally viewed with distaste. People tend to prefer agreement to disagreement (Lipset and Schneider 1987; Sears 1969). Research on interpersonal attraction shows that we like others more when they hold similar attitudes and values to our own (Berscheid 1985; Byrne 1971). A number of psychological theories on the cognitive consistency of attitudes suggests that disagreement creates a negative psychological tension (see Eagly and Chaiken 1993; Petty and Cacioppo 1981). This creates a goal or desire to reduce the tension through one of several means. Both academic and applied subfields have developed to deal exclusively with conflict resolution whether at the interpersonal, organizational, societal, or international level.[1] It seems that people do not prefer to "agree to disagree" as often as they say they do.

1 While the implicit and explicit goal is often to avoid or end social conflict, conflict serves both positive and negative functions for individual development, interpersonal relationships, organizations, and other collectives (see Rahim 1986; Worchel et al. 1993). So conflict is not necessarily bad, but people tend to dislike it.

Spectator Reactions to Social Conflict. In the case of political debate by legislative elites, citizens have no direct role in the conflict. The conflict is primarily between the legislators. In this case, citizens are spectators of political debate by elites.[2] Psychological tendencies to prefer agreement over disagreement refer to participants in the social interaction, not outside observers. Very little is known about how third parties react to social conflict. Research on negotiation and conflict resolution processes have typically focused on the negotiating parties without attending to how others experience the conflict and negotiation process. Past research, then, tells us how people respond when they are directly involved in social conflict but not how they respond to watching other people fight.[3]

It could be that a preference for agreement over disagreement extends to observations of others. So, in addition to preferring agreement over disagreement in our social interactions we might also prefer that others agree in their social interactions. There are a number of psychological tendencies, however, that distinguish between responses involving the self and those involving observation of others (see Gilbert 1998). For example, the fundamental attribution error calls attention to the tendency to make causal attributions for one's own behavior based on situational explanations while causal attributions for other's behavior are based on dispositional, or personality, explanations. Cognitive processes

2 See Price (1992) for a similar view of the public as spectators to political affairs.

3 Political debate is not always experienced as a spectator sport, of course. In another sense, citizens may view the conflict as reflecting a social dissensus between groups whom elites represent. To the extent that citizens care about the issues under debate (whether due to a material interest in the issue or more ideological considerations), they may feel more personally involved in the conflict, albeit still indirectly. In this case, citizens are more like invested observers of the conflict among elites. I would expect reactions in this case to be more akin to those of participants. In particular, invested observers are expected to pay more attention and take a greater interest in the debate. I will not explore the implications of this perspective in detail because it is not clear that greater investment in the debate would influence the direction of emotional response to the debate.

Another wrinkle for understanding public reaction to debate is likely to involve an interaction between beliefs in majoritarian solutions for conflict resolution and a personal investment in the conflict. Given the tendency to view majoritarian solutions to conflict as a fair decision-making rule in the United States, perceptions of social consensus underlying the issue are likely to influence reaction to the debate. Personal investment in the issue is likely to interact with perceptions of social consensus, however. If one's own view is in the minority, I would expect greater support for continuing debate and nonmajoritarian solutions. If one's own view is in the majority, I would expect less support for continuing the debate and more support for majoritarian solutions to the conflict.

that distinguish between personal experience and observations of others suggest that judgments underlying observation of social conflict may differ from those underlying direct participation in conflict.

The Practice of Political Debate and Social Norms for Conflict Resolution

Congressional observers suggest that the practice of debate plays a key role in public dissatisfaction with Congress. Hibbing and Theiss-Morse (1995) point to the "petty haggling" in congressional debate. Elving (1994) suggests that the rancorous floor debates picked up by the media contribute to public dissatisfaction with Congress. The focus on the practice of debate redirects attention to the fairness of the procedures followed in the debate. But rather than focus on voice in decision-making procedures, this suggests we focus on other aspects of fair procedures for social interaction.

What does it mean to "fight fair"? The clues to answering this question come from identifying fights that are unfair; we can recognize the principles of fairness when those principles are violated. Uslaner (1993) points to norms for social interaction within the institution of Congress, especially courtesy and reciprocity, and shows that legislators are increasingly likely to violate these norms compared to past years. These norms tend to apply to social interaction more generally, however. The norm of reciprocity is considered to be one of the most powerful and pervasive across cultures (see Cialdini and Trost 1998). Reciprocity can refer to both material and nonmaterial exchanges as well as positive and negative exchanges. The tit-for-tat behavior pattern is simply one of reciprocity for both positive and negative exchanges. A norm of courtesy in social interaction can also be considered under the rubric of reciprocity. Here, the reciprocal exchange is simply courteous treatment of others. Courteous interactions also appear to influence judgments of procedural fairness. Tyler (1990) finds that judgments of fair procedures in contacts with legal authorities are influenced by the politeness and respect shown to them by the judges, police officers, and other officials.

The practice of debate in Congress often appears to violate these norms for social interaction. Research on retributive justice shows that people dislike rule-breaking by others across a wide variety of contexts and domains (see Tyler, Boeckmann, Smith, and Huo 1997). So, it could be that the rule-breaking in the practice of elite policy debate rather than the conflict, per se, underlies negative response. In particular, policy debate that includes personal animosity is likely to violate norms of courtesy and reciprocity in resolving social conflict. Fighting fair means abstaining from inflammatory personal attacks and instead sticking to the policy issue under debate. Fighting fair means avoiding personal rancor and animosity. Public response to elite policy debate, then, is likely to be influenced by the perceived fairness of elites' behaviors as they seek to resolve their differences.

Rubber-Necking and Social Conflict

The argument that the public has a distaste for conflict in general, or more specifically for the animosity in social conflict, neglects the complexity of reactions to political conflict as a spectator sport. As professional journalists have long recognized, a little conflict appears to pique interest and attention. Olien, Donohue, and Tichenor (1995) suggest a curvilinear relationship between the level of conflict and public interest. Maximum interest occurs at medium rather than high levels of social conflict. Above some threshold, interest in the conflict tapers off. In their studies of media coverage on local policy conflicts, they found that increased coverage of the conflict was related to increased interest in and interpersonal discussion on the issue, as well as a greater likelihood of holding an opinion about the issue. Repeated coverage of the conflict, however, was associated with disinterest in the issue. This is a phenomenon long recognized about public attention to political news stories but rarely documented. It suggests that some political debate by elites is likely to generate interest and attention to the issue. Above some threshold, however, conflict among elites is likely to generate disinterest in the issue. It may be that the threshold involves not just an absolute level of exposure to the debate but rather exposure to the animosity in debate. Minor infractions of the social norms for conflict resolution may pique attention but more substantial infractions will be met with distaste for the rule-breakers.

EVIDENCE OF PUBLIC DISTASTE FOR SOCIAL CONFLICT

I have now joined a number of others in pointing a finger at the conflictual aspects of politics as responsible for negative public reactions to Congress. If the violation of social norms for resolving conflict is at the root of public dissatisfaction, then public response will be directed at the political leaders in Congress. It is the spillover from these judgments that is expected to account for public dissatisfaction with Congress, in general. But we need evidence that is both more direct and more specific about how the conflict in politics influences public reactions.

I report, later, on an experiment that provides an initial test of whether the presence or absence of animosity in congressional policy debate leads to negative affective reactions. This was a "judgment experiment" where participants were randomly assigned to different written descriptions of a congressional debate and asked to make a number of judgments in response to those descriptions. I used a between-subjects design, meaning that each person received only one description of the debate. The experimental comparison, then, is based on comparing mean evaluations in response to two kinds of policy debate—one where animosity is present and one where that animosity is noticeably absent.

This experiment was conducted with a volunteer sample from the greater community of Houston, Texas, in May of 1998. U.S. citizens over twenty-one were solicited from an advertisement in the major newspaper; all were paid $10 for their participation. These participants came from a broad range of age groups and sociodemographic backgrounds. While this sample of respondents is not representative of any particular geographic population, they can be assumed to hold collectively a wide range of experiences with the political world. Relative to a sample of college students, the variation in age, social background, political leanings, and experience suggests that the results may be generalizable to other samples of adults.

The key experimental manipulation was embedded in a written description of changes to Medicare[4] that were recently considered by Congress. The description is meant to mimic that of a newspaper account. It includes a definition of Medicare and the reason changes were being considered by Congress. It, then, describes the debate between those favoring and opposing the bill as either marked by animosity and heated exchange or marked by civility and cordial disagreement. This manipulation is fairly direct. It pits a report of congressional behavior that includes animosity with one where that animosity is notably absent. However, it is also fairly subtle. The manipulation is based on a written description of congressional activity. Written descriptions are not likely to have as much impact as would a videotape or direct observation of debate. Further, the manipulation boils down to portions of only one of the four paragraphs. As experimental manipulations go, this one errs on the weak side. So we can expect the experimental comparisons to understate rather than overstate public response to animosity in debate.

There is some assurance that the experimental manipulations were detected by the respondents and left the intended impression. Ratings of "how well members of Congress get along with each other" based

4 I used Medicare as the issue context because changes to Medicare had been recently considered by Congress and because national surveys indicated that public opinion was often divided in support for the specific alterations being considered.

on this report show a significant difference between those in the animosity condition compared to those in the cordial condition (F (2, 103) = 12.51, p = .0006 for a one-way ANOVA). Responses on this seven-point scale where a high score indicates getting along very well averaged 3.86 for those in the cordial condition and 2.83 for the animosity condition. Neither experimental group thought members got along "very well" on this scale. However, those in the animosity condition saw the members as getting along even less well than those in the cordial condition.

The main hypothesis is that those in the animosity condition will have stronger negative reactions to the debate than those in the cordial behavior condition. A two-item index of negative affective reaction was used as the key dependent variable. Respondents were asked to rate the degree to which they felt angry or disgusted when reading about these activities of Congress. Ratings were made on a seven-point scale and averaged together to form the index (alpha = .68, r = .52).

Results of a one-way ANOVA with the presence or absence of animosity as the independent factor show that affective reactions were consistent with the hypotheses. The differences between groups showed a trend toward significance but did not quite reach a $p < .05$ standard (F (2, 103) = 2.30, p = .13). The mean response for those in the animosity condition was 4.43 on the seven-point index and 3.97 for those in the cordial condition. Those in the animosity condition reported more disgust and anger in reaction to this report.

Multivariate OLS regression analyses show that the tendency of those in the animosity condition to report more negative affect holds even with a number of other factors taken into consideration (see Table 11.1). All of the independent variables in the regression analyses were rescaled to range from 0 to 1 to facilitate the comparison of unstandardized coefficients. A dummy variable is used to represent the experimental conditions; a high score indicates the animosity condition. The analysis controls for greater liking for politics based on a two-item scale (alpha = .82), a three-point measure of greater dislike for arguing, and personal concern for the issue under debate (i.e., Medicare). Another item provides a control for agreement with the proposed changes under consideration by Congress; this item consists of a four-point rating that the changes are likely to improve matters. Controls for gender and party identification were also included.

The OLS analyses show that, on average, those who were exposed to a congressional policy debate where the elites behaved with animosity reacted more negatively than those who were exposed to virtually the same debate where the elites behaved with cordiality. This effect holds even after accounting for a number of other important influences on reac-

Table 11.1. *OLS Regression Estimates of Negative Affect in Response to Congressional Debate*

	Coeff.		SE	|t|
Animosity Present/Absent	0.49	+	.26	1.87
Like Politics	−1.47	*	.57	2.58
Avoid Arguing	−0.20		.37	0.54
Care About Issue	1.00	+	.58	1.73
Proposal Is Improvement	−2.45	*	.64	3.85
Female	0.46	+	.27	1.71
Party Identification (High = Republican)	−0.50		.41	1.25
Intercept	5.19	*	.78	6.65
Adjusted R-sq.	0.25			
N	99			
Model F	5.74		$p = .0001$	

tion to the policy debate. These results provide support for the hypothesis that the animosity present in elite debate leads to negative reactions. This suggests that the violation of social norms in resolving conflict underlie public distaste for political debate.

Individual Differences in Response to Political Debate

It is important to recognize that not everyone is particularly averse to conflict. Individuals differ in their preference for or desire to avoid interpersonal conflict. So it could be that some individuals are more turned off by the animosity in political debate than others. There are a number of differences across cultures in the expression of and response to social conflict, for example. Similarly, men and women are often thought to differ in their willingness to engage in interpersonal conflict, perhaps stemming from differences in sex-role socialization (see Tannen 1998). While conflict avoidance is likely to be correlated with gender, both men and women vary in the extent to which they are willing to engage in conflict. It is, therefore, the difference in preference for or avoidance of conflict, not gender per se, that is relevant here. Past research on individual differences related to conflict generally concerns tendencies for one's own behavior and social interactions rather than observations of social conflict among other parties. If conflict avoidance extends to observations of others, I would expect the more conflict-avoidant individuals to have a stronger negative response to the animosity in political debate relative to the more conflict tolerant.

Table 11.2. *Mean Response to Debate Conditions by Individual Differences in Conflict Avoidance on Index of Negative Affect*

	Debate with Animosity	Debate with Cordiality
Tend to Avoid Arguing	4.5	4.5
Don't Avoid Arguing	4.5	3.7

There is an interaction between individual differences toward conflict and response to animosity in debate. This interaction effect approaches statistical significance in a two-way ANOVA ($F\ (4, 100) = 1.94, p = .166$) and reaches statistical significance in a multivariate OLS regression analysis using the same controls as shown in Table 11.1 ($p < .001$). The findings show that individuals who tend to avoid arguing were equally angry and disgusted by both the animosity and cordial policy debates. Those who were more tolerant of arguing expressed more anger and disgust when the elite debate included animosity compared to when animosity was absent. The mean response to the cordial debate was 4.5 for the conflict-avoidant individuals and 3.7 for the tolerant individuals on the same two-item index of negative affect (see Table 11.2). Looking across debate conditions, those exposed to the animosity condition were uniformly more likely to report anger and disgust after reading this report, regardless of their individual tendencies to avoid arguing. The mean response on the seven-point index for negative affect was 4.5 for both groups. So, people in general respond negatively to animosity in debate. Consistent with expectations for individual differences in response to conflict, however, the conflict-avoidant may be particularly sensitive to the conflict inherent in debate even when it follows norms for cordial behavior.

This interaction has two implications for the interpretation of the experimental results. First, it suggests that people tend to respond negatively to the presence of animosity in elite debate regardless of their individual tendencies to avoid social conflict. Second, it suggests that some people may respond negatively to debate because of their lower tolerance for arguing. This portion of the population will tend to be disinterested in politics. (The correlation between liking for politics and a tendency to avoid arguing was $-.32$, $p < .001$.) Another portion of the public, however, appears to be less bothered by debate. They are bothered more by the animosity in the legislators' behavior than by the debate. This group of people is, in effect, being shooed away from political affairs by the behavior of the politicians. When politicians engage in behaviors that violate the implicit norms or rules for resolving social conflict, public distaste is greater even for those who are more tolerant of social conflict.

SHOOTING THEMSELVES IN THE FOOT . . . REPEATEDLY

As citizens gaze into the fishbowl of elite politics, they do not always like what they see. Public distaste can be found even in response to a single instance of behavior. The experimental findings suggest that the behavior of political leaders engaged in legislative policy debate contributes to public dissatisfaction with government. The experimental data help to specify the aspect of debate that contributes to public dissatisfaction. These findings provide direct evidence that the presence of animosity in elite debate can elicit public anger and disgust.

Conflict among congresspersons is thought to be increasingly open and visible to the public eye (see Brady and Theriault, this volume; Davidson, Kovenock and O'Leary 1968; Elving 1994; Mann and Ornstein 1994; Uslaner 1993). Within Congress, personal attacks of other members have increased over recent years (Uslaner 1993). Similarly, personal attacks have increased in political campaigns. Partly as a result of the changes in politicians' behavior toward one another, an increased number of political leaders is perceived to be involved in "scandals" concerning their personal behavior. The rise in attack journalism further contributes to the salience of incivility and social conflict in politics. Each incident of personal attack might be considered a violation of social norms for behavior between others.

This experiment provides initial support for the hypothesis that the social conflict in policy debate elicits negative reactions. The findings stem from only a single instance of animosity in a reported congressional policy debate. It is the cumulative impact of these elite behaviors, not a single instance, that is hypothesized to affect more general judgments such as overall evaluations of Congress and disinterest in political affairs. It is reassuring to note that general satisfaction with Congress was not affected by the experimental manipulation in the study reported here. So a single instance of behavior is unlikely to account for global evaluations of Congress. As a number of scholars and political observers have argued, however, the cumulative effect of personal attacks, scandal, and incivility among politicians is likely to contribute to a growing disinterest and dissatisfaction with politics (e.g., Dionne 1991; Cappella and Jamieson 1997). In a sense, politicians have been training the public to be cynical about politics. Specific instances of elite behavior contribute to an image of politicians in general. As each new instance matches the stereotype of politicians it only reinforces that image. Specific offenses are seen in the rubric of politicians as "mudslinging liars."

This study has, necessarily, given an incomplete picture of public reaction to the behaviors of leaders engaged in political debate and other processes of governing. Within this limited scope, the results suggest a new direction for understanding public response to elite politics. These insights stem directly from recognizing that elite politics is made up of social interactions, and then using social psychological principles to understand individual response in this social context. Here, I treat the public as spectators to social conflict among elites and consider why observations of social conflict are likely to engender negative public response. Consistent with research on social justice, I suggest that the animosity and incivility among elites in policy debate elicit distaste because the behavior violates social norms or procedural rules for resolving social conflict. While the public distaste for animosity in political debate can be seen in response to a single instance of behavior, it is likely that the cumulative effects of these behaviors spill over to judgments of politicians as a group and politics in general. The prevalence of animosity in elite policy debate is likely to amplify public distaste and contribute to dissatisfaction with politicians and politics.

Past research has largely neglected public reaction to the processes of governing when explaining public satisfaction with government (see Hibbing and Theiss-Morse 1995, 1998). From the public vantage point, however, the world of politics is chock full of information at this more microlevel of behavior. Public response to elites engaged in the processes of governing serve as another component of performance evaluations. While past research has often focused on policy outcome performance, a more comprehensive understanding of public satisfaction with government comes from considering public reaction to "process performance" as well.

Part IV

How Is Dissatisfaction with Government Measured and Incorporated into Political Theory?

In the volume's concluding section, Part IV, the focus of attention shifts from the reasons the American public tends to have negative opinions of government to the most appropriate way to measure public opinion on this matter. Discussions of measurement cannot occur without attention being given to theoretical issues such as the nature, meaning, and consequences of these negative opinions. The three chapters in this part take up the challenge of fitting unfavorable views of government into the larger picture of democratic governance. Investigation of the reasons for people's dissatisfaction with government, after all, puts us in a position to address the following basic question: What is it exactly that Americans want their government to do and to be? It would be a mistake to analyze public attitudes toward government without allowing the findings to bear on these basic measurement and theoretical concerns.

Diana Owen and Jack Dennis squarely confront the task of measuring public attitudes toward government. They are somewhat critical of standard procedures employing the "trust" battery asked every two years by NES. Their main concern is that these items go beyond merely ascertaining levels of trust in government by specifying reasons for trust, thereby confusing "the phenomenon with its antecedents." For example, one of the common items asks if respondents perceive people in government to be "crooked" or not, but it is certainly possible for a person to deny that politicians are crooked but still distrust that government. Even the best question of the lot: "Do you think the government in Washington can be trusted to do what is right," as Owen and Dennis point out, incorporates a reason for distrust and not just measurement of the attitude. After all, if Tyler and Hibbing–Theiss-Morse are correct, distrust may spring not just from the government failing *to do* what is right but from the government failing to do things in the right way.

Owen and Dennis advocate an alternative measurement technique in which public perceptions of the effectiveness of representation become the central element of public opinion toward government. They discovered that a Pew survey conducted in late 1997 actually tapped many of the components of effective representation, so they use it to explain variations in public attitudes as measured by their modified battery of questions. The most powerful explainers of negative attitudes toward government are a belief that government is not particularly relevant to one's life and a belief that government is powerful. The combination of a detached and uncaring but highly influential government is a powerfully negative force on public approval of the political system.

Even if we could all agree on the best way to measure public attitudes toward government, the "so-what" question would remain. Why is it important to know what it is about government that Americans dislike? Practically every chapter in this volume defends the practice of devoting scholarly attention to the goal of understanding attitudes toward government. But after spending a paragraph or two making this defense, the articles quickly return to employing popular attitudes as the dependent variable. Tom Tyler encourages scholars to consider employing those attitudes instead as an explanatory variable so we can discover their consequences. Tyler's specific concern is with the influence of government disapproval on the tendency of people to fail to comply with governmental edicts. The importance of dissatisfaction could hardly be questioned if such attitudes "shape behaviors that are important to the viability of the political system," and what could be more important to system viability in a non–command-and-control polity than voluntary compliance? Drawing on his long-running research agenda, Tyler demonstrates that perceptions of system legitimacy increase compliance with the outputs of that system—even more than judgments about the likelihood of being caught and punished for not complying.

Tyler believes that the typical political science measures of "trust," "confidence," and even "approval" may be targeted more at incumbent office-holders and thus may not actually be measuring legitimacy. The good news is that it should not be assumed, therefore, that the infamous decline in trust will necessarily lead to a collapse in compliance rates. Perhaps this explains Citrin and Luks' observation that "there is little evidence that lower levels of political trust have produced a nation of scofflaws." Thus, attention appropriately turns to the factors that enhance and, more importantly, inhibit legitimacy. Tyler's answer is perception of procedural justice, but what kind of process do people view as just? In investigating people who had interaction with legal authorities, primarily the police, Tyler found that the most influential variables were perceptions of the motives of the authorities, perceptions of the degree to which participants were treated with respect and dignity, and perceptions of the neutrality of authorities. Interestingly, people's judgments of the degree to which they gained or lost in the decisions made by the authorities "had little direct influence upon judgments."

Hibbing and Theiss-Morse bring the volume to a close by suggesting commonalities in several of the chapters. Specifically, they note that, with important exceptions here and there, research attention has come to rest primarily on the public's dissatisfaction with governmental processes. Judging by the topics and hypotheses analyzed in the included chapters, the current conventional wisdom is that the key to understanding "what it is about government that people dislike" is more likely to be found by studying how government does things than by studying what government does. If this interpretation is accurate, it would constitute a considerable evolution from the early days of research in the subfield when Gamson asserted that political distrust could be traced to undesirable policy decisions and outcomes (1968, 178), and when Citrin wrote that "political elites 'produce' policies; in exchange, they receive trust from citizens satisfied with these policies and cynicism from those who are disappointed" (1974, 973). Hibbing and Theiss-Morse endorse this newer emphasis on process, provide further evidence of its usefulness in understanding public attitudes, and outline a larger theoretical perspective that refines and makes sense of the conclusion that many Americans dislike their government not because of what it does but because of the way it goes about its business.

12

Trust in Federal Government
The Phenomenon and Its Antecedents

DIANA OWEN AND JACK DENNIS

Numbered high among the many imperfectly measured political attitudes that social scientists return to again and again is political trust. In everyday language the idea of trusting someone or something is pretty straightforward. The concept of trust conveys a sense of stable expectations, in particular, predictability, credibility, assumed good intentions, and orderly behavior. When we apply this concept to political leaders, individually or collectively, we believe that they will behave in a rightful and just manner that we can anticipate because of our or others' prior experience with them. Sometimes we move beyond the situation of trusting merely a set of individuals in politics and government to the organizations within which they work or even to the system itself. (For some recent examples see Craig 1993, 1996; Bennett and Bennett 1990; Levi 1997; Nye et al. 1997.)

The theoretical issue of political support encompasses questions concerning trust or confidence in political authorities, the political order they operate within, or the wider political community that establishes and maintains a regime (Easton 1965b, 1975; Easton and Dennis 1969). The specific problem that we address here is how to conceptualize and measure the concept of political support. This is not our first attempt to do this, nor is the literature on political support and alienation entirely without clues about how to proceed. However, our goal is to take the discussion one step beyond where it stands at the moment.

Confounding analyses of political trust is the fact that many definitions and operations confuse the phenomenon with its antecedents. Even the best students of trust in government have not always recognized this problem of conflating the causes, symptoms, or consequences with the definition of the phenomenon. Such a definitional strategy is self-defeating because it makes it difficult to test empirically for causes if these are built into how one recognizes the phenomenon itself. As Craig (1993) has observed, leading scholars, such as Easton and Miller, who have done much to develop the theory of political support, nonetheless tend to confuse support or trust with its supposed antecedents and consequences. Craig adds, "In fairness to both Easton and Miller, they are far from alone in their tendency to define away what amounts to empirical questions about the correlates of trust, alienation, and similar orientations" (1993, 25; also see Citrin 1974). If even the best conceptualizers of political support have created untestable propositions because of careless definitions, then it behooves the rest of us to proceed with extreme care when we approach this area of inquiry.

OUR APPROACH

We attempt to attack this problem of definitional ambiguity by employing some survey evidence that gives us a better handle on separating the general concept of support from its causes or consequences than has usually been possible. We begin with the assumption that political support is a latent construct that may be approached with the use of terms from ordinary language, such as trust, confidence, approval, favorable opinion of, or in some sense, the opposite of being politically alienated (see Seeman 1972; Yinger 1973). The concept of support, following Easton, may encompass a continuum of orientations ranging from highly positive, through neutral, to highly negative attitudes (1965b; 1975).

We are concerned primarily with avoiding to the greatest extent possible in this research the use of the kind of definition that characterizes the American National Election Studies (ANES) series of political trust studies. The indicators of trust employed in these studies suffer from the problem of not separating the measurement of support from its putative causes. The ANES's well-established approach dates back in some form to 1958. Despite these studies' great value in giving us a perspective on the changing levels of public confidence in U.S. government over the past fifty years, the measurement problem precludes us from answering some fundamental questions about the reasons for these trends.

We should add at this point that we also endorse the now common view among the laborers in the political trust vineyards that the ANES political trust battery contains another major source of ambiguity beyond the one upon which we focus here. What the famous debate between Citrin and Miller of a quarter century ago revealed, and that subsequent conceptual and measurement attacks on the problem have not completely resolved (e.g. Citrin and Green 1986; Miller and Borrelli 1991; Craig, Niemi, and Silver 1990), is the issue of what respondents have in mind in terms of objects when they answer these questions. Is it the regime of democracy and the whole set of political authorities labeled collectively as "government" (Easton 1965b, 1975; Abramson and Finifter 1981)? Or is it more likely to be only the national government that is focused upon (Miller 1974a, 1974b; Citrin 1974; Craig 1993)? Or is it Congress (Feldman 1983; Davidson and Parker 1972; Dennis 1981; Hibbing and Theiss-Morse 1995), the presidential incumbent (Citrin 1977; Citrin and Green 1986), specific policies and programs (Miller 1974a, 1983; Weatherford 1987; Williams 1985), government officials in general (Weatherford 1988), or something else that rises to public consciousness in the asking of these questions? Thus, the potential objects of support are widely varied. They can include the entire polity, the component parts of government, such as the three major branches (Dennis 1973), agencies, military and civilian bureaucracies and their employees, as well as nongovernmental organizations, such as political parties (Dennis 1966, 1975, 1980, 1986; Dennis and Owen 1997; Owen and Dennis 1996; Owen, Dennis and Klofstad 1998), interest groups (Dennis 1987), the mass media (Cappella and Jamieson 1997; Davis and Owen 1998), religious organizations, labor unions, corporations, and educational institutions.

The problem we address here, however, is a different one. How can we get at people's feelings about federal government without presupposing the reasons they may have had for developing such feelings? This issue is complicated to some extent by the fact that political support is in large degree a measure of government performance. In order to explain political support reliably it is necessary to distinguish between the more general, gut-level feelings about government that may be linked to performance and the specific aspects of government performance that contribute to those feelings.

Indeed, the dominant theme of the usual four or five items of the NES political-trust battery is that performance matters when it comes to political trust. The original single-item measure, first used in the 1958 NES, asks respondents whether they think the government in Washington can be trusted *to do what is right* (emphasis ours; see NES Website, toptables/tab 5A.1). Trust thus becomes performance in this question. Still, this item taps a general orientation rather than a specific cause of political support. It can be employed successfully as a dependent variable. The other four items that have typically been used in the trust battery focus on more specific criteria of performance evaluations. Rather than measuring support per se, these items may be more meaningfully conceptualized as antecedents of support.

We advocate an approach to measuring and explaining political support that begins with a more specific analysis of the possible reasons people may have for being politically supportive or resistant. We suspect that the core processes of judgment in the U.S. at the present time revolve around the concept of representation. A darker public mood relating to government is likely to coincide with citizens feeling that they are inadequately represented (e.g., Ryden 1996; Rosenthal 1998).

The recent literature on political trust gives us a variety of clues about the specifics of such feelings. (We draw here especially upon the work of Easton 1975; Jennings 1998; Hibbing and Theiss-Morse 1995; Owen 1997; Tyler et al. 1989; Tyler et al. 1997; Levi 1997; Braithwaite and Levi 1998; Craig 1993; Nye et al. 1997; Kinder 1986; Rahn and Clore 1994; Miller and Borrelli 1991; Putnam 1993; Cappella and Jamieson 1997; and Smith et al. 1979).

We identify six major criteria of effective representation that come into play when people make judgments about the trustworthiness of government or its officials. Each of these general factors is associated with specific criteria related to support as well. The following outline delineates these likely criteria:

1. *Perceptions that there are effective linkages between citizens and government.* This criterion taps the degree of perceived responsiveness of officials or other political actors to the needs, concerns, values, interests, and demands of citizens. It encompasses the extent of perceived accountability for decisions made or actions taken, as well as the degree of representativeness of those who govern relative to the traits, attitudes, memberships, or identifications of those being represented.
2. *Perceptions of government decision makers as having good qualifications.* Related to trust is the extent to which citizens believe officials have the requisite competence, skill, intelligence, expertise, and experience. It taps decision makers' demonstrated effectiveness, leadership capacity, vision, take-charge attitude, and performance.
3. *Perceptions of government decision makers as having good personal qualities.* This criterion pertains to the extent to which decision makers are law abiding and exhibit virtue, proper motives, good character, morality, veracity, and ethical standards. It takes into account the degree of sympathy, empathy, compassion, and concern for citizens that leaders demonstrate.
4. *Perceptions of the fairness of the political decision-making process, especially in the sense of using appropriate procedures and practices.* Citizens may be concerned about leaders' seriousness in addressing problems comprehensively and objectively. This includes such practices as holding balanced hearings that allow the

airing of arguments on all sides, and the maintenance of the possibility of further peaceful opposition, dissent, or criticism after decisions have been made or actions taken.

5. *Perception of effective outputs that address and resolve major societal problems.* Citizens assess the extent to which societal resources are properly allocated to solve problems, the degree of proper standards of performance evaluation, and the extent to which unanticipated or undesirable consequences are avoided.
6. *Perception of fair outcomes of public policy.* This criterion assesses whether or not desired benefits are achieved. It taps the extent to which appropriate standards of equality, fairness, justice, equity, or compensation are applied, and whether undeserved disadvantages and deprivations result.

These criteria suggest that people's reasons for judging the trustworthiness of officials or government institutions may arise in connection with different phases of the policy process—either at the beginning with the representing officials and what they are like, in the middle with perceptions of processes and procedures, or at the end with outputs and outcomes.

When we apply these categories of public response to the NES political trust items, we see that they cover relatively little of this domain of reactions to the perceived quality of representation of citizens. One of the NES questions—whether we can trust the government in Washington to do what is right—is a dependent variable. In a highly pragmatic society, diffuse support and perceived general performance are apt to be virtually synonymous. The other four ANES political-trust items are statements of the reasons one might or might not have for approving the performance of, and thus determining the more general state of legitimation of, the government or its officials.

One of the four items, which we believe to be more properly constituted as an independent measure, asks whether "the government is run by a few big interests looking out for themselves or that it is run for the benefit of all the people." This question is in our view a measure of criterion 6, specifically addressing the extent to which appropriate and fair standards are applied. Another item asks how many of "the people running the government are crooked." This question pertains to criterion 3, which references the moral character of public officials. A third item in this series asks how much of the money we pay in taxes the people in the government waste, which we interpret to be an indicator of criterion 5, reflecting a concern about the proper allocation of societal resources. The last of the NES index items—which in recent NES surveys has been discarded—taps whether government officials are smart people who know what they are doing. This is an application of our criterion 2 as it specifically relates to perceptions of competence.

Thus, the NES taps only limited aspects of three of the six major categories of reasons that we postulate people might have for feeling confident or not about the representational performance of government and officials. From a psychometric perspective, we fear that such a slim coverage of the territory may well lead to problems of validity, quite aside from the fact that the objects of perception in this index are also ambiguously presented, and notoriously so. In new work on these matters, which we in this essay and our cocontributors in this volume attempt to provide, such limitations of the traditional NES approach need to be taken into account.

THE EVIDENCE

Given our theoretical and empirical purposes, ideally we need a survey in which there is a rich body of questions pertaining to government support, plus good coverage of at least the main varieties of antecedent variables that we believe are central to our analysis. We discovered one series of surveys, conducted by the Pew Research Center for the People and The Press in 1997 and 1998, that is suitable for our purposes. In this research, we focus in particular on the Pew "trust in government" survey conducted in September and October 1997.[1] While the initial trust in government survey in this series does not have all that we might wish for, especially in terms of providing the basis for multi-item indexes for measuring the reasons for trust/mistrust, it includes enough of this content to be quite suggestive for our investigative purposes.

The Concept of Political Support: The Dependent Variables

We consider now the operationalizations of some general constructs of government support. The Pew data allow us to distinguish support for a political object, such as the federal government, from its performance-related causes, including the application of specific criteria such as fairness, efficiency, rectitude, or competence. Further, unlike the NES, the Pew data base includes a large battery of items that we can employ to

1 Together, this survey and six others in the same Pew series are overviewed in the Pew Research Center publication, *Deconstructing Distrust: How Americans View Government* (Washington, D.C., 1998).

construct multi-item indexes of general support for government and of federal government officials that we employ as dependent variables in regression analyses designed to examine the antecedents of political support. (A complete listing of all the measures employed in this study appears in the Appendix[2]).

General Support for the Federal Government. Our measure of general support taps respondents' basic feelings about the federal government. It consists of four items that take into account favorable or unfavorable opinions of the federal government in Washington, opinions about federal departments and agencies, trust in the federal government, and whether the government evokes feelings of contentment, frustration, or anger. Direct references to government job performance are absent from these measures. When combined into an additive scale, the reliability is relatively strong (alpha = .75). A high score on this scale indicates strong support for the federal government.

Support for Federal Officials. Aside from general evaluations of the national government and the job it is doing, citizens express their opinions about government in terms of the officials who wield authority at the federal level. As Hibbing and Theiss-Morse (1995) remind us, it is important to ascertain whether people's trust in government is directed more at institutions and agencies or at the people in authority. Thus, we need to examine separately how people feel about government personnel.

We employ three indicators to measure support for federal officials. These include respondents' favorable or unfavorable opinions of elected officials, their belief that most elected officials are trustworthy, and their rating of the ethical and moral practices of federal officials.[3] When combined into an additive scale, a high score on this measure indicates a high

2 To determine the relationship of each of the survey items to the underlying support constructs, we performed a confirmatory factor analysis. The model indicates a good fit between the measured variables and the two unobserved political support concepts. Further information about the data or the analysis that is not included in this report can be obtained by e-mailing the authors at *DMOwen@ibm.net.*

3 The ethical and moral rating of officials is difficult to segregate empirically from the concept of general support for public officials. Conventional bivariate analysis reinforces the fact that the correlation between this variable and the underlying concept is extremely high. Therefore, we treat it as an integral part of the general support measure rather than as a separate cause.

level of support for federal officials. Again, the scale reliability is respectable (alpha = .71).

Antecedents

Unlike the early days of empirical research on matters of political support in the 1960s, we have today a long list of suspects for antecedent variables. The survey data-based treatment of the putative causes of trust or mistrust has grown ever more extensive. While we cannot examine all of these causes here,[4] we focus on some prominent antecedents in relation to our four measures of political support.

Factors Related to Political Pragmatism and Classical Liberalism. Some of the sources of citizen attitudes toward government are rooted in major themes of American culture. One set of factors, consisting of causes linked to specific aspects of government performance, is a product of our ingrained pragmatism. Trustworthiness is linked to good performance evaluations in a variety of domains. The strong pragmatic strain focuses on performance both at the level of generally meeting citizens' expectations and in the application of specific criteria to performance evaluations. The latter includes the perceived fairness in how decisions are made (Levi 1997; Tyler et al. 1989), unrepresentativeness in how government institutions operate (Hibbing and Theiss-Morse 1995), and assorted other criteria—outlined previously—such as incompetence, immorality, inefficiency, corruption, arrogance, and lack of accountability.

In this study, we are able to analyze a variety of these plausible antecedents of support. The Pew data set includes variables that tap the influence of the perceived fairness of government in terms of it being run for the benefit of all the people, the belief that the government is inefficient and wasteful, the view that government has the wrong priorities, and the respondents' feelings regarding whether they pay too much in taxes for what they get in return. In addition, we incorporate into our analysis a measure of whether respondents view the condition of the country as being positive or negative.

4 For example, there is a whole range of social or external influences and agencies that we expect to affect people's attitudes toward authorities and government that we cannot test directly here. Some of these begin to have effects early in life, such as family, schools, peer groups, neighborhood, or religious organizations (Easton and Dennis 1969; Hess and Torney 1967; Greenstein 1965; Hyman 1959; Dawson and Prewitt 1969; Jennings and Niemi 1974, 1981). In adulthood, additional sources of images about government may come into play (see Sigel 1989), such as voluntary associations and the workplace.

By contrast, another main source of feelings about government lies in the cultural theme of individualism or classical liberalism. From the side of limiting government, we may judge the federal government as much on how well it preserves the rights and freedoms of individuals as on how well it does its job of solving societal problems. Such liberalism also means that we may be affected by how relevant we see government to be in our daily lives. We are perhaps less likely to regard government as intrusive, and thus untrustworthy, if we find it salient (Craig 1993) as a focus for our demands. If we do not expect government to do much (Sniderman and Brody 1977), then we are unlikely to become less supportive if it fails to act.

To some degree, a classically libertarian perspective on the role of government conditions our expectations about what the federal government, or other governments, are supposed to be like. One impact may be a vision of a narrowed sphere within which government is seen to be relevant. Another is some preference for keeping the role of the authorities bounded in terms of their relative power. While we may generally prefer some form of representative government to that of full-scale participatory democracy (Aberbach et al. 1981; Devine 1972; but see Citrin 1996), we still want our representatives to play by the rules, to face the recurrent possibility of being turned out of office by popular vote, and to be responsive to citizens' demands while in office. We thus put some real limits on how much status and privilege we are willing to accord to those who would wield power over us (Mitchell 1959). We resist at least any overt signs of official arrogance, permanence of tenure, lack of responsiveness, arbitrariness, and lack of accountability. In an individualistic society (Bellah et al. 1985; Hartz 1955), we are especially prone to mistrust those who want to loom too large in our lives (Lipset and Schneider 1987).

For purposes of our analysis, we take into account citizens' concern with the power of government and the relevance that they feel government has in their lives. We include a scale that taps the degree to which people feel the government has too much power. We also use a variable that measures how much people believe the government affects their lives. This indicator ranges from the perception of the government having a strong positive to a strong negative effect on one's life.

It is important to consider the complexities of the dynamic surrounding the influence of pragmatic and liberal based factors related to support. There is a sense in which the public's trustful or mistrustful perceptions may come into conflict. On pragmatic grounds we may want the government to get the job done. However, on classical libertarian grounds, we want to be assured that government's efforts are nonetheless constrained by limits on its potential for hyperactivity, and thus that there are safeguards for the maintenance of individual freedom. We can test for the relative strength of this variety of factors in our regression analyses.

Personal Factors. People's personal outlooks and orientations in a variety of areas also are likely to be relevant to their feelings about government. One's personal political identities and attitudes, such as partisanship, ideology, policy preferences, or images of highly visible officials, may affect one's willingness to trust (King 1997; Peterson and Wrighton 1998). Thus, we take into account an individual's partisan identification in our analysis. It may well be the case that people are more willing to trust government if those in power share their partisan orientations, although this relationship is complex (Craig 1993).

At an even more general level, one's perceived quality of life might be connected to support for government, especially if government is seen to have some role in the creation of life satisfaction. A citizen's sense of political efficacy also may be linked to supportive or nonsupportive attitudes, as those who feel they can influence government may be more trusting. Finally, people who participate more in politics, such as turning out to vote, are also likely to hold a more favorable view of government (Teixeira 1992; Verba, Schlozman, and Brady 1995; Bennett and Bennett 1990). We include measures of the respondents' perceived quality of life, political efficacy, and regularity of voting in our regression analyses.

Communication Factors. Mass media are among the culprits blamed for the increased public cynicism that we have witnessed over the past two decades. The pervasive negative, often vitriolic, messages about politics disseminated via mass media have led scholars to investigate this connection, which is somewhat difficult to establish empirically. Recent evidence, however, suggests that the hypothesized linkage between exposure and attention to mass media and political distrust may be valid (see Chaffee and Yang 1990; Capella and Jamieson 1997; Kerbel 1995). There are indications that the talk radio audience, in particular, holds especially negative opinions about government, as it is both exposed to and participates in the creation of highly inflammatory political discourse (Davis and Owen 1998).

The Pew data provide a battery of questions about the respondents' media use habits, including how regularly they watch television news, read the newspaper, listen to radio news, tune into talk radio, and log onto the Internet. The survey also asks whether people's impression of government is influenced most by things they have heard or read, or by things they have personally experienced. We examined all of these variables in relation to the political support measures, although only two—talk-radio listening and the source of people's impressions about government—remained in the final multivariate model.

Trust in Other Citizens. Finally, political support may be linked to whether people in general are regarded as being capable of making political judgements properly (Dennis 1993). We include two measures of individuals' faith in their fellow citizens. The first is more general and deals with the respondents' views about human nature being basically good or bad. The second asks how much trust and confidence individuals have in the wisdom of the American people when it comes to making political decisions.

FINDINGS

In order to examine the antecedents of political support empirically, we used OLS regression to estimate identical models for each of the dependent variables—support for the federal government and for federal officials. The findings appear in Table 12.1.

Demographic Controls

The existing lore on support for political structures gives us a large list of other suspects beyond the primary ones. At a fairly simple yet often mysterious level, a variety of demographic variables are significantly related to political support measures in certain contexts. Race, for example (Abramson 1977, 1983; Flanigan and Zingale 1998), has been shown since the mid-1960s to affect one's degree of political trust when the NES items are employed. African Americans, in particular, have a lower level of confidence in officials and in government. Social class, especially education, income, and occupation, also are related to some indicators of trust, as are sex and age (Craig 1993; Luttbeg and Gant 1995). Age-related variations in political support are evident, even though they are not always the expected ones. Generation X, for example, tends to be more supportive of government than are older generational cohorts (Owen 1997).

We include controls for sex, age, race, education, and income in our models. Bivariate analyses revealed statistically significant relationships for all of these demographic variables with at least one of our dependent

Table 12.1. *Multiple Regression Analysis (OLS) of Institutional Support*

	Federal Government	Federal Officials
Sex	.023	.011
Age	.032	–.078**
Race	–.058**	–.001
Education	.020	.037
Income	.028	.044
Govt. Power	–.183**	–.114**
Fairness	.170**	.244**
Relevance	.219**	.125**
Inefficient	–.134**	–.094**
Priorities	–.081**	–.073**
Taxes	–.021	–.056**
Condition US	–.161**	–.113**
Quality of Life	–.051**	–.026
Party ID	–.023	.029
Efficacy	–.110**	–.186**
Vote	–.017	.046*
Heard/Read	–.041*	–.036
Talk Radio	.006	.059**
Human Nature	–.021	–.025
Wisdom	.052**	.123**
Adjusted R^2	.531**	.442**
N	1,219	1,287

Note: Entries are standardized regression coefficients. * $p < .05$. ** $p < .01$.

measures. For the most part, these relationships do not hold up when additional variables are introduced into the analysis.[5] As Table 12.1 indicates, the demographic variables generally do little to explain differences in political support in the multivariate analyses, with a few exceptions. Nonwhites are less trustful of the federal government than are whites. In addition, younger adults are more likely to hold positive evaluations of federal officials than are those who are older, which we expected to find given earlier age-cohort analyses of political trust.

5 Women and younger people are more supportive of the federal government than are other citizens. People with higher levels of education and income hold less favorable opinions than those with lower education and income. In addition, controls for other demographic factors, including religion, religiosity, born-again Christians, and employment status were not related statistically to either dependent measure (see Craig 1993; Wilson 1975; Teixeira 1996; Wald 1997).

Trust in Federal Government

Our Main Predictors

Table 12.1 presents as its second block of predictors variables tapping the antecedents related to notions of pragmatism and liberalism. We discover that almost every one of these hypothesized reasons for trust or mistrust is significant for our dependent trust measures. Overall, the most powerful of the predictors are those associated with classical liberal views of democracy. The measure of the personal relevance of government to the respondent is the strongest of the antecedent factors included in our model. Individuals who find the federal government to be highly relevant to their lives in a negative sense are less supportive of government than are those who find government to be a highly relevant, yet positive, force. Next most potent is our measure of perceived government power. As we anticipated, if people do not see the federal government as being too powerful, they tend to rate its performance as high.

The reasons for trusting government associated with pragmatism also have significant, if somewhat less powerful, individual effects. Thus, the criteria of fairness, efficiency, having the right programmatic priorities, taxing fairly, and perceiving a positive state of the nation are related to our indexes in the expected direction. People who believe that the government is run for the benefit of all, that government is not inefficient or wasteful, that it has the right priorities,[6] and that the tax burden is fair have a favorable view of the federal government and federal officials. Further, a positive perception of the state of the nation corresponds to good feelings about government.

In terms of the personal factors we included in the analysis, there are small, but significant, effects of one's perceived quality of life, political efficacy, and how often one votes. Those who sense that they have higher life satisfaction, that officials respond, and who vote regularly are more supportive of the federal government. The latter finding does not hold for citizens' feelings about federal officials, where those who say they vote regularly are less trusting of officials.

6 The Pew data-base question used to tap the belief that the government has wrong priorities is double barreled. We treated it as a dummy variable in the regression analyses, where 1 indicates that the government has the wrong priorities and 0 indicates that the government has the right priorities but runs programs inefficiently. When the dummy coding was reversed so that the priorities issue was confounded by the inefficiency issue, and the variable entered into the regression equation, we found that people who believed the government had the right priorities, but who also felt government was inefficient, were distrustful. The correlation between this variable and our other indicator of inefficiency was extremely low (.118).

Party identification was not a significant predictor of support for either of the federal government measures in the regression analyses. Bivariate correlations indicate that Republicans are significantly more likely to hold negative evaluations of the federal government and officials than are Democrats.[7] However, these relationships wash out when more powerful predictors are introduced into the equation.

With respect to communication processes, two variables show patterns of causal significance across our range of support measures. Those who say they have heard or read things that have influenced their impression of government—versus those who have relied more on their personal experience—trust federal government more.

We examined the range of media-use variables in the survey and found that only talk-radio listening was related to our support measures. Those who listen to talk radio regularly are more likely to give low ratings to federal officials. Talk-radio listening is surprisingly unrelated to support for the federal government (Owen 1996; Davis and Owen 1998). However, the findings regarding federal officials are expected given the negative, highly personalized rhetoric that characterizes political talk radio.

Finally, we show in Table 12.1 some effects of attitudes toward other people on government support. Regarding trust in other citizens, or what on the downside psychologists term "misanthropy," the usual hypothesis posits that those who take a more pessimistic view of human nature are less likely to trust government. Such an orientation of interpersonal mistrust does not pertain for our measures of trust in the federal government or officials.

We also include a question that asks respondents how much confidence they have in the wisdom of the general populace in making political decisions. Those who lack faith are more likely to be mistrustful on both of our dependent variables. This finding makes sense if one assumes that the government in operation is seen to be a product of democratic processes. To put the matter another way, to mistrust our government is also to mistrust ourselves.

DISCUSSION

We have revisited, in the present essay, the concept of political support using some recent national survey evidence. The data we have employed have the special advantage of containing a rich set of measures useful

7 The bivariate correlation between party identification and federal government support is −.209 and for federal officials it is −.081.

for unscrambling some of the ambiguities contained in our usual index of political trust or confidence. We make here several basic distinctions, both conceptually and operationally, that we then use to test a range of predictors of government support of various types. While the survey we use is not as rich in terms of providing a basis for creating multi-item indexes of the antecedent variables (excepting perceived power of the federal government), it nonetheless allows us to make some improvements over the usual way of measuring the dependent variables.

The most robust of our antecedents of political trust come out of a classically liberal theme of our political culture, which has to do with the personal relevance and perceived power of government. While there may be other senses in which these two cultural themes combine (Anderson 1990), we find that pragmatism and liberalism as premises each makes a contribution to our explanations. Still, there are a variety of other reasons people may have for developing their levels of confidence in government. These include some personal life experiences and political attitudes, such as life satisfaction and a sense of political efficacy, and more general feelings about other people, such as interpersonal trust and confidence in "the wisdom of the multitude." In addition, we see some impact of communication processes, such as for those who are more exposed to the mass media for their knowledge of politics versus those who rely more on their own experience with government as a premise for evaluation. Talk-radio listening appears to influence perceptions of public officials.

Where Next?

We do not propose here that we have fully resolved these problems of conceptualization and measurement. Cleaner measures of support could still be produced than the ones we were able to devise here in the course of our secondary analysis of others' evidence. We think that newer techniques of measuring emotions versus cognition in these kinds of attitudes will prove especially useful (Rahn and Clore 1994; Marcus and Rahn 1990; Hibbing and Theiss-Morse 1998). One needs to begin to take more into account a greater range of specific emotions. The latter may well include, on the downside, hate (Dionne 1991), anger (Tolchin 1996), fear or anxiety versus boredom (Marcus and MacKuen 1993), or depression (Rahn and Clore 1994). While we have not as yet come very far from the earliest attempts to measure these things (e.g., Agger et al. 1961), nonetheless there has been some progress. As we begin to disaggregate these phenomena even more, according to the new theories of social psychology, we should be able to move well beyond the stage of research at which our only useful conceptual handles were confined to various derivations of alienation theory (e.g., Wright 1976; Gamson 1968; Finifter 1972; Muller 1979; Schwartz 1973; Gilmour and Lamb 1975).

APPENDIX

Institutional Support Dependent Variables

General Support for Federal Government. Do you have a very favorable, mostly favorable, mostly unfavorable, or very unfavorable opinion of the federal government in Washington? (Q3)

Some people say they are basically content with the federal government, others say they are frustrated, and others say they are angry. Which of these best describes how you feel? (Q7)

Would you say you basically trust the federal government in Washington or not? (Q6)

Generally speaking, what is your opinion of departments and agencies of the federal government? Is it very favorable, mostly favorable, mostly unfavorable, or very unfavorable? (Q27B)

Scale alpha = .75 (Scored so that a high value indicates high support)

Support for Federal Officials. Most elected officials are trustworthy. Completely agree, mostly agree, mostly disagree, completely disagree. (Q31C)

Generally speaking, what is your opinion of elected federal officials? Is it very favorable, mostly favorable, mostly unfavorable, or very unfavorable? (Q27A)

Generally, how would you rate the ethical and moral practices of federal government officials? Would you give them an excellent, good, only fair, or poor rating? (Q32A)

Scale alpha = .71 (Scored so that a high value indicates high support for federal officials)

Independent Variables

Government Power. The federal government is interfering too much in state and local matters. Completely agree, mostly agree, mostly disagree, completely disagree. (Q24B)

The federal government is too powerful. Completely agree, mostly agree, mostly disagree, completely disagree. (Q24F)

Which one of the following statements comes closest to your views about government power today? The federal government has too much power. The federal government is now using about the right amount of power for meeting today's needs. The federal government should use its powers even more vigorously to promote the well-being of all segments of the people. (Q35)

The federal government controls too much of our daily lives. Completely agree, mostly agree, mostly disagree, completely disagree. (Q31A)

If 1 represents someone who generally believes that, on the whole, federal government programs should be cut back greatly to reduce the power of government, and 6 represents someone who feels that federal government programs should be maintained to deal with important problems, where on the scale of 1 to 6 would you place yourself? (Q8)

Scale alpha = .68 (Scored so that a low value indicates the government has too much power)

Fairness. The government is really run for the benefit of all the people. Completely agree, mostly agree, mostly disagree, completely disagree. (Q24E)

Personal Relevance. In general, is the federal government's effect on your life positive or negative? (DAYTODAY)

Government Inefficient. When something is run by the government it is usually inefficient and wasteful. Completely agree, mostly agree, mostly disagree, completely disagree. (Q24D)

Wrong Priorities. What do you personally feel is the bigger problem with government? Government has the wrong priorities, OR government has the right priorities but runs programs inefficiently? (Q13 recoded into GOVPRI2, where 1 = wrong priorities, 0 = all other responses)

More than Fair Share of Taxes. Considering what you get from the federal government, do you think you pay more than your fair share of taxes, less than your fair share, or about the right amount? (Q33 recoded into PAYTAX, where 1 = more than fair share, 0 = all other responses)

Quality of Life. First, let's talk about the quality of your life. Imagine a ladder with steps numbered from 0 at the bottom to 10 at the top. Suppose the top of the ladder represents the best possible life for you; and the bottom, the worst possible life for you. On which step of the ladder do you feel you personally stand at the present time? You can name any number between 0 and 10. (Q1)

Condition of U.S. Still thinking about the ladder (with steps numbered from 0 at the bottom to 10 at the top), suppose the top represents the best possible situation for our country; and the bottom, the worst possible situation. Please tell me on which step of the ladder you think the United States is at the present time? You can name any number between 0 and 10. (Q2)

Political Efficacy. Public officials don't care what people like me think. Completely agree, mostly agree, mostly disagree, completely disagree. (Q31B)

Party Identification. Republican (1), Independent (2), Democrat (3) (PARTYID)

Vote. How often would you say you vote? Always, nearly always, part of the time, or seldom? (Q37)

Influenced Impression of Government—Heard/Read or Personal Experience. What has most influenced your impression of the federal government . . . what you've heard or read OR things you've personally experienced? (Q5 recoded into GOVIMPR1, where 1 = heard/read, 0 = all other responses)

Talk Radio. How often do you listen to talk radio shows that invite listeners to call in to discuss current events, public issues, and politics? Regularly, sometimes, hardly ever, or never? (Q34D, recoded into TALKRAD)

Human Nature. Please tell me whether the first statement or the second statement comes closer to your views, even if neither is exactly right. Human nature is basically bad, and you can't be too careful in your dealings with people; OR Human nature is basically good, and people can be trusted. (Q14, recoded into HUMNAT, where 1 = basically bad, 2 = neither, 3 = basically good)

Wisdom of the American People. In general, how much trust and confidence do you have in the wisdom of the American people when it comes to making political decisions? A very great deal, a good deal, not very much, or none at all? (Q36)

13

The Psychology of Public Dissatisfaction with Government

TOM R. TYLER

The focus of the essays in this volume is on public dissatisfaction with government. The work outlined reflects a number of sophisticated efforts to understand trust and distrust in government, usually focused on "trust" as it is indexed by the widely studied "trust in government" scale. My own work on satisfaction and dissatisfaction has had a somewhat different focus. I have been concerned with the feelings of obligation that people feel they have to obey laws and accept the decisions of legal and political authorities. However, these feelings of obligation are also an important type of public beliefs that might potentially shape the viability of state authorities.

My perspective upon this different aspect of satisfaction suggests potentially interesting insights about two issues concerning the general study of public dissatisfaction with government. First, it suggests some potentially new issues about the focus of the study of distrust in government; issues that develop from an examination of the behavioral consequences of various possible types of dissatisfaction with the political system. Second, it helps us to expand our understanding of the antecedents of dissatisfaction—the factors that lead people to be dissatisfied with government.

The roots of my own approach to public views about the government lie in my early work with Jack Citrin and David Sears (Sears et al. 1978). In that work we examined the influence of attitudinal support for the government upon the willingness of the public to make personal sacrifices during a "crisis"—a national energy shortage. In response to this crisis the government asked citizens to behave in ways that involved personal sacrifices in the interest of society. The sacrifices requested by the government at that time involved deference to a variety of government requests to use less energy by turning off lights, conserving water, using carpool lanes, and so forth.

This initial study of citizen behavior helped me to frame what I have regarded as the key issue regarding political dissatisfaction. That issue is understanding how public attitudes about the political system and political authorities shape behaviors that are important to the viability of the political system. This issue is a core question of concern to political scientists who have long studied the influence of popular beliefs on the viability of democratic societies (Almond and Verba 1963, 1980; Dahl 1971, 1989; Inglehart 1990). For example, Dahl (1971) noted five public beliefs that he argued facilitated the development of democracy: (1) belief in the legitimacy of government institutions; (2) beliefs about the nature of authority relationships between government and governed; (3) confidence in the ability of government to deal with problems effectively; (4) political and interpersonal trust; and (5) belief in the possibility and desirability of political cooperation.

In the case of our study of the energy crisis the citizen behavior we studied was the willingness to voluntarily conserve energy. The government calls upon citizens to make a wide variety of types of sacrifice, ranging from obeying laws, serving in the military (Levi 1997), and paying taxes, as well as to engage in many types of proactive political behaviors, such as helping others in one's community and voting. My concern is with the role of satisfaction or dissatisfaction with government in shaping citizen willingness to engage in these various types of behaviors.

THE CONSEQUENCES OF DISSATISFACTION: WHICH POLITICAL BEHAVIORS ARE AFFECTED BY ATTITUDINAL DISSATISFACTION?

As my comments suggest, I believe that the importance of dissatisfaction with government stems from its impact upon the willingness of the public to engage in important civic behaviors. However, which civic behaviors are important? To address this issue, we must consider the impact of various types of citizen behaviors on the viability and effectiveness of legal and political authority. As the recent experience of societies such as Russia and Yugoslavia makes clear, political and legal systems are not automatically effective. Government is not always able to manage the problems within a society, and societies sometimes crumble, fragment, and descend into civil war and possible collapse. Hence, we need to be concerned about understanding what type of citizen behavior is needed for a system of political or legal authority to be effective. We should then explore the impact of dissatisfaction upon that behavior.

My own work has focused on one key behavior that is central to the viability of authority systems. That behavior is citizen compliance with the laws, rules, and policies established by legal and political authorities. We need this particular type of behavior from citizens for authorities to be able to manage a society. If noncompliance is widespread, the system of government that has been created to manage society's problems will not be able to do so effectively (Tyler 1990). Hence, the ability to gain compliance is central to political viability.

Of course, compliance with everyday laws is not the only important public behavior. Gibson (1996) studies the willingness to support a coup attempt in Russia—another type of politically important behavior—and finds that it is linked to public beliefs about law and government. Other political scientists study behaviors such as the willingness to strike, to occupy factories, to protest, and so forth (Muller and Jukam 1977). All of these involve the willingness of citizens to accept and follow, as opposed to disputing and potentially disobeying, rules. A fundamentally different type of behaviors is proactive behaviors that involve taking actions that help the political system, actions such as joining political groups, voting, and so forth. These behaviors have been more typically studied when political dissatisfaction is of concern, but they have not been the focus of my work.

There are several motivations that can lead citizens to comply with rules. The most direct is instrumental—people seek rewards and resources for themselves or the groups to which they belong for complying, or they fear punishment or the deprivation of resources to themselves or the groups to which they belong for failing to comply. While such instrumental behaviors influence people's compliance with the law to some degree, they are generally an inefficient system for producing effective governance. Society is seldom in a position to provide groups with desired resources, and is least able to provide such resources during times of emergency and crisis when citizen cooperation is most needed (Tyler 1990, 1996–7, 1997a). Further, the costs of the surveillance of public behavior required by punishment-based deterrence strategies are prohibitive.

In the case of the already mentioned energy crisis, the government saw some success in gaining desired behaviors through providing incentives, such as car-pool lanes, but had difficulty trying to monitor people's use of gasoline, electricity, and water. Because of the difficulties associated with such instrumental approaches, societies typically benefit from, and may ultimately depend upon, their ability to find other motivations that will encourage citizen behavior (Tyler 1990, 1996–7, 1997a).

An important source of additional motivation for citizen behavior lies in the internal values that lead citizens to voluntarily act on behalf of the state. For example, in the case of compliance with state authority, people's judgment that state authorities are legitimate and ought to be obeyed has been found to have an important influence upon their compliance behavior (Tyler 1990). This compliance is particularly important because it is voluntary and does not depend upon threats or promises from state authorities. Because of its voluntary character, such compliance behavior is especially important to the viability of the state. In other words, government authorities especially benefit from the consent and cooperation of those being governed. Beyond simple compliance, societies gain from voluntary deference to rules.

In my own work I focus on such voluntary compliance. Hence, my interest in attitudes about the legitimacy of government, a citizen attitude reflecting the belief that authorities are entitled to be obeyed, comes from the demonstration that legitimacy shapes voluntary compliance behavior (Tyler 1990). Consistent with the perspective I have outlined, my research suggests that legitimacy has an influence upon compliance that is independent of concerns about being caught and punished for wrongdoing. In other words, legitimacy motivates voluntary compliance with rules. Hence, having citizens who view authorities as legitimate facilitates effective governance by leading to widespread voluntary obedience to the law.

Strikingly, legitimacy has a stronger independent influence upon rule-following behavior than do judgments about the likelihood of being caught and punished for breaking rules. This suggests that legal and political authorities benefit from the existence of supportive attitudes in two ways. First, those supportive attitudes facilitate the voluntary acceptance of rules and decisions, lessening the need for command and control strategies that seek to shape citizen behavior via promised rewards or actual or threatened punishments. Second, these internal values have a stronger influence upon behavior than the influence that develops from command and control strategies based upon rewards and actual or threatened punishments. Both of these findings suggest that political and legal authorities may function less effectively if citizens distrust them (Tyler 1997b; 1998).

Beyond my own research focus, I think there is an important point to be drawn from my work for our understanding of the general framework that might be used in the study of citizen dissatisfaction with government. We can potentially study a wide variety of citizen attitudes, including trust in political authorities, trust in other people, views about the legitimacy of authorities, and support for the rule of law. Ultimately, the attitudes that are of concern to us depend upon the behaviors that we feel are central to the viability of the government. We are concerned about people's attitudes because we think they influence citizens' political behaviors. Hence, the attitudes we study should depend upon their behavioral consequences. Our concern with dissatisfaction with government needs to be grounded in assessments of the impact of such dissatisfaction upon citizen behavior.

Much of the research currently being conducted by political scientists has the level of "trust in government" as its ultimate concern. However, the behavioral consequences of trust are often unclear. Instead of focusing upon attitudes per se, I suggest that we need to focus upon identifying the behaviors that are key to societal functioning. We can then identify the attitudes that are the antecedents of such behaviors. It is those attitudes that ought to be the focus of our attention and concern.

I will illustrate the potential advantage of such an approach by distinguishing between trust in incumbent authorities and trust in the institutions and rules of government. The work on the energy crisis, which I have already outlined, drew upon this key distinction that was originally made by David Easton (Easton 1965b) between support for incumbent authorities ("specific" system support) and support for the underlying institutions and rules of government ("diffuse" system support). My own subsequent work has focused upon the support for rules, laws, and institutions that is the core feature of "diffuse" system support. I distinguish that support from evaluations of the performance of authorities.

In my work on attitudes toward legal authorities, I find that public attitudes about incumbent authorities and about rules and institutions can be empirically distinguished. One set of attitudes involves performance evaluations of current authorities—satisfaction or dissatisfaction with their ability to provide help or solve problems, as well as with their decisions and policies. This corresponds to the idea of "specific system support"—the evaluation of incumbent performance. The second type of attitudes are linked to assessments of the legitimacy of institutions and authorities—the feeling that their decisions ought to be respected and obeyed. These attitudes are more directly linked to "diffuse system support." I typically find that these two types of attitudes are correlated, but that they can be measured and studied separately.

When we separate performance evaluations and attitudes about rules and institutions, we find that these two types of attitudes lead to different types of behavior (Tyler 1998). As already mentioned, legitimacy leads to voluntary compliance with rules and decisions. Interestingly, however, performance evaluations do not influence voluntary compliance with rules. Further, performance evaluations are only weakly linked to legitimacy—the belief that one ought to obey. In other words, whether people feel that the police and courts are doing a good job does not influence whether they feel that those authorities ought to be obeyed, or whether they actually are voluntarily obeyed by those citizens.

The separation of performance evaluations from feelings of obligation to obey the law is not surprising, since obligation is an attitude that develops during the childhood socialization process, along with other basic political and social attitudes and values such as party identification, authoritarianism, attitudes toward ethnic groups and foreigners, and so forth. As a consequence, it is distinct from the later evaluations of policies and performance that are part of ongoing adult evaluations of particular incumbent authorities.

While they do not influence deference to rules, performance evaluations do influence people's willingness to take their problems before legal authorities. Those who think the police and courts do their jobs well are more likely to indicate that they go to the police or courts with problems or in emergencies. They also shape citizen willingness to empower legal authorities by giving them discretionary authority to decide how to handle crime and criminals, to hold suspects, to question citizens, and to make discretionary decisions about sentencing and parole. Hence, performance evaluations have important attitudinal and behavioral consequences of a different type.

These findings suggest that we should not assume that all attitudes toward authorities have the same behavioral consequences. In particular, attitudes of "specific" and "diffuse" system support represent two distinct aspects of satisfaction with authorities. For us to know which of these attitudes should be the focus of our concern, we need to better understand which of the behaviors that they influence are important to the viability of legal and political authority and, through that viability, the viability of society.

This behavioral perspective is important because, within the political science literature on public dissatisfaction with government, the conceptual nature of the dissatisfaction being studied has been unclear. This lack of clarity has developed because dissatisfaction is typically studied using items measuring "trust in government." These items do not clearly represent either "specific" or "diffuse" support. Instead, they can be interpreted as reflecting either construct, and their conceptual status has been the subject of debate (Citrin 1974). My work suggests the value of more clearly differentiating between these two aspects of public attitudes toward government authorities and institutions and of exploring the behavioral consequences of each.

The differentiation among these various types of attitudinal dissatisfaction also has another important possible gain. It might help us to develop a more differentiated view of citizens' changing orientations toward government. Based on the use of trust in government items, it has been widely suggested that people are becoming increasingly distrustful of government. However, it is not clear that people are increasingly viewing the government as illegitimate, in the sense of feeling less respect for the rules and institutions of government. Hence, it is not clear that voluntary compliance and deference toward law and public policies is declining. To address this question it is important to assess public dissatisfaction with incumbent authorities, as well as feelings about the institutions and rules of government.

Consider the example of attitudes concerning the legitimacy of legal and political authorities. Attitudes about the legitimacy of government authorities differ from incumbent evaluations, meaning that most efforts to study dissatisfaction using national surveys do not directly assess legitimacy. Hence, we need to more clearly distinguish "specific" and "diffuse" evaluations of government and to measure each separately on national surveys. This will help to clarify, over time, how citizens' views toward government are changing.

As this discussion of my approach makes clear, I have studied public dissatisfaction from a different perspective than that of most political scientists. My work suggests that political scientists might benefit from more broadly examining the behavioral consequences of various types of dissatisfaction. Such an examination, in the context of my own work, suggests that different types of dissatisfaction have different behavioral consequences.

Hence, my work suggests the value of defining the types of citizen behavior that shape the viability of the government as a first step in a strategy designed to identify the types of attitudinal dissatisfaction that should be the focus of our study.

THE ANTECEDENTS OF DISSATISFACTION: WHY ARE CITIZENS DISSATISFIED?

Interestingly, my research suggests that both "specific" and "diffuse" attitudes of support for the legal system have the same psychological roots. My studies of people's evaluations of legal and political authorities indicate that both performance evaluations and attitudes about the legitimacy of legal authorities are linked to evaluations of the fairness of the procedures used by authorities to make decisions and determine policies. This procedural justice effect suggests that the roots of public support for law and government lie in citizen assessments of the manner in which government authorities exercise their authority.

One example of these procedural justice effects is found in studies of personal experiences with the police and the courts. Tyler (1990) studied 652 citizens of Chicago with recent personal experiences with the police and courts. He explored the impact of experience on performance evaluations and evaluations of the legitimacy of the police and courts. The

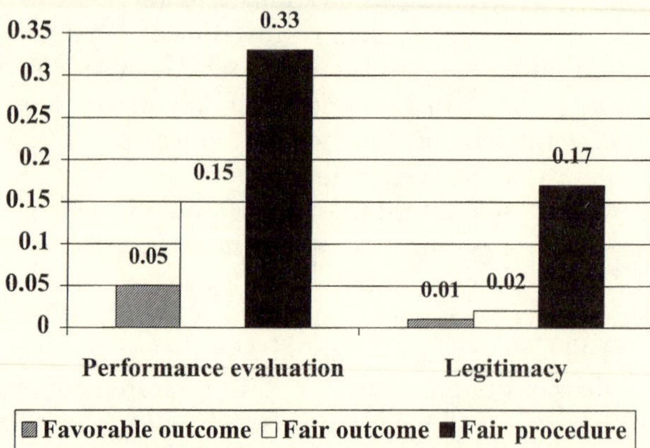

Figure 13.1. The Impact of Experience on the Evaluation of Legal Authorities.

study considered subjective assessments of three aspects of experience: the favorability of the outcomes or decisions of the authority with whom people were dealing; the fairness of the outcome people received from those authorities; and the fairness of the decision-making procedures the authorities used to make their decisions about how to handle the issues or problems of concern.

The results of this study are shown in Figure 13.1. The numbers shown are beta weights reflecting the relative independent influence of the various factors on the dependent variable, when all factors are simultaneously included within a regression equation. The results shown in Figure 13.1 indicate that procedural justice was the primary factor shaping the influence of experience upon both performance evaluations and attitudes about the legitimacy of legal authorities. In other words, people did not react to the degree to which they received a personally beneficial decision. Instead, they reacted to how fairly the decision was made by the authority.

This procedural justice effect is widely found. It occurs when people are dealing with authorities about substantial sums of money (Lind, Kulik, Ambrose, de Vera Park 1993), about serious possible deprivations of liberty (Casper, Tyler, Fisher 1988), and about personally important decisions such as child custody and divorce (Kitzmann and Emery 1993).

The studies that I have outlined explore the influence of procedural justice in situations in which people have direct personal experience with the authorities. This situation differs from the typical situation of political satisfaction. In that situation citizens are asked to evaluate authorities with whom they have had little or no direct personal experience. Few citizens have dealt with their congressperson, with the president, or with

Table 13.1. *The Role of Procedural Justice in Shaping Evaluations of the Legitimacy of the Supreme Court*

	Legitimacy of the Court's Institutional Responsibility to Interpret the Constitution	Obligation to Obey Government	Willingness to Empower the Court to Make Abortion Decisions
Agree with Court Decisions/ Policies	.04	.03	.16*
Fairness of Court Decisions	.08	–.03	.26*
Justice of Court Decision-Making Procedures	.13*	.31*	.43*

Note: The entries are beta weights reflecting the independent influence of each factor in an equation in which all terms are entered along with background factors. For a detailed discussion of this analysis, see Tyler and Mitchell (1994). * Coefficients significantly different from zero.

national-level authorities such as Supreme Court justices. Hence, their evaluations are typically based upon abstract impersonal judgments of those government agencies and officials.

Tyler and Mitchell (1994) explore the basis of the legitimacy of one national institution: the United States Supreme Court. They do so using interviews conducted with a random sample of the citizens of the San Francisco bay area. Those citizens were asked about their views concerning the legitimacy of the institutional role of the Court, their perceived obligation to obey government decisions, and their willingness to empower the Court to make controversial policy decisions in the area of abortion. The results of their analysis are shown in Table 13.1 (drawn from Tyler and Mitchell 1994, 768). This table shows the relative independent influence of agreement with decisions, assessments of decision fairness, and evaluations of procedural fairness in shaping indices of the Court's legitimacy. They indicate that all three indices of legitimacy were primarily responsive to evaluations of the procedural fairness of Court decision making.

Tyler (1994) conducts a similar analysis of the legitimacy of the United States Congress. This analysis is based upon a different sample of citizens from the San Francisco bay area, stratified to include a disproportionate number of minority citizens. In this analysis the procedural justice of congressional decision making was established by asking citizens to evaluate four elements of decision making: voice, neutrality, trustworthiness, and respect for citizen rights ("standing"). These procedural

Table 13.2. *The Role of Procedural Justice in Shaping Evaluations of Congress*

	Trust in Congress	Obligation to Obey Congressional Decisions
Degree to Which You Agree with Congressional Decisions/Policies	.23*	.04
Degree to Which You Are Allowed to Make Arguments about What Policy Should Be (Voice)	–.02	–.10*
Neutrality of Congress	.24*	.26*
Trust in the Motives of Congressional Decision Makers	.17*	.06
How Concerned is Congress with Citizen Rights?	.21*	.11*
Adjusted R-Squared	.45	.21

Note: Trust in Congress is measured using traditional trust in government items. Obligation reflects citizen feelings that they ought to obey the laws and policies of the Federal government. For a detailed discussion of the results, see Tyler (1994). Entries are beta weights reflecting the relative independent influence of the factors, when controls are made on background factors. * Significant entries.

elements are discussed in more detail later in this chapter. The influence of these four elements of procedural fairness is compared to that of the favorability of the decisions made by Congress. The dependent variables are evaluations of the quality of Congress as an institution of government ("performance evaluations"), and judgments about whether one is obligated to follow the rules enacted by Congress.

The results of this analysis of citizen evaluations of Congress are shown in Table 13.2 (these findings are drawn from Tyler 1994, 825). They indicate that performance evaluations of Congress are shaped by both the favorability of congressional policies and by independent evaluations of (1) congressional neutrality, (2) trust in the motives of the members of Congress, and (3) respect for citizen rights. Evaluations of citizen obligation to obey congressional rules and decisions are shaped by procedural evaluations, particularly assessments of the neutrality of Congress and its respect for citizen rights. Obligation is not influenced by agreement with congressional decisions.

These findings, together with those already outlined concerning the Supreme Court, suggest that procedural justice influences are strong when the focus of attention is citizen evaluations of national political and legal authorities. With both the Supreme Court and Congress, citizen evaluations of legitimacy and obligation are strongly influenced by assessments of the fairness of institutional decision making. These findings support those based upon citizens' personal experiences with government authorities in arguing for the centrality of procedural justice judgments as an antecedent to attitudes of support for government authorities and institutions.

PROCEDURAL JUSTICE AND THE DEVELOPMENT AND MAINTENANCE OF INTERNAL VALUES

As I have noted, one especially important issue is exploring what shapes the development and maintenance of supportive attitudes toward authorities and institutions. Studies suggest that procedural justice has a strong positive influence upon people's attitudes about authorities and rules (Korsgaard, Schweiger, and Sapienza 1995; Tyler, Casper, and Fisher 1989). Hence, the use of fair procedures leads to attitudinal support for law and legal and political authorities. As this finding would suggest, procedural justice is found to produce behavior change that persists over time (Paternoster, Brame, Bachman, and Sherman 1997; Pruitt et al. 1993).

These findings suggest that both "specific" system support and "diffuse" system support are shaped by judgments about the fairness of government procedures. That is, irrespective of whether we are concerned with the legitimacy of government institutions and rules or with people's attitudes toward particular incumbent authorities or officials, we should focus upon people's understanding of the manner in which those authorities make their decisions.

WHAT ELEMENT OF PROCEDURES LEADS THEM TO BE VIEWED AS FAIR?

This concern about procedures leads us to want to understand what procedural justice means to citizens dealing with government authority. In my own work, I explore the influence of five judgments upon people's views about the fairness of the decision making they have experienced when dealing with legal authorities (i.e., police officers and judges). Those judgments are the favorability of the outcome (the amount lost/gained), the degree to which people are given an opportunity to make arguments (voice), people's trust in the motives of authorities, the degree to which people feel that the authorities treat them with respect, and people's assessments of the neutrality of the government authorities with whom they are dealing.

The influence of judgments about these five aspects of personal experience when dealing with legal authorities on assessments of the fairness of the decision-making procedures utilized are shown in Figure 13.2.

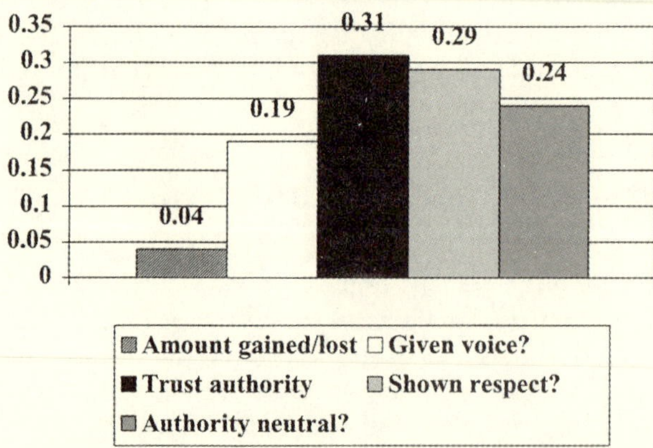

Figure 13.2. Influences on Judgments About the Fairness of a Legal Procedure.

They indicate that the primary issues people considered when evaluating the police and the courts were their trust in the motives of authorities, the degree to which they felt treated with respect and dignity by those authorities, and their assessment of the neutrality of the authorities. I refer to these issues as "relational" issues (Tyler and Lind 1992) because they represent people's judgments about the quality of their relationships with legal authorities. Interestingly, people did not judge the fairness of legal procedures by the degree to which they gained or lost from those procedures; that is, whether or not they received effective help when they called the police, were arrested or received a ticket when stopped by the police, or won or lost their case when they went to court.

It is also possible to explore the direct impact of these judgments about procedural elements upon attitudes about the quality of the performance of legal authorities and about their legitimacy. Figure 13.3 shows the results of such an analysis. It indicates that the primary direct influence upon both judgments of performance evaluation and legitimacy comes from judgments about the trustworthiness of authorities.

These findings further support the argument that the roots of specific and diffuse support lie within the same psychological model. It has already been shown that both judgments are responsive to assessments of the fairness of the decision-making procedures used by the authorities. This analysis further suggests that both performance evaluations and judgments about legitimacy are linked to judgments about the trustworthiness of authorities.

These analyses can be expanded by considering the previously outlined studies of citizen evaluations of national-level legal and political institutions. First, consider the Supreme Court. Table 13.3 shows the results of

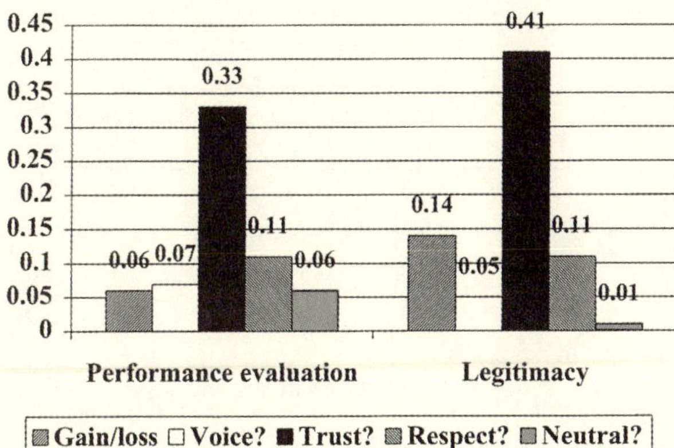

Figure 13.3. Aspects of Experience Influencing Performance Evaluations and Legitimacy.

Table 13.3. *Elements of Fair Decision-Making Procedures: The Supreme Court*

	Procedural Justice of the Supreme Court
Ability to Influence the Decisions of the Court	–.13
Neutrality	.48*
Trustworthiness of the Members of Congress	.34*
Respect for the Rights of Citizens	.10
Adjusted R-Squared	.60

Note: The entries are beta weights reflecting the independent influence of each factor in an equation in which all terms are entered along with background factors. For a detailed discussion of this analysis, see Tyler and Mitchell (1994). * Coefficients significantly different from zero.

a regression analysis exploring the antecedents of citizen judgments about the fairness of Supreme Court decision-making procedures (Tyler and Mitchell 1994, 775). The results suggest that both neutrality and the trustworthiness of the motives of the justices shape evaluations of the fairness of their decision making. Agreement with decisions or judgments about the ability to influence those decisions had no influence upon procedural fairness judgments. A similar analysis of Congress shows that evaluations of the fairness of its decision-making procedures are linked to assessments of congressional neutrality, trust in the motives of

Table 13.4. *Elements of Fair Decision-Making Procedures: Congress*

	Procedural Justice of Congress
Degree to Which You Agree with Congressional Decisions/Policies	.10*
Degree to Which You Are Allowed to Make Arguments about What Policy Should Be (Voice)	.03
Neutrality of Congress	.31*
Trust in the Motives of Congressional Decision Makers	.25*
How Concerned Is Congress with Citizen Rights?	.14*
Adjusted R-Squared	.44

Note: For a detailed discussion of the results, see Tyler (1994). Entries are beta weights reflecting the relative independent influence of the factors, when controls are made on background factors. * Significant entries.

Congress members, and evaluations of the respect Congress shows for citizen rights (see Table 13.4, from Tyler 1994, 825). Agreement with congressional decisions has a minor independent influence upon procedural justice judgments.

What is the model that these analyses support? A model that suggests that people's judgments about the fairness of the procedures authorities use to make decisions are based upon issues that reflect the nature of their relationship with authorities. People do not judge decision-making procedures by determining whether they agree with the decisions made. Their judgments seem more strongly linked to issues that reflect the character of the authorities. In particular, trust in the motives of the authorities is typically found to be central to evaluations of procedures.

What aspect of the character of authorities is important? We can distinguish between two aspects that are potentially important: judgments of competence and judgments of benevolence. Competence refers to the ability to solve problems effectively. Benevolence refers to having a concern about treating citizens with dignity and respect and being sincerely interested in their needs, problems, and concerns. These two elements in authorities are related but can be distinctly assessed and measured.

Using the data collected by Tyler (1990) on citizen evaluations of the police and courts, these two aspects of citizen evaluations can be separately assessed on two levels: (1) as a general evaluation among all citi-

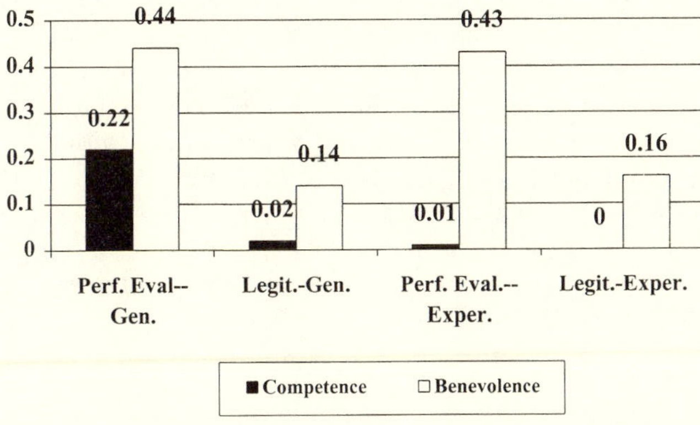

Figure 13.4. Competence and Benevolence as Antecedents of Evaluation.

zens ($n = 1{,}575$), irrespective of whether or not they have had recent personal experience with legal authorities; and (2) as evaluations of two distinct aspects of people's personal experiences with legal authorities among those citizens ($n = 652$) with recent personal experience with the police or courts. In each case, we can examine the relative independent impact of each judgment upon performance evaluations and judgments about the legitimacy of legal authorities.

The results of an examination of the impact of competence and benevolence upon performance evaluations and judgments about legitimacy are shown in Figure 13.4. They suggest that, irrespective of whether people are making general judgments or judgments based upon personal experience, judgments of benevolence dominate their performance evaluations and their assessments of legitimacy. This suggests that people are primarily reacting to legal authorities by determining the degree to which they feel those authorities are sincerely trying to be responsive to their needs and concerns. They are less directly influenced by judgments about the competence of the authorities—that is, the extent to which those authorities are effective in making decisions and handling problems.

Summary. These findings about the psychological antecedents of dissatisfaction suggest that people evaluate government officials through an ethical frame. In particular, they are concerned about whether officials make decisions in ways that show a sensitivity and concern to the rights of citizens, a concern with their welfare, and an absence of bias or favoritism. If made in this way, decisions are viewed as fair and are deferred to by members of the public. This is true both of the police officers and judges with whom the public has personal experience and of the national-level leaders known primarily via indirect means.

The findings highlight the centrality of the ethical climate of government to the development and maintenance of supportive public attitudes toward the law and government. People's evaluations of government are clearly tied to ethical judgments. They are not primarily a response to feeling that one has gained or lost when dealing with government, or that government policies are desired or not desired. Instead, people engage in a much broader ethical evaluation of how government functions by evaluating the actions of political leaders and institutions against criteria of justice that are distinct from personal gain/loss or personal judgments about the desirability of government decisions and policies.

14

The Means Is *the End*

JOHN R. HIBBING AND ELIZABETH THEISS-MORSE

Explanations for Americans' unhappiness with government are as plentiful as grains of sand. Even among the contributors to this volume, a remarkable diversity of suspected causes is apparent. This is as it should be since there are undoubtedly multiple explanations for such a complex phenomenon. How could we expect there to be a single reason for the sentiments of so many different people toward so many different governmental referents over so many different eras, years, and days? Suggesting that a common theme can be observed among the chapters in this volume is a risky endeavor. The authors utilize different methodologies, data sets, theories, and interpretations, and their work should and does stand on its own. The last thing we as editors wish to do is to cram anyone's work into a theoretical perspective with which he or she may not be totally comfortable.

PROCESS MORE THAN POLICY

This being said, when taken as a whole, the strategies and findings of the contributors do seem to point toward a certain set of explanations and away from another set. More specifically, we are struck by the frequency with which theories and findings suggest explanations based on the way government works and not explanations based on what government produces. Readers will need to look closely to find instances in which a researcher hypothesizes and then finds supportive evidence that particular governmental outputs or even societal outcomes and conditions are the source of public dissatisfaction with government.

Perhaps the closest we come is Citrin and Luks' suspicion that economic conditions and similar "contextual" factors affect the public's mood toward government, but they hasten to point out the instances in which these conditions fail to account for shifts in public attitudes. Alford's imaginative explanation might also be interpreted as an instance of a policy success leading government to be less popular. The United States wins the Cold War and is therefore deprived of a clear and consistent outside threat, which in turn leads people to be less likely to unite in support of our government.

Elsewhere, output and outcome variables fare much worse. Chanley, Rudolph, and Rahn find that "trust and responsiveness are not . . . directly influenced by . . . measures of policy outcomes." If the condition of the country were a dominant influence on public attitudes toward government, why, as Richardson, Houston, and Hadjiharalambous show, does approval vary so much across different institutions at the same point in time? (In fairness, they do find that economic conditions affect attitudes toward the president, though not the other branches.) Bernstein finds little support for the "partisan control" theory that holds that we like government when our fellow partisans are in power and can produce policies we like. In fact, Bernstein finds that approval of a Republican president is actually associated positively with approval of a Democratic Congress. At best, Uslaner finds "weak" support for a connection between partisanship, perceptions of government performance, and approval of government. More directly, Hetherington and Nugent find absolutely no support for the expectation that the performance, capabilities, and efficiency of government (in the case of their study, state government) has any impact on public evaluations of government. Brady and Theriault stress that public opinion of Congress suffers because many members skate around tough issues, use extreme and hyperbolic rhetoric, and bash the institution. In fact, Brady and Theriault find that the actual centrist accomplishments of Congress are often obscured from public view by noncentrist members' dominance of the airwaves. Again, it is not what government does but how it does it that seems to be telling. This is precisely the finding, at least, of Funk's experimental work as she discovers that subjects are more turned off by acrimonious debate than by cordial debate.

All this is quite consistent with Tyler's long-standing emphasis on the public's desire for "procedural justice." His research on people's sentiments toward the police and other legal authorities with whom they had recently interacted indicates that attitudes "are linked to evaluations of the fairness of the procedures used by authorities." Surprisingly, people "did not react to the degree to which they received a personally beneficial decision." Additional survey work by Tyler, albeit with a non-national sample, suggests that perceptions of fairness are also central to people's evaluations of institutions such as the Supreme Court and Congress. Our own previous research on public attitudes toward Congress leads us to conclude that "people's views of the political system . . . are shaped not just by policy outcomes . . . but primarily by the processes employed" (Hibbing and Theiss-Morse 1995, 145). Assuming for the sake of argument that previous theorizing (see especially Levi 1998) as well as the findings presented here and elsewhere (see especially Tyler's work) are somewhat convincing in calling attention to the importance of process, the obvious question becomes which particular processes lead people to feel better about their government?

VOICE AND ACCOUNTABILITY, NO: EMPATHETIC AND OBJECTIVE DECISION MAKERS, YES

What political processes people prefer is an issue we have addressed elsewhere at some length (see Hibbing and Theiss-Morse 2002), so here we will only draw attention to the conclusion of ours that is probably the most counterintuitive. Conventional wisdom holds that Americans love democracy and respond favorably to any opportunity to give ordinary people a greater role in the political decision-making process. Witness Americans' fondness for initiatives and referenda, their predilection for making every governmental position an elective position, their desire to open all corners of the polity to public view, and their establishment of a nearly universal primary election system. As Fishkin (1995) notes, anything the founders set up as remotely nondemocratic, such as the electoral college and indirect Senate elections, has eventually been eroded by popular pressure. Surely Anthony King has it right when he observes that "the American people are, and have been for a very long time, the western world's 'hyperdemocrats.' They are keener on democracy than almost anyone else and are more determined that democratic norms and practices should pervade every aspect of national life" (1997, 52). In investigating people's preferences, one of Tyler's first instincts is that people will be more favorable toward procedures in which they have been provided a voice. Is it not likely that if a process allows us to put in "our two cents worth," we will view that process as being more legitimate?

We acknowledge that such beliefs are widespread. Everyone seems eager to find ways of getting the people more involved with the governing process (see Headlam 1933; Dahl 1970; Etzioni 1972; MacDonald 1986; the Jefferson Center 1988; and Fishkin 1995). One of the main reasons for doing so is the belief that public involvement, especially involvement in meaningful deliberation, will enhance system legitimacy (see Cohen 1989; Dryzek 1990; Gutmann and Thompson 1996; and Manin 1987). But we would like to close this volume with a plea that observers refrain from assuming automatically that the connection between participatory deliberation and approval of government is positive.

Sometimes if people are allowed to make their case they will be more upset with the eventual decision than if they had never been in a position to speak to the issue in the first place. By participating and being forced into some form of contact with people of divergent opinions, people may actually become bitter and estranged rather than become newly invigorated and more favorably disposed. Consider the following comment volunteered to us by Ernie, a focus group participant in 1997.

> I know the only kind of political background I had was my senior year of civics, really, and when I took [indecipherable] at a junior college. But it was never an interest. . . . And then the last election [1996] was the first time I just said, 'hey, you know, I'm always bitching about this and this and that.' So I registered and voted. You know and I think that out of . . . all the changes that I wanted, I think only one of them happened, you know . . . I could care less right now because it's just like everything you wanted to see changed still hasn't happened.

As is apparent, Ernie's foray into participatory politics had clear negative consequences. He went from someone who was basically out of touch with government to someone who was disgusted with it. Ernie "could care less right now" because of his experience. In this case, at least, participation most definitely did *not* lead to a more favorable view of government.

But perhaps this is because Ernie only voted; he did not really get involved in a meaningful, deliberative forum. Maybe weak democratic acts like voting do not have positive repercussions for attitudes toward the political system, but strong democratic acts like discussing issues and working with compatriots on those issues will indeed generate approval, support, and legitimacy (Barber 1984). The evidence for such beliefs consists mostly of unsubstantiated assertions and, in fact, systematic analysis suggests the relationship may be just the opposite. Consider Jane Mansbridge's careful observations of a New England town meeting. When she talked to people who had just participated in this version of strong democracy, eight townspeople gave the following descriptions of participatory democracy (Mansbridge 1980, 60–65):

> Well to me, all it is is more or less a fight . . . a big argument.
> You get quarreling and a big hubbub.
> It's just bickering back and forth.
> There are too damn many arguments.
> People knowingly going against one another, that is what I don't like.
> No one likes each other.
> They get so darned personal at town meetings.
> There are too many personalities involved.

Seeing the process up close or even being involved in that process frequently creates negative feelings toward the process. These feelings are particularly obvious among those who are most in need of governmental attention, as face-to-face deliberative democracy often "accentuates rather than redress(es) the disadvantage of those with least power in a society" (Mansbridge 1980, 277). As one farmer put it, "There's a few people who really are brave enough to get up and say what they think in town meetings . . . now myself, I feel inferior, in ways, to other people . . . a lot of [people] feel that way" (1980, 60).

If face-to-face deliberative democracy is the key to reconnecting people to politics as so many communitarians and deliberative democrats claim, why in those instances where people have the real opportunity to deliberate with their neighbors are people disconnecting themselves as fast as they can? Hampson documents the epidemic decline in attendance, interest, and debate in New England town meetings. He notes that "in the old days" there would be 900 people at town meetings, even 200 a few years ago, but that now you are lucky to get 50, "and nearly half of them are town employees or school board members" (Hampson 1996). In Hampton, Connecticut, "the highlight of the political year used to be the town meeting where the budget was voice-voted up or down. But for the past five years voters have insisted the Hampton budget be approved via referendum" (Hampson 1996).

Tyler's research contains tantalizing support for these contentions. Though he hypothesizes that the perceived ability to "make arguments to" or to "influence decisions of" a political body (such as Congress or the Supreme Court) should lead an individual to be more favorable toward that body, this relationship does not materialize. In fact, the coefficients for these relationships are usually negative (see his Tables 13.2 and 13.3 in this volume) and sometimes reach statistical significance in the negative direction. This suggests that the greater a person's perceived involvement with a political entity, the less the person tends to like or respect that entity. This finding is completely at odds with traditional claims concerning the benefits of participation for system legitimacy. It is, however, perfectly consistent with our revisionist view that more participation does not elevate the public's evaluations of government and may very well harm those evaluations.

Even such supporters of deliberative democracy as Gutmann and Thompson concede that "extending the domain of deliberation has the risk of creating even greater conflict than it is intended to solve" (1996, 44). More colloquially, one of Morris Rosenberg's ordinary interviewees from Ithaca, New York, in the early 1950s said that he stayed away from politics because "there is no harm in avoiding unnecessary conflicts" (1954–5, 350).

The key to creating a process that makes people feel good about government is not finding ways to get people more involved in politics. Many ordinary Americans are surprisingly eager to have someone else make political decisions, as is illustrated by the sentiments of this focus group participant:

> When I leave here [the focus group session], when I walk out this door, I'm not going to volunteer for anything. I'm not going to get involved in anything. I mean I know this. I'm not going to pretend I'm some political activist. I'm lazy. I'm not going to do it. I'm too busy obsessing on other things going on in my life. ... So somebody's got to do it. I want them [politicians] to do [it]. ... I don't want the job. I'm not interested in it.

But here is the kicker. Although most people would rather defer political discussions and decision-making power to somebody else, they are very concerned that those who end up making the decisions are not in a position to benefit directly from those decisions. The public is less concerned than is typically imagined with decision makers doing exactly as the people wish on all issues. Indeed, most people recognize quite candidly that they do not follow issue debates carefully enough to make such a process work. They just want to be secure in the belief that whatever decisions have been made were taken in the interests of the people and not in the self-interest of the decision makers.

This sentiment explains why Tyler consistently finds strongest support for variables such as perceptions of the "neutrality" of the decision-making body, trust in the motives of those making the decisions, and perceptions of the body's level of concern for citizens (again, see Tables 13.2 and 13.3 in this volume). He demonstrates that these concepts are strongly and positively related to people's approval of the pertinent governmental body. This is why the Supreme Court is viewed much more favorably than other political bodies. The Court, after all, makes many decisions (for example, flag burning) that the public believes to be seriously wrong-headed but are well-regarded by the public because of the perception that judges make their mistakes honestly; that is, they do not profit materially from their decisions. Congress and special interests, on the other hand, are placed at the epicenter of what the public dislikes about government because they are seen to be self-interested.

The public categorically rejects the vision of most elite observers that pluralistic competition among interests quite appropriately leads to enlightened, brokered solutions that capture and integrate the diverse sentiments of people across the country. "You ordinary people might not realize it but you are all represented by special interests and many of you belong to special interests," elite observers persist in saying. Elite observers might just as well save their breath. The people's vision is that there is the public interest and then there are special interests. Special interests, by their very nature, are concerned with their own interests. The public interest, by its very nature, is concerned with the welfare of all salt-of-the-earth Americans. The popular perception is that these two camps—special interests and the public interest—are locked in a zero-sum struggle that transcends ideology. Whether special interests are best seen as residing on the left or the right of the political spectrum is immaterial. All that matters to the people is that it appears as though the special interests are winning—and have been winning since the late 1960s when diversity, discord, cynical reporting, and big money involvement in politics gave birth, or at least new life, to the special interests–public interest dichotomy.

CONCLUSION

We believe the American public's desire for empathetic, non–self-interested decision makers (rather than for certain policies and policy outcomes) allows us to integrate many, though certainly not all, of the research contained in this volume. It helps to explain why attitudes toward government fell off the table in the late 1960s/early 1970s, and why specific conditions of the country and specific governmental achievements do not seem to explain longitudinal variations in those attitudes (see Citrin and Luks, Alford, Bennett, and Chanley, Rudolph, and Rahn).

It helps to explain why approval of certain institutions, like the Court, is higher and is explained by a different set of factors than approval of other institutions, such as Congress, even though all institutions operate in the same overall societal climate and policy mix (see Richardson, Houston, and Hadjiharalambous). It helps to explain why the match between the particular party in control of institutions (like the Congress and the presidency) and the party affiliation of an ordinary person does not make more difference in that person's evaluations of those institutions (see Bernstein). It helps to explain both why people are generally warmer toward state and local government that, relative to the federal government, they believe to be in a position to be more empathetic toward and in touch with the concerns of ordinary people, and why variations in support are driven less by partisan and ideological preferences (see Uslaner) and more by a belief that anything is better than the special-interest–dominated mess in Washington (Hetherington and Nugent).

It helps to explain why actions of politicians that can be interpreted as furthering divisions, acrimony, partisanship, ideological extremism, and, generally, the self-interest of politicians (see Fried and Harris, Brady and Theriault, and Funk) all diminish government in the eyes of the people. It helps to explain why Owen and Dennis found evaluations of government to be most damaged by people's perceptions that government is not relevant to their own lives and that government has much power. (Indeed, traditional explanations would be hard-pressed to account for why respondents would care about the government at all if it were perceived to be irrelevant, but if people's concerns are not for favorable policies but for non–self-interested governmental decisions, the power of Government becomes crucial regardless of its perceived relevance.) As we noted earlier, it is perfectly consistent with Tyler's finding that voice does not help and may damage evaluations of government but that decision makers who are perceived to be altruistically motivated have a powerful positive impact on those evaluations (but see Tyler, Rasinski, and Spodick 1985).

Of course, the situation is nowhere near as tidy as we have just implied. No complex phenomenon such as public attitudes toward government can be neatly explained. But we do believe that the research contained here, on balance, favors procedural rather than policy explanations for Americans' dissatisfaction with government *and* greatly advances our understanding of the kinds of procedures and procedural arrangements that people prefer. If our interpretation of this general thrust is correct, then the public's negativity toward government is unlikely to be corrected by a series of policy decisions that could in some sense be deemed as wise or even by societal conditions that could in some sense be deemed as favorable. Moreover, public negativity is unlikely to be corrected by attempts to facilitate public involvement in the political process. Rather, the best strategy for improving public attitudes toward government is to enact reforms that would make it difficult or impossible for decision makers to feather their own nests by virtue of the decisions they render. The people's apparent clamoring for populist or even direct democracy has misled too many reformers into thinking empowering the people is the answer. In actuality, the preference for people-power is merely a manifestation of the public's aversion to being taken advantage of by special interests and self-interested politicians, and therefore suggests an entirely different reform strategy.

References

Aberbach, Joel, Robert D. Putnam, and Bert A. Rockman. 1981. *Bureaucrats and Politicians in Western Democracies.* Cambridge, MA: Harvard University Press.

Abramowitz, Alan I. 1980. "The United States: Political Culture under Stress." In Gabriel A. Almond and Sidney Verba, eds., *The Civic Culture Revisited.* Boston: Little, Brown.

Abramson, Paul R. 1977. *The Political Socialization of Black Americans: A Critical Evaluation of Research on Efficacy and Trust.* New York: The Free Press.

Abramson, Paul R. 1983. *Political Attitudes in America: Formation and Change.* San Francisco: Freeman.

Abramson, Paul R., and Ada W. Finifter. 1981. "On the Meaning of Political Trust: New Evidence from Items Introduced in 1978." *American Journal of Political Science* 25:297–307.

Advisory Commission on Intergovernmental Relations. 1990. *State Fiscal Capacity and Effort.* Washington, DC: ACIR.

Agger, R. E., M. N. Goldstein, and S. A. Pearl. 1961. "Political Cynicism: Measurement and Meaning." *Journal of Politics* 23:477–506.

Almond, Gabriel A., and Sidney Verba. 1963. *The Civic Culture: Political Attitudes and Democracy in Five Nations.* Princeton, NJ: Princeton University Press.

Almond, Gabriel A., and Sidney Verba, eds. 1980. *The Civic Culture Revisited.* Boston: Little, Brown.

Anderson, Charles W. 1990. *Pragmatic Liberalism.* Chicago: University of Chicago Press.

Apple, R. W., Jr. 1998. "The Testing of a President: The Assessment." *New York Times*, September 22, 17.

Balz, Dan, and Ronald Brownstein. 1996. *Storming the Gates: Protest Politics and the Republican Revival.* Boston: Little, Brown.

Barber, Benjamin R. 1984. *Strong Democracy: Participatory Politics for a New Age.* Berkeley: University of California Press.

Barber, Bernard. 1983. *The Logic and Limits of Trust.* New Brunswick, NJ: Rutgers University Press.

Barry, John M. 1990. *The Ambition and the Power.* New York: Penguin.

Beck, Paul A., Hal G. Rainey, and Carol Traut. 1990. "Disadvantage, Disaffection, and Race as Divergent Bases for Citizen Fiscal Policy Preferences." *Journal of Politics* 52:71–93.

References

Beer, Samuel H. 1993. *To Make a Nation: The Rediscovery of American Federalism*. Cambridge, MA: Belknap Press.

Bellah, Robert N., Richard Madsen, William M. Sullivan, Ann Swidler, and Steven M. Tipton. 1985. *Habits of the Heart: Individualism and Commitment in American Life*. Berkeley: University of California Press.

Bennett, Linda L. M., and Stephen Earl Bennett. 1990. *Living with Leviathan: Americans Coming to Terms with Big Government*. Lawrence, KS: University Press of Kansas.

Berscheid, Ellen. 1985. "Interpersonal Attraction." In G. Lindzey and E. Aronson, eds., *Handbook of Social Psychology*, third ed. New York: Random House.

Blendon, Robert J., J. M. Benson, R. Morin, D. E. Altman, M. Brodie, M. Brossard, and M. James. 1997. "Changing Attitudes in America." In Joseph S. Nye, Jr., Philip D. Zelikow, and David C. King, eds., *Why People Don't Trust Government*. Cambridge, MA: Harvard University Press.

Bloom, Howard S., and H. Douglas Price. 1975. "Voter Response to Short-Run Economic Conditions: The Asymmetric Effect of Prosperity and Recession." *American Political Science Review* 69:1240–54.

Bok, Derek. 1997. "Measuring the Performance of Government." In Joseph S. Nye, Jr., Philip D. Zelikow, and David C. King, eds., *Why People Don't Trust Government*. Cambridge, MA: Harvard University Press.

Born, Richard. 1990. "The Shared Fortunes of Congress and Congressmen: Members May Run from Congress, But They Can't Hide." *Journal of Politics* 52:1223–41.

Bourdieu, Pierre. 1977. *Outline of a Theory of Practice*. Trans. Richard Nice. Cambridge: Cambridge University Press.

Bowman, Ann O'M., and Richard C. Kearney. 1986. *The Resurgence of the States*. Englewood Cliffs, NJ: Prentice-Hall.

Brady, David W., and Craig Volden. 1998. *Revolving Gridlock: Politics and Policy from Carter to Clinton*. Boulder, CO: Westview Press.

Braithwaite, Valerie, and Margaret Levi, eds. 1998. *Trust and Governance*. New York: Russell Sage.

Brehm, John, and Wendy Rahn. 1997. "Individual-Level Evidence for the Causes and Consequences of Social Capital." *American Journal of Political Science* 41:999–1023.

Broder, David S., and Dan Balz. 1999. "Scandal's Damage Wide, If Not Deep." *Washington Post* (February 11): A1.

Bryce, James. 1888. *The American Commonwealth, 3 vols*. London: MacMillan and Co.

Burnham, Walter Dean. 1997. "Bill Clinton: Riding the Tiger." In Walter Dean Burnham, William McWilliams, and Gerald M. Pomper, eds., *The Election of 1996*. Chatham, NJ: Chatham House.

Byrne, Donn. 1971. *The Attraction Paradigm*. New York: Academic Press.

Caldeira, Gregory A. 1986. "Neither the Purse nor the Sword: Dynamics of Public Confidence in the Supreme Court." *American Political Science Review* 80:1209–26.

Caldeira, Gregory A., and James L. Gibson. 1992. "The Etiology of Public Support for the Supreme Court." *American Journal of Political Science* 36:635–64.

Campbell, Angus, Philip E. Converse, Warren E. Miller, and Donald E. Stokes. 1960. *The American Voter*. New York: Wiley.

Cappella, Joseph N., and Kathleen Hall Jamieson. 1997. *Spiral of Cynicism*. New York: Oxford University Press.

Casey, Gregory. 1974. "The Supreme Court and Myth: An Empirical Investigation." *Law and Society Review* 8:385–419.

Casper, J. D., T. R. Tyler, and B. Fisher. 1988. "Procedural Justice in Felony Cases." *Law and Society Review* 22:483–507.

Chaffee, Steven H., and Seung-Mock Yang. 1990. "Communication and Political Socialization." In Orit Ichilov, ed., *Political Socialization, Citizenship Education, and Democracy*. New York: Teacher's College Press.

Chubb, John E. 1988. "Institutions, the Economy, and the Dynamics of State Elections." *American Political Science Review* 82:133–54.

Cialdini, Robert B., and Melanie R. Trost. 1998. "Social Influence: Social Norms, Conformity and Compliance." In D. T. Gilbert, S. T. Fiske, and G. Lindzey, eds., *The Handbook of Social Psychology*, fourth ed. New York: McGraw-Hill.

Citrin, Jack. 1974. "Comment: The Political Relevance of Trust in Government." *American Political Science Review* 68:973–88.

Citrin, Jack. 1977. "Political Alienation as a Social Indicator: Attitudes and Action." *Social Indicators Research* 4:381–419.

Citrin, Jack. 1996. "Who's the Boss? Direct Democracy and Popular Control of Government." In Stephen C. Craig, ed., *Broken Contract*. Boulder: Westview Press.

Citrin, Jack, and Donald Philip Green. 1986. "Presidential Leadership and the Resurgence of Trust in Government." *British Journal of Political Science* 16:431–53.

Citrin, Jack, Donald Philip Green, and Beth A. Reingold. 1987. "The 'Soundness of Our Structure': Political Confidence in the Reagan Years." *Public Opinion* 10(5).

Citrin, Jack, and Samantha C. Luks. 1998. "The Problem of Political Trust." A report prepared for the Pew Charitable Trusts, Philadelphia, PA.

Citrin, Jack, Herbert McClosky, John M. Shanks, and Paul Sniderman. 1975. "Personal and Political Sources of Political Alienation." *British Journal of Political Science* 5:1–31.

Clift, Eleanor, and Tom Brazaitis. 1996. *War Without Bloodshed*. New York: Scribner.

Cohen, Joshua. 1989. "Deliberation and Democratic Legitimacy." In Alan Hamlin and Philip Pettit, eds., *The Good Polity: Normative Analysis of the State*. Oxford: Basil Blackwell.

Cohen, Richard. 1995. "Always the National News." *Washington Post*, 2 May, A19.

Cole, Richard L. 1973. "Toward a Model of Political Trust: A Causal Analysis." *American Journal of Political Science* 17:809–18.

Converse, Philip. 1964. "The Nature of Belief Systems in Mass Publics." In David Apter, ed., *Ideology and Discontent*. New York: Basic Books.

Converse, Philip E. 1972. "Change in the American Electorate." In Angus Campbell and Philip E. Converse, eds., *The Human Meaning of Social Change*. New York: Russell Sage.

Converse, Philip E., Aage R. Clausen, and Warren E. Miller. 1965. "Electoral Myth and Reality: The 1964 Election." *American Political Science Review* 59:321–36.

Cook, Timothy E. 1979. "Legislature vs. Legislator: A Note on the Paradox of Congressional Support." *Legislative Studies Quarterly* 4:43–52.

Cook, Timothy E. 1989. *Making Laws and Making News: Media Strategies in the U.S. House of Representatives.* Washington, DC: The Brookings Institution.

Council of State Governments. 1996–7. *The Book of the States, 1996–7.* Lexington, KY: CSG.

Craig, Stephen C. 1993. *The Malevolent Leaders: Popular Discontent in America.* Boulder, CO: Westview Press.

Craig, Stephen C., ed. 1996. *Broken Contract: Changing Relationships between Americans and their Government.* Boulder, CO: Westview Press.

Craig, Stephen C. 1996. "The Angry Voter: Politics and Popular Discontent in the 1990s." In Stephen C. Craig, ed., *Broken Contract: Changing Relationships between Americans and Their Government.* Boulder, CO: Westview Press.

Craig, Stephen C., Richard G. Niemi, and Glenn E. Silver. 1990. "Political Efficacy and Trust: A Report on the NES Pilot Study Items." *Political Behavior* 12:289–314.

Crozier, Michel, Samuel P. Huntington, and Jōji Watanuki. 1975. *The Crisis of Democracy: Report on the Governability of Democracies to the Trilateral Commission.* New York: New York University Press.

Dahl, Robert A. 1966. "The American Oppositions: Affirmation and Denial." In Robert A. Dahl, ed., *Political Oppositions in Western Democracies.* New Haven: Yale University Press.

Dahl, Robert A. 1970. *After the Revolution: Authority in a Good Society.* New Haven: Yale University Press.

Dahl, Robert A. 1971. *Polyarchy.* New Haven: Yale University Press.

Dahl, Robert A. 1989. *Democracy and Its Critics.* New Haven: Yale University Press.

Davidson, Roger H., and Glenn R. Parker. 1972. "Positive Support for Political Institutions: The Case of Congress." *Western Political Quarterly* 25:600–12.

Davidson, Roger H., David M. Kovenock, and Michael K. O'Leary. 1966. *Congress in Crisis: Politics and Congressional Reform.* Belmont, CA: Wadsworth.

Davis, Richard, and Diana Owen. 1998. *New Media and American Politics.* New York: Oxford.

Dawson, Richard E., and Kenneth Prewitt. 1969. *Political Socialization.* Boston: Little, Brown.

Delli Carpini, Michael X., and Scott Keeter. 1996. *What Americans Know about Politics and Why It Matters.* New Haven: Yale University Press.

Dennis, Jack. 1966. "Support for the Party System by the Mass Public." *Political Science Review* 60:600–15.

Dennis, Jack. 1973. "Public Support for American Political Institutions." Presented at the Conference on Public Support for the Political System, Madison, Wisconsin.

Dennis, Jack. 1975. "Trends in Public Support for the American Party System." *British Journal of Political Science* 5:179–222.

Dennis, Jack. 1980. "Changing Public Support for the American Party System." In William J. Crotty, ed., *Paths to Political Reform.* Lexington, MA: D.C. Heath—Lexington.

Dennis, Jack. 1981. "Public Support for Congress." *Political Behavior* 3:319–50.

Dennis, Jack. 1986. "Public Support for the Party System, 1964–84." Presented at the Annual Meeting of the American Political Science Association, Washington, DC.

Dennis, Jack. 1987. "Groups and Political Behavior: Legitimation, Deprivation and Competing Values." *Political Behavior* 9:323–73.

Dennis, Jack. 1993. "Do We Believe Aristotle? A Study of American Beliefs About Democracy." Presented at the Annual Meeting of the Midwest Political Science Association, Chicago.

Dennis, Jack, and Diana Owen. 1997. "The Partisanship Puzzle: Identification and Attitudes of Generation X." In Stephen C. Craig and Stephen Earl Bennett, eds., *After the Boom: The Politics of Generation X*. Lanham, MD: Rowman & Littlefield.

Devine, Donald J. 1972. *The Political Culture of the United States*. Boston: Little, Brown.

Diggins, John Patrick. 1988. *The Proud Decades: America in War and Peace, 1941–1960*. New York: Norton.

Dionne, E. J., Jr. 1991. *Why Americans Hate Politics*. New York: Simon & Schuster.

Donahue, John D. 1997. *Disunited States*. New York: Basic Books.

Drew, Elizabeth. 1996. *Showdown: The Struggle between the Gingrich Congress and the Clinton White House*. New York: Simon & Schuster.

Dryzek, John S. 1990. *Discursive Democracy*. Cambridge: Cambridge University Press.

Duncan, Philip D., and Christine C. Lawrence with CQ's Political Staff. 1995. *Politics in America 1996*. Washington: CQ Press.

Durr, Robert H. 1993. "What Moves Policy Sentiment?" *American Political Science Review* 87:158–70.

Durr, Robert H., John B. Gilmour, and Christina Wolbrecht. 1997. "Explaining Congressional Approval." *American Journal of Political Science* 41:175–207.

Eagly, Alice H., and Shelly Chaiken. 1993. *The Psychology of Attitudes*. New York: HBJ.

Easton, David. 1965a. *A Framework for Political Analysis*. Englewood Cliffs, NJ: Prentice-Hall.

Easton, David. 1965b. *A Systems Analysis of Political Life*. New York: Wiley.

Easton, David. 1975. "A Re-Assessment of the Concept of Political Support." *British Journal of Political Science* 5:435–57.

Easton, David, and Jack Dennis. 1969. *Children in the Political System: Origins of Political Legitimacy*. New York: McGraw-Hill.

Easton, David, and Robert D. Hess. 1962. "The Child's Political World." *Midwest Journal of Political Science* 6:229–46.

Edsall, Thomas Byrne, and Mary D. Edsall. 1991. *Chain Reaction: The Impact of Race, Rights, and Taxes on American Politics*. New York: W. W. Norton.

Edwards, George C., III, and Stephen J. Wayne. 1994. *Presidential Leadership: Politics and Policy Making*. New York: St. Martin's Press.

Ehrenhalt, Alan. 1991. *The United States of Ambition: Politicians, Power, and the Pursuit of Office*. New York: Times Books.

Elazar, Daniel J. 1966. *American Federalism: A View from the States*. New York: Crowell.

Elving, Ronald D. 1994. "Brighter Lights, Wider Windows: Presenting Congress in the 1990s." In Thomas E. Mann and Norman J. Ornstein, eds., *Congress, the Press, and the Public*. Washington, DC: American Enterprise Institute and The Brookings Institution.

Engelberg, Stephen, Jeff Gerth, and Katharine Q. Stell. 1995. "Files Show How Gingrich laid a Grand G.O.P. Plan." *New York Times* (December 3): 1.

Erskine, Hazel. 1973–4. "The Polls: Corruption in Government." *Public Opinion Quarterly* 37:628–44.

Etzioni, Amitai. 1972. "Minerva: An Electronic Town Hall." *Policy Sciences* 3:457–74.

Evans, C. Lawrence, and Walter J. Oleszek. 1997. *Congress Under Fire: Reform Politics and the Republican Majority*. Boston: Houghton Mifflin Company.

Fallows, James. 1996. *Breaking the News: How the Media Undermine American Democracy*. New York: Pantheon.

Feldman, Stanley. 1983. "The Measurement and Meaning of Trust in Government." *Political Methodology* 9:341–54.

Felten, Eric. 1993. *The Ruling Class: Inside the Imperial Congress*. Special Abridged Edition. Washington, DC: The Heritage Foundation.

Fenno, Richard F. 1975. "If, as Ralph Nader Says, Congress is 'The Broken Branch,' How Come We Love our Congressmen So Much?" In Norman J. Ornstein, ed., *Congress in Change: Evolution and Reform*. New York: Praeger.

Fenno, Richard F., Jr. 1977. "U.S. House Members in Their Constituencies: An Exploration." *American Political Science Review* 71:883–917.

Fenno, Richard F., Jr. 1978. *Home Style: House Members in Their Districts*. New York: HarperCollins.

Fenno, Richard F., Jr. 1997. *Learning to Govern: An Institutional View of the 104th Congress*. Washington, DC: Brookings Institution.

Ferguson, Thomas. 1995. *Golden Rule: The Investment Theory of Party Competition and the Logic of Money-driven Political Systems*. Chicago: University of Chicago Press.

Finifter, Ada W. 1972. *Alienation and the Social System*. New York: Wiley.

Fiorina, Morris P. 1981. *Retrospective Voting in American National Elections*. New Haven: Yale University Press.

Fiorina, Morris P. 1996. *Divided Government*. Second ed. Needham Heights, MA: Allyn and Bacon.

Fishkin, James S. 1995. *The Voice of the People*. New Haven: Yale University Press.

Flanigan, William H., and Nancy H. Zingale. 1998. *Political Behavior of the American Electorate*, ninth ed. Washington, DC: CQ Press.

Fowler, Linda L., and Robert D. McClure. 1989. *Political Ambition: Who Decides to Run for Congress*. New Haven: Yale University Press.

Freeman, John R. 1983. "Granger Causality and the Time Series Analysis of Political Relationships." *American Journal of Political Science* 27:337–58.

Freeman, John R., Daniel Houser, Paul M. Kellstedt, and John T. Williams. 1998. "Long-Memoried Processes, Unit Roots, and Causal Inference in Political Science." *American Journal of Political Science* 42:1289–327.

Freeman, John R., John T. Williams, and Tse-min Lin. 1989. "Vector Autoregression and the Study of Politics." *American Journal of Political Science* 33:842–77.

Fried, Amy. 1997. *Muffled Echoes: Oliver North and the Politics of Public Opinion*. New York: Columbia University Press.

Gamson, William A. 1968. *Power and Discontent*. Homewood, IL: The Dorsey Press.

Germond, Jack W., and Jules Witcover. 1994. "Blame Today's Cynicism on Watergate." *National Journal* 26(August 13):1937.
Gibson, James L. 1996. "A Mile Wide But an Inch Deep(?): The Structure of Democratic Commitments in the Former USSR." *American Journal of Political Science* 40:396–420.
Gibson, James L., and Gregory A. Caldeira. 1992. "Blacks and the United States Supreme Court: Models of Diffuse Support." *Journal of Politics* 54(4):1120–45.
Gibson, James L., Gregory A. Caldeira, and Vanessa A. Baird. 1998. "On the Legitimacy of National High Courts." *American Political Science Review* 92:343–58.
Gilbert, Daniel T. 1998. "Ordinary Personology." In D. T. Gilbert, S. T. Fiske, and G. Lindzey, eds., *The Handbook of Social Psychology*, fourth ed. New York: McGraw-Hill.
Gilmour, Robert S., and Robert B. Lamb. 1975. *Political Alienation in Contemporary America*. New York: St. Martin's Press.
Ginsberg, Benjamin, and Martin Shefter. 1990. *Politics by Other Means: The Declining Importance of Elections in America*. New York: Basic Books.
Gitlin, Todd. 1987. *The Sixties: Years of Hope, Days of Rage*. New York: Bantam.
Gold, Steven D. 1996. "Issues Raised by the New Federalism." *National Tax Journal* 44:273–87.
Goulden, Joseph C. 1976. *The Best Years: 1945–50*. New York: Athenaeum.
Graber, Doris A. 1997. *Mass Media and American Politics*. Washington, DC: CQ Press.
Graves, W. Brooke. 1936. *American State Government*. Boston: D. C. Heath and Company.
Gray, Virginia, and David Lowery. 1996. *The Population Ecology of Interest Representation: Lobbying Communities in the American States*. Ann Arbor: University of Michigan Press.
Greenstein, Fred I. 1965. *Children and Politics*. New Haven: Yale University Press.
Greider, William. 1992. *Who Will Tell the People? The Betrayal of American Democracy*. New York: Simon and Schuster.
Gurwitt, Rob. 1996. "Comes the Devolution: Covering State Capitals." *Columbia Journalism Review* 35:52–5.
Gutmann, Amy, and Dennis Thompson. 1996. *Democracy and Disagreement*. Cambridge, MA: Harvard University Press.
Hammond, Michael E., and Peter M. Weyrich. 1988. "Legislative Lords: Gag Rules and Permanent Staff." In Gordon S. Jones and John A. Marini, eds., *The Imperial Congress*. New York: Pharos Books.
Hampson, Rick. 1996. "Decline of the Town Meeting." *Lincoln Journal Star* (14 October 1996):2A.
Hardin, Russell. 1993. "The Street-Level Epistemology of Trust." *Politics and Society* 21:505–29.
Harris, Fred R. 1995. *In Defense of Congress*. New York: St. Martin's Press.
Harris Poll. 1996. New York: Louis Harris and Associates.
Hart, Vivien. 1978. *Distrust and Democracy: Political Distrust in Britain and America*. Cambridge: Cambridge University Press.
Hartz, Louis. 1955. *The Liberal Tradition in America*. New York: Marvest.
Hayek, F. A. 1960. *The Constitution of Liberty*. Chicago: University of Chicago Press.

Haynes, George H. 1938. *The Senate of the United States: Its History and Practice, 2 vols.* Boston: Houghton Mifflin.

Headlam, James Wycliffe. 1933. *Election by Lot at Athens, Second Edition.* Cambridge: Cambridge University Press.

Hemingway, Ernest. 1932. *Death in the Afternoon.* New York: Charles Scribner's Sons.

Henry J. Kaiser Family Foundation. 1996. "Why Don't Americans Trust The Government?" Menlo Park, CA.

Hess, David. 1998. "Congress Hibernating Till Fall." *Houston Chronicle* (19 March):8A.

Hess, Robert D., and Judith V. Torney. 1967. *The Development of Political Attitudes in Children.* Chicago: Aldine.

Hess, Stephen. 1986. *The Ultimate Insiders: U.S. Senators in the National Media.* Washington, DC: The Brookings Institution.

Hetherington, Marc J. 1997. "Political Trust's Effect on the Presidential Vote: 1968–1992." Presented at the Annual Meeting of the Midwest Political Science Association, Chicago, IL.

Hetherington, Marc J. 1998. "The Political Relevance of Political Trust." *American Political Science Review* 92:791–808.

Hetherington, Marc J. 1999. "The Effect of Political Trust on the Presidential Vote, 1968–96." *American Political Science Review* 93:311–26.

Hibbing, John R. 1983. "Washington on 75 Dollars a Day: Members of Congress Voting on Their Own Tax Break." *Legislative Studies Quarterly* 8:219–30.

Hibbing, John R., and Elizabeth Theiss-Morse. 1995. *Congress as Public Enemy: Public Attitudes Toward American Political Institutions.* New York: Cambridge University Press.

Hibbing, John R., and Elizabeth Theiss-Morse. 1998. "The Media's Role in Public Negativity Toward Congress: Distinguishing Emotional Reactions and Cognitive Evaluations." *American Journal of Political Science* 42:475–98.

Hibbing, John R., and Elizabeth Theiss-Morse. 2001. "Process Preferences and American Politics: What the People Want Government to Be." *American Political Science Review* 95: forthcoming.

Hibbing, John R., and Elizabeth Theiss-Morse. 2002. *Stealth Democracy: Americans' Beliefs about How Government Should Work.* Cambridge: Cambridge University Press.

House, James S., and William M. Mason. 1975. "Political Alienation in America, 1952–68." *American Sociological Review* 2:123–47.

Howard, Margaret. 1998. "Attention to News and Knowledge of Politics." Ph. D. diss., University of Michigan.

Huntington, Samuel P. 1981. *American Politics: The Promise of Disharmony.* Cambridge, MA: Harvard University Press.

Huntington, Samuel P. 1996. *The Clash of Civilizations and the Remaking of World Order.* New York: Simon & Schuster.

Hyman, Herbert. 1959. *Political Socialization.* Glencoe: Free Press.

Hyman, Herbert H., and Paul B. Sheatsley. [1950] 1954. "The Current Status of American Public Opinion." In Daniel Katz, Dorwin Cartwright, Samuel Eldersveld, and Alfred McClung Lee, eds., *Public Opinion and Propaganda: A Book of Readings.* New York: Holt, Rinehart & Winston.

Inglehart, Ronald. 1990. *Culture Shifts in Advanced Industrial Societies.* Princeton, NJ: Princeton University Press.

Inglehart, Ronald. 1997. "Postmaterialist Values and the Erosion of Institutional Authority." In Joseph S. Nye, Philip D. Zelikow, and David C. King, eds., *Why People Don't Trust Government.* Cambridge, MA: Harvard University Press.

Iyengar, Shanto, and Donald R. Kinder. 1987. *News that Matters: Television and American Opinion.* Chicago: University of Chicago Press.

Jacobs, Lawrence R., and Robert Y. Shapiro. 1995. "Don't Blame the Public for Failed Health Care Reform." *Journal of Health Politics, Policy and Law* 21:411–23.

Jacobson, Gary C. 1992. *The Politics of Congressional Elections.* Third ed. New York: HarperCollins.

Jamieson, Kathleen Hall. 1992. *Dirty Politics: Deception, Distraction, Democracy.* New York: Oxford University Press.

Jefferson Center. 1988. "Electoral Juries to Rejuvenate Presidential Politics." Minneapolis, MN: The Jefferson Center for New Democratic Processes.

Jennings, M. Kent. 1998. "Political Trust and the Roots of Devolution." In Valerie Braithwaite and Margaret Levi, eds., *Trust in Governance.* New York: Russell Sage.

Jennings, M. Kent, and Richard G. Niemi. 1974. *The Political Character of Adolescence: The Influence of Families and Schools.* Princeton, NJ: Princeton University Press.

Jennings, M. Kent, and Richard G. Niemi. 1981. *Generations and Politics: A Panel Study of Young Adults and Their Parents.* Princeton, NJ: Princeton University Press.

Jennings, M. Kent, and Harmon Zeigler. 1970. "The Salience of American State Politics." *American Political Science Review* 64:523–35.

Jensen, Merrill. 1950. *The New Nation: A History of the United States during the Confederation, 1781–1789.* New York: Vintage Books.

Johnson, Haynes, and David S. Broder. 1996. *The System: The American Way of Politics at the Breaking Point.* New York: Little, Brown.

Jones, Gordon S., and John A. Marini, eds. 1988. *The Imperial Congress: Crisis in the Separation of Powers.* New York: Pharos Books.

Kazee, Thomas A., and Susan Roberts. 1998. "Eroding Political Trust in America: An Assessment of Its Nature and Implications." Presented at the 1998 Annual Meeting of the American Political Science Association, Boston, MA.

Kenski, Henry C. 1977. "The Impact of Economic Conditions on Presidential Popularity." *Journal of Politics* 39:764–73.

Kerbel, Mathew Robert. 1995. *Remote and Controlled: Media Politics in a Cynical Age.* Boulder, CO: Westview Press.

Kernell, Samuel. 1978. "Explaining Presidential Popularity." *American Political Science Review* 72:506–22.

Kettering Foundation. 1991. *Citizens and Politics: A View from Main Street America.* Dayton, OH: Kettering Foundation.

Key, V. O. 1966. *The Responsible Electorate: Rationality in Presidential Voting.* New York: Vintage Books.

Kiewiet, D. Roderick. 1981. "Policy-Oriented Voting in Response to Economic Issues." *American Political Science Review* 75:448–59.

Kimball, David C., and Samuel C. Patterson. 1997. "Living Up to Expectations: Public Attitudes Toward Congress." *Journal of Politics* 59:701–28.

Kincaid, John. 1998. "The Devolution Tortoise and the Centralization Hare." *New England Economic Review* (May/June):13–40.

Kinder, Donald R. 1986. "Presidential Character Revisited." In Richard R. Lau and David O. Sears, eds., *Political Cognition*. Hillsdale, NJ: Lawrence Erlbaum.

Kinder, Donald R., and D. Roderick Kiewiet. 1979. "Economic Discontent and Political Behavior: The Role of Personal Grievances and Collective Economic Judgments in Congressional Voting." *American Journal of Political Science* 23:495–527.

King, Anthony. 1997. *Running Scared*. New York: Free Press.

King, David C. 1997. "The Polarization of American Political Parties and Mistrust of Government." In Joseph S. Nye, Philip D. Zelikow, and David C. King, eds., *Why People Don't Trust Government*. Cambridge, MA: Harvard University Press.

Kingdon, John W. 1993. "Politicians, Self-Interest and Ideas." In George E. Marcus and Russell L. Hanson, *Reconsidering the Democratic Public*. University Park, PA: Pennsylvania State University Press.

Kitzmann, K. M., and Emery, R. E. 1993. "Procedural Justice and Parent's Satisfaction in a Field Study of Child Custody Dispute Resolution." *Law and Human Behavior* 17:553–67.

Koch, Jeffrey W. 1998. "Political Rhetoric and Political Persuasion: The Changing Structure of Citizens' Preferences on Health Insurance during Policy Debate." *Public Opinion Quarterly* 62:209–29.

Kornberg, Allan, and Harold D. Clarke. 1992. *Citizens and Community: Political Support in a Representative Democracy*. New York: Cambridge University Press.

Korsgaard, M. A., D. M. Schweiger, and H. J. Sapienza. 1995. "Building Commitment, Attachment, and Trust in Strategic Decision-Making Teams: The Role of Procedural Justice." *Academy of Management Journal* 38:60–84.

Kovaleski, Serge F., and Charles R. Babcock. 1994. "Gingrich & Co. Fund a Megaphone for Ideas." *Washington Post* (December 21):A19.

Krehbiel, Keith. 1998. *Pivotal Politics*. Chicago: University of Chicago Press.

Krosnick, Jon A., and Donald R. Kinder. 1990. "Altering the Foundations of Support for the President Through Priming." *American Political Science Review* 84:497–512.

Ladd, Everett Carl, ed. 1995. *America at the Polls 1994*. Storrs, CT: The Roper Center for Public Opinion Research.

Lane, Robert E. 1962. *Political Ideology: Why the American Common Man Believes What He Does*. New York: Free Press.

Lane, Robert E. 1965. "The Politics of Consensus in an Age of Affluence." *American Political Science Review* 59:874–95.

Lane, Robert E. 1966. "The Decline of Politics and Ideology in a Knowledgeable Society." *American Sociological Review* 31:649–62.

Lawrence, Robert Z. 1997. "Is It Really the Economy, Stupid?" In Joseph S. Nye, Jr., Philip D. Zelikow, and David C. King, eds., *Why People Don't Trust Government*. Cambridge, MA: Harvard University Press.

Levi, Margaret. 1997. *Consent, Dissent and Patriotism*. New York: Cambridge University Press.

Levi, Margaret. 1998. "A State of Trust." In Valerie Braithwaite and Margaret Levi, eds., *Trust and Governance*. New York: Russell Sage.

Lewis, Gregory B. 1993. "Women, Occupations, and Federal Agencies: Occupational Mix and Interagency Differences in Sexual Inequality in Federal White-Collar Employment." *Public Administration Review* 54:271–6.

Lijphart, Arendt. 1980. "The Structure of Inference." In Gabriel A. Almond and Sidney Verba, eds., *The Civic Culture Revisited.* Boston: Little, Brown.

Lijphart, Arendt. 1984. *Democracies: Patterns of Majoritarian and Consensus Government in Twenty-One Countries.* New Haven: Yale University Press.

Lind, E. A., C. T. Kulik, M. Ambrose, and M. de Vera Park. 1993. "Individual and Corporate Dispute Resolution: Using Procedural Fairness as a Decision Heuristic." *Administrative Science Quarterly* 38:224–51.

Lind, E. Allan, and Tom R. Tyler. 1988. *The Social Psychology of Procedural Justice.* New York: Plenum.

Lipset, Seymour Martin. 1990. *Continental Divide: The Values and Institutions of the United States and Canada.* New York: Routledge.

Lipset, Seymour Martin. 1995. "Malaise and Resiliency in America." *Journal of Democracy* 6(3):4–18.

Lipset, Seymour Martin. 1996. *American Exceptionalism: A Double-Edged Sword.* New York: W. W. Norton.

Lipset, Seymour Martin, and William Schneider. 1987. *The Confidence Gap: Business, Labor, and Government in the Public Mind.* Baltimore: Johns Hopkins University Press.

Lodge, Milton, and Bernard Tursky. 1979. "Comparisons Between Category and Magnitude Scaling of Public Opinion Employing SRC/CPS Items." *American Political Science Review* 73:50–66.

Lowi, Theodore J., and Benjamin Ginsberg. 1996. *American Government: Freedom and Power.* Fourth ed. New York: W. W. Norton.

Luks, Samantha. 1998. "What Has Our Country Done for Us Lately? How Political Awareness Influences Political Trust." Presented at the Annual Meeting of the American Political Science Association, Boston, MA.

Luks, Samantha C., and Jack Citrin. 1997. "Revisiting Political Trust in an Angry Age." Presented at the Annual Meeting of the Midwest Political Science Association, Chicago, IL.

Luskin, Robert C. 1987. "Measuring Political Sophistication." *American Journal of Political Science* 31:856–99.

Luttbeg, Norman R., and Michael M. Gant. 1995. *American Electoral Behavior 1952–1992.* Second ed. Itasca, IL: Peacock.

MacDonald, Gus. 1986. "Election 500." In Ivor Crewe and Martin Harrop, eds., *Political Communications: The General Election Campaign of 1983.* Cambridge: Cambridge University Press.

MacKuen, Michael B., Robert S. Erikson, and James A. Stimson. 1992. "Peasants or Bankers? The American Electorate and the U.S. Economy." *American Political Science Review* 86:597–611.

Madsen, Douglas. 1987. "Political Self-Efficacy Tested." *American Political Science Review* 81:571–81.

Magleby, David B. 1995. "Governing by Initiative: Let the Voters Decide? An Assessment of the Initiative and Referendum Process." *Colorado Law Review* 66:13–46.

Manin, Bernard. 1987. "On Legitimacy and Political Deliberation." *Political Theory* 15:338–68.

Mann, Thomas E., and Norman J. Ornstein, eds. 1994. *Congress, the Press, and the Public.* Washington, DC: American Enterprise Institute and The Brookings Institution.

Mansbridge, Jane J. 1980. *Beyond Adversary Democracy.* New York: Basic Books.

Maraniss, David, and Michael Weisskopf. 1996. *"Tell Newt to Shut Up!"* New York: Simon & Schuster.

Marcus, George E., and Michael B. MacKuen. 1993. "Anxiety, Enthusiasm and the Vote: On the Emotional Underpinnings of Learning and Involvement During Presidential Campaigns." *American Political Science Review* 87:672–85.

Marcus, George E., and Wendy Rahn. 1990. "Emotions and Democratic Politics." In Samuel Long, ed., *Research in Micro-politics 3*. Greenwich, CT: JAI Press.

Markus, Gregory B. 1988. "The Impact of Personal and National Economic Conditions on the Presidential Vote: A Pooled Cross-Sectional Analysis." *American Journal of Political Science* 32:137–54.

Mason, William M., James S. House, and Steven S. Martin. 1985. "On the Dimensions of Political Alienation in America." In Nancy Brandon Tuma, ed., *Sociological Methodology, 1985*. San Francisco: Jossey-Bass.

McClosky, Herbert. 1964. "Consensus and Ideology in American Politics." *American Political Science Review* 58:361–82.

McClosky, Herbert, Paul J. Hoffman, and Rosemary O'Hara. 1960. "Issue Conflict and Consensus among Party Leaders and Followers." *American Political Science Review* 54:406–27.

Miller, Arthur H. 1974a. "Political Issues and Trust in Government, 1964–1970." *American Political Science Review* 68:951–72.

Miller, Arthur H. 1974b. "Rejoinder to 'Comment' by Jack Citrin: Political Discontent or Ritualism?" *American Political Science Review* 68:989–1001.

Miller, Arthur H. 1983. "Is Confidence Rebounding?" *Public Opinion* 6:16–20.

Miller, Arthur H., and Stephen A. Borrelli. 1991. "Confidence in Government During the 1980s." *American Politics Quarterly* 19:147–73.

Miller, Arthur H., Edie N. Goldenberg, and Lutz Erbring. 1979. "Type-Set Politics: Impact of Newspapers on Public Confidence." *American Political Science Review* 73:67–84.

Miller, Warren E., Arthur H. Miller, and Edward J. Schneider. 1980. *Data Sourcebook, 1952–1978*. Cambridge, MA: Harvard University Press.

Mitchell, William C. 1959. "The Ambivalent Social Status of the American Politician." *Western Political Quarterly* 12:683–98.

Monroe, Kristen R. 1978. "Economic Influences on Presidential Popularity." *Public Opinion Quarterly* 42:360–9.

Morin, Richard, and Dan Balz. 1996. "Americans Losing Trust in Each Other and Institutions." *Washington Post* (28 January):A1, A6–A7.

Morone, James A. 1990. *The Democratic Wish: Popular Participation and the Limits of American Government*. New York: Basic Books.

Mueller, John E. 1970. "Presidential Popularity from Truman to Johnson." *American Political Science Review* 64:18–34.

Mueller, John E. 1973. *War, Presidents, and Public Opinion*. New York: Wiley.

Muller, Edward. 1979. *Aggressive Political Participation*. Princeton, NJ: Princeton University Press.

Muller, Edward, and T. O. Jukam. 1977. "On the Meaning of Political Support." *American Political Science Review* 71:1561–95.

Naff, Katherine C. 1994. "Through the Glass Ceiling: Prospects for the Advancement of Women in the Federal Civil Service." *Public Administration Review* 54:503–14.

Natchez, Peter B. 1985. *Images of Voting/Visions of Democracy: Voting Behavior and Democratic Theory.* New York: Basic Books.

Nathan, Richard P. 1996. "The Devolution Revolution: An Overview." In Michael J. Malbin, ed., *Rockefeller Institute Bulletin: American Federalism Today.*

Nelson, Michael. 1995. "Evaluating the Presidency." In Michael Nelson, ed., *The Presidency and the Political System.* Fourth ed. Washington, DC: CQ Press.

Newton, Kenneth. 1998. "Social and Political Trust." In Pippa Norris, ed., *Critical Citizens: Global Support for Democratic Government.* Oxford: Oxford University Press.

NORC. 1944. "The Public Looks at Politics and Politicians." Denver: National Opinion Research Center, University of Denver. Report No. 20 (March).

Norris, Pippa. 1998. "The Growth of Critical Citizens." In Pippa Norris, ed., *Critical Citizens: Global Support for Democratic Government.* Oxford: Oxford University Press.

Nye, Joseph S., Jr., Philip D. Zelikow, and David C. King, eds. 1997. *Why People Don't Trust Government.* Cambridge, MA: Harvard University Press.

Nye, Joseph S. 1997. "Introduction: The Decline of Confidence in Government." In Joseph S. Nye, Philip D. Zelikow, and David C. King, eds., *Why People Don't Trust Government.* Cambridge, MA: Harvard University Press.

Oakley, J. Ronald. [1986] 1990. *God's Country: America in the Fifties.* New York: Dembner.

Olien, Clarice N., George A. Donohue, and Phillip J. Tichenor. 1995. "Conflict, Consensus, and Public Opinion." In T. L. Glasser and C. T. Salmon, eds., *Public Opinion and the Communication of Consent.* New York: Guilford.

O'Neill, William. 1986. *American High: The Years of Confidence, 1945–1960.* New York: Free Press.

Ornstein, Norman J., Thomas E. Mann, and Michael J. Malbin, comps. 1998. *Vital Statistics on Congress 1997–1998.* Washington, DC: CQ Press.

Orren, Gary. 1997. "Fall from Grace: The Public's Loss of Faith in Government." In Joseph S. Nye, Philip D. Zelikow, and David C. King, eds., *Why People Don't Trust Government.* Cambridge, MA: Harvard University Press.

Owen, Diana. 1996. "Who's Talking? Who's Listening? The New Politics of Radio Talk Shows." In Stephen C. Craig, ed., *Broken Contract: Changing Relationships Between Americans and Their Government.* Boulder, CO: Westview Press.

Owen, Diana. 1997. "Mixed Signals: Generation X's Attitudes Toward the Political System." In Stephen C. Craig and Stephen Earl Bennett, eds., *After the Boom: The Politics of Generation X.* Lanham, MD: Rowman & Littlefield.

Owen, Diana and Jack Dennis. 1996. "Anti-Partyism in the USA and Support for Ross Perot." *European Journal of Political Research* 29:383–400.

Owen, Diana, Jack Dennis, and Casey Klofstad. 1998. "Public Support for the Party System in the United States in the Late 1990s." Paper presented at the Annual Meeting of the American Political Science Association, Boston, MA.

Parker, Glenn R. 1977. "Some Themes in Congressional Unpopularity." *American Journal of Political Science* 21:93–109.

Parker, Glenn R. 1981. "Can Congress Ever Be a Popular Institution?" In Joseph Cooper and G. Calvin Mackenzie, eds., *The House at Work.* Austin, TX: University of Texas Press.

Parker, Glenn R., and Roger H. Davidson. 1979. "Why Do Americans Love Their Congressmen So Much More Than Their Congress?" *Legislative Studies Quarterly* 4:54–61.

Pateman, Carole. 1980. "The Civic Culture: A Philosophical Critique." In Gabriel A. Almond and Sidney Verba, eds., *The Civic Culture Revisited.* Boston: Little, Brown.

Paternoster, R., R. Brame, R. Bachman, and L. W. Sherman. 1997. "Do Fair Procedures Matter? The Effect of Procedural Justice on Spouse Assault." *Law and Society Review* 31:163–204.

Patterson, James T. 1996. *Grand Expectations: The United States, 1945–1974.* New York: Oxford University Press.

Patterson, Samuel C., and Michael K. Barr. 1995. "Congress Bashing and the 1992 Congressional Election." In Herbert F. Weisberg, ed., *Democracy's Feast: Elections in America.* Chatham, NJ: Chatham House.

Patterson, Samuel C., and Gregory A. Caldeira. 1990. "Standing Up for Congress: Variations in Public Esteem Since the 1960s." *Legislative Studies Quarterly* 15:25–47.

Patterson, Samuel C., Randall B. Ripley, and Stephen V. Quinlan. 1992. "Citizens' Orientations Toward Legislatures: Congress and the State Legislature." *Western Political Quarterly* 45:315–38.

Patterson, Thomas. 1994. *Out of Order.* New York: Vintage Books.

Peterson, Geoff, and J. Mark Wrighton. 1998. "Expressions of Distrust: Third Party Voting and Cynicism in Government." *Political Behavior* 20:17–34.

Peterson, George E. 1984. "Federalism and the States: An Experiment in Decentralization." In John L. Palmer and Isabel V. Sawhill, eds., *The Reagan Record.* Cambridge: Ballinger.

Petty, Richard E., and John T. Cacioppo. 1981. *Attitudes and Persuasion: Classic and Contemporary Approaches.* Dubuque, IA: Wm. C. Brown.

Pew Research Center. 1998. *Deconstructing Distrust: How Americans View Government.* Philadelphia: Pew Research Center for People and the Press.

Piper, J. Richard. 1991. "Presidential–Congressional Power Prescriptions in Conservative Political Thought Since 1933." *Presidential Studies Quarterly* 21:35–54.

Piper, J. Richard. 1994. "'Situational Constitutionalism' and Presidential Power: The Rise and Fall of the Liberal Model of Presidential Government." *Presidential Studies Quarterly* 24:577–94.

Price, Vincent. 1992. *Public Opinion.* Newbury Park, CA: Russell Sage.

Prosser, Gabriel. 1988. "Comes the Revolution." In Gordon S. Jones and John A. Marini, eds., *The Imperial Congress.* New York: Pharos Books.

Prothro, James, and Charles Grigg. 1960. "Fundamental Principles of Democracy: Bases of Agreement and Disagreement." *Journal of Politics* 22:276–94.

Pruitt, D. G., R. S. Peirce, N. B. McGillicuddy, G. L. Welton, and L. M. Castrianno. 1993. "Long-Term Success in Mediation." *Law and Human Behavior* 17:313–30.

Putnam, Robert D. 1993. *Making Democracy Work.* Princeton, NJ: Princeton University Press.

Putnam, Robert D. 1995a. "Bowling Alone: America's Declining Social Capital." *Journal of Democracy* 6:65–78.

Putnam, Robert D. 1995b. "Tuning In, Tuning Out: The Strange Disappearance of Social Capital in America." *PS: Political Science & Politics* 28:664–83.

Rae, Nicol C. 1998. *Conservative Reformers: The Republican Freshmen and the Lessons of the 104th Congress.* Armonk, NY: M. E. Sharpe.

Rahim, M. Afzalur. 1986. *Managing Conflict in Organizations.* New York: Praeger.

Rahn, Wendy, and Gerald L. Clore. 1994. "Public Mood: Structure, Origins, and Individual Differences." Presented at the Annual meeting of the Southern Political Science Association, Atlanta.

Rakove, Jack N. 1997. *Original Meanings: Politics and Ideas in the Making of the Constitution.* New York: Alfred A. Knopf.

Reeves, Mavis Mann. 1985. *The Question of State Government Capability.* Washington, DC: Advisory Commission on Intergovernmental Relations.

Reich, Robert B. 1997. *Locked in the Cabinet.* New York: Alfred A. Knopf.

Ripley, Randall B., Samuel C. Patterson, Lynn Maurer, and Stephen V. Quinlan. 1992. "Constituents' Evaluations of U.S. House Members." *American Politics Quarterly* 20:442–56.

Roeder, Phillip W. 1994. *Public Opinion and Policy Leadership in the American States.* Tuscaloosa, AL: University of Alabama Press.

Rose, Lisle A. 1999. *The Cold War Comes to Main Street: America in 1950.* Lawrence, KS: University Press of Kansas.

Rosenberg, Morris. 1954–5. "Some Determinants of Political Apathy." *Public Opinion Quarterly* 18:349–66.

Rosenstone, Steven J., and John Mark Hansen. 1993. *Mobilization, Participation, and Democracy in America.* New York: Macmillan.

Rosenthal, Alan. 1998. *The Decline of Representative Democracy.* Washington, DC: CQ Press.

Rossiter, Clinton, ed. 1961. *The Federalist Papers.* New York: Mentor.

Ryden, David K. 1996. *Representation in Crisis.* Albany, New York: SUNY Press.

Schattschneider, E. E. 1960. *The Semi-Sovereign People.* New York: Holt, Rinehard and Winston.

Schneider, William. 1997. "A Crime that Made Cynicism the Rule." *National Journal* 20 21:1306.

Scholz, John T., and Mark Lubell. 1998. "Trust and Taxpaying: Testing the Heuristic Approach to Collective Action." *American Journal of Political Science* 42:398–417.

Scholz, John, and Neal Pinney. 1995. "Duty, Fear, and Tax Compliance: The Heuristic Basis of Citizenship Behavior." *American Journal of Political Science* 39:490–512.

Schrag, Peter. 1998. *Paradise Lost: California's Experience, America's Future.* New York: New Press.

Schwartz, David C. 1973. *Political Alienation and Political Behavior.* Chicago: Aldine.

Sears, David O. 1969. "Political Behavior." In G. Lindzey and E. Aronson, eds., *Handbook of Social Psychology*, second ed. Reading, MA: Addison-Wesley.

Sears, David O., Tom R. Tyler, Jack Citrin, and Donald R. Kinder. 1978. "Political System Support and Public Response to the Energy Crisis." *American Journal of Political Science* 22:56–82.

Seeman, Melvin. 1972. "Alienation and Engagement." In Angus Campbell and Philip E. Converse, eds., *The Human Meaning of Social Change.* New York: Russell Sage.

Seligman, Adam B. 1992. *The Idea of Civil Society.* Princeton, NJ: Princeton University Press.

Shafer, Byron E., ed. 1997. *Present Discontents: American Politics in the Very Late Twentieth Century.* Chatham, NJ: Chatham House.

Shils, Edward A. 1960. *Political Development in the New States.* The Hague: Mouton.

Sigel, Roberta S. 1965. "Assumptions about the Learning of Political Values." *Annals of the American Academy of Political and Social Science* 361:1–9.

Sigel, Roberta, ed. 1989. *Political Learning in Adulthood: A Sourcebook of Theory and Research.* Chicago: University of Chicago Press.

Skocpol, Theda. 1996. *Boomerang: Health Care Reform and the Turn Against Government.* New York: W. W. Norton.

Smith, Tom W., D. Garth Taylor, and Nancy Mathiowitz. 1979. "Public Opinion and Public Regard for the Federal Government." In Carol H. Weiss and Allen H. Barton, eds., *Making Democracies Work.* Beverly Hills, CA: Russell Sage.

Sniderman, Paul M. 1981. *A Question of Loyalty.* Berkeley, CA: University of California Press.

Sniderman, Paul M., and Richard A. Brody. 1977. "Coping: The Ethic of Self-Reliance." *American Journal of Political Science* 21:501–21.

Squire, Peverill, Raymond E. Wolfinger, and David P. Glass. 1987. "Residential Mobility and Voter Turnout." *American Political Science Review* 81:45–65.

Stanley, Harold W., and Richard G. Niemi, comps. 1992. *Vital Statistics on American Politics*, third ed. Washington, DC: CQ Press.

Stimson, James A. 1991. *Public Opinion in America: Moods, Cycles, and Swings.* Boulder, CO: Westview Press.

Stimson, James A., Michael B. MacKuen, and Robert S. Erikson. 1995. "Dynamic Representation." *American Political Science Review* 89:543–65.

Stokes, Donald E. 1962. "Popular Evaluations of Government: An Empirical Assessment." In Harlan Cleveland and Harold D. Lasswell, eds., *Ethics and Bigness: Scientific, Academic, Religious, Political, and Military.* New York: Harper.

Sundquist, James L. 1980. "The Crisis of Competence in Our National Government." *Political Science Quarterly* 95:183–208.

Tanenhaus, Joseph, and Walter F. Murphy. 1981. "Patterns of Public Support for the Supreme Court: A Panel Study." *Journal of Politics* 43:24–39.

Tannen, Deborah. 1998. *The Argument Culture.* New York: Random House.

Tannenwald, Robert. 1998. "Come the Devolution, Will States be Able to Respond?" *New England Economic Review* (May/June):53–72.

Teixeira, Ruy A. 1992. *The Disappearing American Voter.* Washington, DC: The Brookings Institution.

Teixeira, Ruy A. 1996. "Economic Change and the Middle-Class Revolt Against the Democratic Party." In Stephen C. Craig, ed., *Broken Contract.* Boulder, CO: Westview Press.

Theriault, Sean. 1998. "Moving Up or Moving Out: Career Ceilings and Congressional Retirement." *Legislative Studies Quarterly* 23:419–34.

Thompson, Michael, Richard Ellis, and Aaron Wildavsky. 1990. *Cultural Theory.* Boulder, CO: Westview Press.

Tolchin, Susan J. 1996. *The Angry American: How Voter Rage Is Changing the Nation.* Boulder, CO: Westview Press.

Tyler, Tom R. 1990. *Why People Obey the Law*. New Haven: Yale University Press.

Tyler, Tom R. 1994. "Psychological Models of the Justice Motive: Antecedents of Distributive and Procedural Justice." *Journal of Personality and Social Psychology* 67:850–63.

Tyler, Tom R. 1994. "Governing Amid Diversity: Can Fair Decision-Making Procedures Bridge Competing Public Interests and Values?" *Law and Society Review* 28:701–22.

Tyler, Tom R. 1996–7. "Compliance with Intellectual Property Laws: A Psychological Perspective." *Journal of International Law and Politics* 29:219–36.

Tyler, Tom R. 1997a. "Procedural Fairness and Compliance with the Law." *Swiss Journal of Economics and Statistics* 133:219–40.

Tyler, Tom R. 1997b. "Citizen Discontent with Legal Procedures: A Social Science Perspective on Civil Procedure Reform." *American Journal of Comparative Law* 45:871–904.

Tyler, Tom R. 1998. "Public Mistrust of the Law: A Political Perspective." *University of Cincinnati Law Review* 66:847–75.

Tyler, Tom R., and E. A. Lind. 1992. "A Relational Model of Authority in Groups." *Advances in Experimental Social Psychology* 25:115–91.

Tyler, Tom R., R. J. Boeckmann, H. J. Smith, and Y. J. Huo. 1997. *Social Justice in a Diverse Society*. New York: Westview Press.

Tyler, Tom R., Jonathan D. Casper, and Bonnie Fisher. 1989. "Maintaining Allegiance Toward Political Authorities: The Role of Prior Attitudes and the Use of Fair Procedures." *American Journal of Political Science* 33:629–52.

Tyler, Tom R., and Peter Degoey. 1995. "Collective Restraint in Social Dilemmas: Procedural Justice and Social Identification Effects on Support for Authorities." *Journal of Personality and Social Psychology* 69:482–97.

Tyler, Tom R., and Peter Degoey. 1996. "Trust in Organizational Authorities: The Influence of Motive Attributions on Willingness to Accept Decisions." In Roderick M. Kramer and Tom R. Tyler, eds., *Trust in Organizations*. Thousand Oaks, CA: Russell Sage.

Tyler, Tom R., and G. Mitchell. 1994. "Legitimacy and the Empowerment of Discretionary Legal Authority: The United States Supreme Court and Abortion Rights." *Duke Law Journal* 43:703–814.

Tyler, Tom R., K. Rasinski, and N. Spodick. 1985. "The Influence of Voice on Satisfaction with Leaders: Exploring the Meaning of Process Control." *Journal of Personality and Social Psychology* 48:72–81.

Uslaner, Eric M. 1993. *The Decline of Comity in Congress*. Ann Arbor: University of Michigan Press.

Uslaner, Eric M. 1997. Review of John R. Hibbing and Elizabeth Theiss-Morse, *Congress as Public Enemy: Public Attitudes toward American Institutions, Public Opinion Quarterly* 61:667–9.

Uslaner, Eric M. 1998. *The Moral Foundations of Trust*. Manuscript in preparation, University of Maryland—College Park.

Van Horn, Carl E. 1989. "The Quiet Revolution." In Carl E. Van Horn, ed., *The State of the States*. Washington, DC: Congressional Quarterly Press.

Verba, Sidney, Kay Lehman Schlozman, and Henry E. Brady. 1995. *Voice and Equality: Civic Voluntarism in American Politics*. Cambridge, MA: Harvard University, Press.

Wald, Kenneth D. 1997. *Religion and Politics in the United States*, third ed. Washington, DC: CQ Press.

Washington Post. 1997. "New Evidence of Public Distrust." (24 March).

Wattenberg, Martin P. 1996. *The Decline of American Political Parties, 1952–1994*. Cambridge, MA: Harvard University Press.

Weatherford, M. Stephen. 1984. "Economic 'Stagflation' and Public Support for the Political System." *British Journal of Political Science* 14:187–205.

Weatherford, M. Stephen. 1987. "How Does Government Performance Influence Political Support?" *Political Behavior* 9:5–28.

Weatherford, M. Stephen. 1988. "Are the Traditional Measures of Political Trust as Bad as They Look?" Presented at the Annual Meeting of the Midwest Political Science Association, Chicago, IL.

Weingast, Barry R., Thomas W. Gilligan, and William J. Marshall. 1989. "Regulation and the Theory of Legislative Choice: The Interstate Commerce Act of 1887." *Journal of Law & Economics* 32:35–61.

Weingast, Barry R., and Daniel B. Rodriguez. 1995. "Legislative Rhetoric, Statutory Interpretation, and the History of the 1964 Civil Rights Act." Unpublished Manuscript. Stanford, California.

West, Thomas G. 1988. "Restoring the Separation of Powers." In Gordon S. Jones and John A. Marini, eds., *The Imperial Congress*. New York: Pharos Books.

White, Stephen, Richard Rose, and Ian McAllister. 1997. *How Russia Votes*. Chatham, NJ: Chatham House.

White, Theodore H. 1982. *America in Search of Itself: The Making of the President, 1956–1980*. New York: Harper & Row.

Wiatr, Jerzy J. 1980. "The Civic Culture from a Marxist Sociological Perspective." In Gabriel A. Almond and Sidney Verba, eds., *The Civic Culture Revisited*. Boston: Little, Brown.

Williams, John T. 1985. "Systemic Influences on Political Trust: The Importance of Perceived Institutional Performance." *Political Methodology* 11:125–42.

Wilson, James Q. 1975. "The Riddle of the Middle Class." *The Public Interest* 39:125–9.

Wood, Gordon S. 1969. *The Creation of the American Republic, 1776–1787*. New York: W. W. Norton.

Worchel, Stephen, Dawna Coutant-Sassic, and Frankie Wong. 1993. "Toward a More Balanced View of Conflict: There Is a Positive Side." In Stephen Worchel, ed., *Conflict Between Groups and People*. Chicago: Nelson-Hall.

Woshinsky, Oliver H. 1995. *Culture and Politics: An Introduction to Mass and Elite Political Behavior*. Englewood Cliffs, NJ: Prentice Hall.

Wright, James D. 1976. *The Dissent of the Governed: Alienation and Democracy in America*. New York: Academic Press.

Yinger, J. Milton. 1973. "Anomie, Alienation and Political Behavior." In Jeanne N. Knutson, ed., *Handbook of Political Psychology*. San Francisco: Jossey-Bass.

Young, William H. 1958. "The Development of the Governorship." *State Government* (Summer):178–83.

Zaller, John R. 1992. *The Nature and Origins of Mass Opinion*. Cambridge: Cambridge University Press.

Zeller, Richard A., and Edward G. Carmines. 1980. *Measurement in the Social Sciences: The Link between Data and Theory*. Cambridge: Cambridge University Press.

Zellner, A. 1963. "Estimators of Seemingly Unrelated Regressions: Some Exact Finite Sample Results." *Journal of the American Statistical Association* 58:977–92.

Zis, Michael, Lawrence R. Jacobs, and Robert Y. Shapiro. 1996. "The Elusive Common Group: The Politics of Public Opinion and Healthcare Reform." *Generations* 20:7–13.

Index